JACK ROTHMAN
University of Michigan

Social R & D
research and development in the human services

PRENTICE-HALL, INC., *Englewood Cliffs, New Jersey 07632*

Library of Congress Cataloging in Publication Data

Rothman, Jack.
  Social research and development in the human services.

  Bibliography: p.
  Includes index.
    1. Social science research.   2. Social sciences
  —Methodology.   3. Evaluation research (Social
  action programs)   I. Title.
  H62.R676   300'.1'8   79-15302
  ISBN 0-13-818112-8

© 1980 *by* PRENTICE-HALL, INC., *Englewood Cliffs, N.J. 07632*

PRINTED IN THE UNITED STATES OF AMERICA

10   9   8   7   6   5   4   3   2   1

editorial/production supervision and interior design: Cathie Mick Mahar
cover design: Jerry Pfeifer
manufacturing buyer: Ray Keating

PRENTICE-HALL INTERNATIONAL, INC., *London*
PRENTICE-HALL OF AUSTRALIA PTY. LIMITED, *Sydney*
PRENTICE-HALL OF CANADA, LTD., *Toronto*
PRENTICE-HALL OF INDIA PRIVATE LIMITED, *New Delhi*
PRENTICE-HALL OF JAPAN, INC., *Tokyo*
PRENTICE-HALL OF SOUTHEAST ASIA PTE. LTD., *Singapore*
WHITEHALL BOOKS LIMITED, *Wellington, New Zealand*

The ideas in this book hold, it seems to me, promise of social progress. For this reason I would like to dedicate it to my children Amy, Dan and Josh—and to young people generally.

Contents

part three

ORGANIZATIONAL STRUCTURE
FOR SOCIAL R&D   *215*

11

STRUCTURES AND RESOURCES FOR CENTERS OF SOCIAL R&D   *217*

part four

CONCLUSIONS AND PROSPECTUS   *242*

12

SOCIAL R&D IN ACTION: THE CIP EXPERIENCE   *243*

Foreword

The issue this book raises could not be more timely. We have entered the third leg of a dialectic process in the movement from Big Government, to Anti-Government, to Effective and Responsive Government. In the late Fifties, and most of the Sixties, the thesis was advanced that government could be relied upon to act as the major agent of social change, to provide both collective cures and personal services to encompass practically all human aspects.

The late Sixties and most of the Seventies were characterized by a reaction against the excessive optimism invested in the Great Society programs. For a while, this period of anti-thesis seemed like *the* trend, with such code words as "Proposition 13," "constitutional amendment to balance the budget," and "a move to the right" flagging the nation that the government was an inept and inappropriate, if not corrupt and corrupting, agent.

However, throughout this reaction, it was evident that, while most of the public were down on the government *as it was,* they had a long and impressive list of matters they wished the government to provide for—for instance, support for college students and National Health Insurance. They were not actually so much against government, but against a government dedicated to services for the few at the cost of the majority; a government which is wasteful rather than effective; and a government which is abusive rather than sensitive. The next step is, hence, the golden mean, the quest for less but more government, a smaller budget, fewer regulations, fewer civil servants, less paper work—but more delivery of services, more responsive to more people.

It is here that social R&D will have its key role. It had a limited place in an age in which billions of dollars were easily appropriated on the basis of a memo, a position paper, a promising experiment at a few sites. It had a similar limited place in the age of across-the-board cutbacks and give-backs. Now, as we are entering the third stage—trying to ferret out what works, and what works *well*—R&D will acquire a central role because it is the only way to find out—without massive waste, coercion, and alienation—which programs work effectively and are responsive.

As Professor Jack Rothman points out, it is not just that social sciences are weak. No science can bring into being a concrete, in-the-world, service program without a full process of development.

This accounts for the particular value of this book at this time. There is always a great need for being concerned with the processes through which social ideas become effective programs. In the era in which we find ourselves, such concern is essential and unavoidable.

Drawing both on a thorough search of the literature and on practical experience, Professor Rothman presents in this volume the action guidelines which must be followed if effective program development is to be achieved. It does not matter whether the reader completely agrees that these are the correct guidelines or would rather follow a somewhat different mix. (I, personally, would pay more attention to the role of power and its proper use.) The main achievement is that we have before us a very necessary set of guidelines; that these are systematic and encompassing—not sporadic or anecdotal; and that they are pitched at the proper level of abstraction—dealing with concrete systems rather than "functions" or "pattern variables."

We must take it from here—either to improve social programs as we heed these guidelines, or to further develop them as we work with them. In either case, we are all in Professor Rothman's debt for having set us on the road to social development—and for having launched the voyage with his systematic volume.

AMITAI ETZIONI

Columbia University
and Director, Center for Policy Research

Acknowledgements

Social R&D is a complex human enterprise that requires the collective skills and competencies of many hands and heads. The work of the Community Intervention Project, which forms the main experiential base for this book, spanned more than a ten year time period and was divided into three different phases involving different objectives and tasks.

Over that time, three individuals stand out for their critical roles in implementing the project and achieving its objectives. Joseph G. Teresa served as director of research operations during the middle or "development" phase of CIP and as assistant director during the later diffusion phase. His contributions to methodological issues in social R&D were invaluable, particularly regarding strategies of statistical treatment and data analysis generally. He also played a leading role in developing various project instruments, and the protocols and procedures associated with them. Dr. Teresa's influence is felt especially in Chapters 6–10 and in Part IV. He was a co-author of the project Technical Report, DEVELOPING EFFECTIVE STRATEGIES FOR SOCIAL INTERVENTION: A RESEARCH AND DEVELOPMENT METHODOLOGY, which emphasized methodological questions. This was drawn upon in writing portions of the aforementioned chapters. He was also a co-author of the project handbook which is used illustratively in Chapter 9.

John L. Erlich was director of field operations during the development phase of the project. His sensitivity and skill in working with practitioners based in community agencies was a crucial factor in permitting the action-research design to be implemented successfully in the field. Mr. Erlich also participated actively in developing many of the procedures and instruments described in Part IV, and in introducing them into the field situation. His unique contributions are evidenced in the practitioners' handbook and manual that were produced of which he is a co-author, and which are used illustratively in Chapter 9. His work implicates chapters concerned with field-related matters in development, particularly portions of Chapters 6, 7 and 8. He, too, is a co-author of the Technical Report which was a resource for the preparation of those chapters.

Gershom Clark Morningstar was editorial consultant and editor through the diffusion phase of the project and into the summing-up period. His proficiency and sophistication as a practitioner of communication has been felt in varied project publications. He has brought clarity, coherence and style to unruly subject matter and helped shape effective communications addressed to multiple audiences of practitioners, researchers and applied social scientists. His most thorough-going work is embodied in this book and in the Technical Report. His identification with the concepts involved in this book and his dedication to the task of helping to convey them to others has been out of the ordinary.

Other individuals who may be singled out for notable aid during different project phases are indicated below:

RETRIEVAL AND CONVERSION PHASE: Marsha Kahn was the first staff member and her splendid back-up helped me get the project started during my first sabbatical leave. Lou Ferman was kind enough to provide seed money to an uncertain venture. Jack Weiner of NIMH came through with more long-range support. Joseph Katan, Lynne Morris and Celeste Sturdevant helped oversee a small army of reviewers of research studies. Chuck Chomet began a long-standing association with the project, initially as a study reviewer. Preliminary reports synthesizing existing bodies of research were prepared by Joseph Katan, Lynne Morris, Harry Finkelstein, David Fram, Ron Beck, and Paul McNeal. These formed the basis for our first publication, PLANNING AND ORGANIZING FOR SOCIAL CHANGE.

DEVELOPMENT PHASE: Joseph Teresa and John Erlich were my main sources of support during this period. We were buoyed additionally by the fine work of Chuck Chomet, Betty Deshler and Angie Current, as field practitioners who implemented action guidelines and as unit supervisors assisting other practitioners. Betty stayed on through the conclusion of the next phase. Basic field tasks were carried out by some thirty practitioners, too numerous to mention, who were situated in field agency settings. Their dedicated "on-the-line" performance generated the raw experience and data of development work. Sue Rasher and Vivian Roeder managed the demanding clerical side of things. Sue Martin's calm and capable perseverance saw us through the formidable data processing operation. Karen Kirkhart was our highly-informed and meticulous evaluation specialist. Judy Hartoog and Alan Gordon performed other important and well-appreciated research tasks. A useful editorial stint was carried out by Jan Eckstein in connection with the manual.

DIFFUSION PHASE: Joseph Teresa served as my assistant director and as acting director for a brief period during a sabbatical leave. Terry Kay, our research assistant, performed remarkably well in many different ways as a young auxiliary staffer. Betty Deshler and Chuck Chomet, together with Alan Gordon and Ralph Paterson led diffusion workshops in urban centers around the country. Betty also conducted sensitive field interviews with agency directors. Vivian Roeder functioned admirably in the many-sided roles of office manager, research assistant and administrative aide to the director. Sue Martin kept the data processing side going. Ben Crane lent editorial assistance in preparation of the handbook, followed in the editorial role by the intrepid Gersh Morningstar.

The School of Social Work at the University of Michigan, with its established interest in the integration of social practice and social science, was a nurturing and stimulating organizational base. Thanks are due to Deans Fedele F. Fauri and Phillip Fellin for seeing value in the venture. Dean Fellin was my earliest collaborator, having aided in the pilot testing of procedures by students in a course we co-taught back in 1967. Also thanks are due to colleagues at the School who helped create an atmosphere conducive to this type of experimental inquiry, in particular, Edwin J. Thomas, Henry J. Meyer, Jesse Gordon, Eugene Litwak and Tony Tripodi. Other important intellectual influences have come from Ronald Havelock, Everett Rogers, Ronald Lippitt and Richard Schutz (from educational R&D).

NIMH gave substantial financial and moral support to this research endeavor over a considerable period of time. Without that commitment this work would not have materialized.

The idea of this generalized form of presentation of the R&D framework in textbook style originated with my Prentice-Hall editor, Edward Stanford. Chris Sherman typed the final manuscript with dispatch and in a flawless fashion.

R&D is a large-scale team activity intertwining multiple intellectual and technical efforts within a creative mileau. The CIP undertaking required and benefited from many devoted professionals and students who lent their talents to fulfill its purposes. To them all let this signify recognition of their vital contributions and gratitude for the good spirit in which they were given.

JACK ROTHMAN

University of Michigan

1

Introduction to Social Research and Development

It is fairly standard practice in the engineering of new spacecraft, weapons, airplanes, even toys, to move systematically from a theoretical concept to a pencil-and-paper design, to a small scale model that is subject to various tests, leading to the production of one or a few full-scale prototypes—all before mass production is authorized. Normally, at each stage modifications are made on the basis of experience gained . . . New government [social] programs need to go through a full and as careful a process of research and development as new technologies.

Amitai Etzioni
Human Behavior, Dec. 1976

In Gilbert and Sullivan's opera *The Yeomen of the Guard,* Jack Point, a strolling jester, poses the following riddle: "Why is a cook's brain-pan like an overwound clock?" The answer, alas, is never forthcoming; and generations of Savoyards have been left to puzzle out on their own some possible solutions to this curious conundrum. No satisfactory answer has ever been found. In the social realm the posing of what appear to be equally insoluble riddles is an ongoing process. We call these riddles "questions concerning the addressing of social problems." Our strategy for solving the social problems we observe around us is both as well understood and as ritualistic as a traditional Japanese *No* drama. The continuance of this strategy lends credence to the saying that the only true lesson of history is that no one ever learns from the lesson of history. In its simplest form this strategy commonly consists of such things as forming a committee, fact finding, legislating more funds and programs, and issuing a report (written or verbal) explaining the failure of the strategy. It has mattered very little in the past that such an approach is costly (and getting more expensive all the time), inefficient, and cruel to those whom we would purport to serve through our social problem solving. We persist with the process, presumably, only because we are familiar with it.

In this book we shall present an alternate approach to human problem solving, and the providing of services to people. Frankly, it is not an approach with which those of a traditional orientation to social science or social programming will be initially comfortable. Failing to examine this approach carefully may lead one to the false impression that what we are recommending is both far too mechanistic and too unrealistic to deal effectively with human needs. Our ultimate retort is that it works.

What we have done, and what we are recommending, is on its face very simple: the application of industrial research and development techniques to problem solving in the human services. We are not the first to see the possibilities of R&D for matters of social concern, nor are we the first to recommend its application to such matters. We have, however, spent the better part of a decade in a sustained action-research examination of the R&D process, adapting the concepts and techniques of industrial R&D to provide tools for human services professionals. We have attempted to apply this formulation in detail and as an integrated whole to real world problem situations. We have concluded that it offers great potential for moving toward a systematic methodology of applied social science.

The method works. In the course of a single program year (September through June) we recorded literally dozens of examples of successful purposive interventions by human service practitioners. We saw task forces established and begin work directed toward criminal justice, education, poverty and unemployment. We saw outreach services provided at the neighborhood level to clients of a health clinic. We saw tenants from isolated public housing sites organize and use bus service to shopping centers. We saw the establishment of a new curriculum, "Poverty: The American Experience," as part of the social studies classes for students from tenth grade through junior college in seven schools in a tri-county area. We saw the development of a planned, structured program of preventive health education for enrollees in an innovative pre-paid health plan. We saw a supplementary enriched education program for school age parents develop, gain administrative approval, and attain funding. We saw the establishment of a rotating library of toys, equipment, books, records, and films for the cooperative use of ten child care facilities. Many of these episodes have been documented in a previously published work (Rothman, Erlich, and Teresa, 1976).

Our studies were specifically designed to promote small scale, proximate implementations for research purposes. Though we were not able to bring about the elimination of poverty or mental illness, the establishment of social equity, or the bursting forth of racial harmony, the catalogue of tangible, goal-specific accomplishments was impressive. Small fragments of much larger social problems were addressed with an encouraging rate of success. There is no reason to believe that wider applications could not have been made.

In this presentation we add our voice to those of such persuasive and important figures as Amitai Etzioni (1976) who, in an article in *Human Behavior* observes:

We have learned from the social programs of the 60's, the campaigns against drug abuse, crime and cancer and the recent drive to develop new energy resources, that in trying to use national resources to overcome our social problems, highly ambitious projects have often been attempted without a sufficient knowledge base or back up. Multibillion-dollar programs, conceived in Washington, D.C. were introduced based on verbal concepts and with little testing or prior research. We cannot afford, in human or financial terms, the expensive wrecks that result. We need fewer but better-researched and developed government programs. (p. 11)

This book starts essentially where many others leave off. It assumes that there is a concrete technology for converting social science research and theory into practical tools that can be put to work by professionals in the human service fields. Further, it projects a model of such technology by drawing upon the highly successful research and development methods used in the physical sciences and in industry for product development purposes. Our assumptions are that the research and development process can be conceptualized in such a way as to be relevant to both the physical and the social sciences, and further that R&D techniques used in such diverse areas as fabricating new commercial products and exploring space can be carried over (selectively and with sensitivity) to assist in attacking problems faced by human service agencies. R&D methods can aid the design of both large scale programs for aggregate client populations and also clinical techniques for the treatment of individuals.

Such a formulation, we believe, constitutes a significant conceptual breakthrough for the application of social science knowledge. We have also developed, through our studies, a methodological counterpart that operationalizes the model in its specifics. The methodology has emerged in the Community Intervention Project through investigations of the research utilization process conducted over the past ten years at the University of Michigan under the sponsorship of the National Institute of Mental Health. The project had the objective of developing research-based strategies and techniques to enhance community problem solving and provide field-tested intervention tools to human service professionals. Procedures for effective research and development in the human services have been concretized, some key operational problems have been identified, and a number of these problems have been solved. This book will present what has been learned about translating theory into practice through this long-term investigation.

This work has proceeded in a series of functionally linked steps. The initial three years (1968–1971) involved a broad search of social science and professional literature. We sought to retrieve research findings pertinent to community and organizational intervention. Based on the empirical research findings, we developed a sizable number of generalizations and sub-generalizations. We then converted each of these to an applied form. This produced a series of "Action Guidelines," or strategies, for use by professional change agents, practitioners, agency administrators, and planners. The full set is given elsewhere (Rothman, 1974).

In our second phase (1971–1974) we implemented a limited number of these Action Guidelines in a field test. In this test we sought to operationalize and to evaluate the guidelines in realistic application settings. In addition, we sought to produce a practitioners' guidebook that would present specific steps, resources, personal and organizational contacts, and so forth (Rothman, Erlich, and Teresa, 1976) needed to implement these guidelines in human service agencies. That book incorporated operational guides for practitioners which were formulated from data drawn from the field studies.

Our next phase (1974–1977) centered upon the development of a revised handbook geared specifically to the needs of mental health personnel (Rothman, Teresa and Erlich, 1978). We also employed, on an experimentally controlled basis, varying approaches to diffusing the products of social R&D throughout the population of potential users (Division of Research Development and Administration, 1977).

Ultimately we aim to consolidate the R&D methods that have emerged from the project experience into an ongoing R&D laboratory attached to a national human services delivery system. The lab will receive problems of the system and employ a crystallized, coordinated research utilization/R&D technology to fabricate solutions quickly and feed these back into the system in the form of operationalized strategies, techniques, and procedures.

The discussions that follow will provide intellectual explication of the process that was followed. What we have outlined should give sufficient understanding of the empirical base underlying the R&D overview emerging in this book. From time to time examples from project work will be introduced for purposes of illustration. In addition, in the concluding chapters a succinct case presentation of the CIP experience will be given as a way of demonstrating how social R&D works in action.

In a companion technical report we have presented the elaborated details of the development methodology (Rothman, Teresa and Erlich, 1977). In that volume we focus on the technical facets of social R&D. In these pages, we emphasize conceptual and theoretical aspects of R&D in terms of its applicability to human services. Those who are interested in a comprehensive technical treatment of the social R&D methodology employed are referred to the companion volume.

All these project publications inform the current work. The first publication (Rothman, 1974) provides the basis for the theoretical overview discussed in chapters 1, 2 and 3, and for the retrieval and conversion/-design concepts presented in chapters 4 and 5. It also constitutes an earlier version of the communication principles and illustrations found in chapter 9. The handbook (Rothman, Teresa and Erlich, 1978) and the manual (Rothman, Erlich and Teresa, 1976) likewise support that chapter. The CIP technical report (Rothman, Teresa and Erlich, 1977) is used and sometimes replicated in portions of chapters 6, 7 and 8. It also forms the basis for much of Part IV in the same way. A forthcoming volume on diffusion by Rothman, Teresa, Kay and Morningstar is reflected in chapter 10. The present book summarizes and synthesizes these previous writings, integrating them within a coherent R&D theoretical framework that has crystallized as the work progressed. There is overlap of ideas and text among these various works as the concepts are interrelated. However, the arrangement and presentation here are new, and a great deal of additional conceptual and illustrative material has been introduced, making this a distinct and comprehensive theoretical statement on social R&D.

We acknowledge that the R&D concept we articulate is not a cure-all for bringing social science to bear on all areas of social concern. At this time it must be considered to be in a highly formative stage. The implementation of social R&D should, however, make for an increment in the utilization of the knowledge of the social sciences in the larger society.

The quotation by Etzioni at the beginning of this chapter conveys an R&D perspective along lines similar to those which we will advance. In recent years there has been an upswing of applied studies in areas of policy research and program evaluation using bits and pieces of the methods proposed here: pilot tests, field experiments, strict program assessment, active dissemination. What remains is the assembly within a unified framework of the diverse steps and methods which are necessary in implementing social change, i.e., knowledge and knowledge building, programming and policy development, program operation and program evaluation, dissemination and utilization. Without such a holistic and integrated process the pieces often fall by the wayside without follow-through or impact. This process constitutes a powerful means of systematically linking research and application.

Typically, researchers and action people berate one another for failures in communication and defects in application. These *ad hominem* accusations result from lack of recognition that there is a basic structural problem—an absence of a linking technology and related instrumentalities connecting social theory with social practice. The vast, complex network of engineering roles and institutions characteristic of the physical sciences is completely missing in the social field. It is as though the theoretical physicist at Princeton were expected to state his propositions and theorems in a form that could immediately be put to use by the factory foreman in Bayonne. The need for a profession and technology of engineering in the social sciences has somehow been overlooked.

Gouldner (1968) has stated the matter in a cogent way:

Traditionally, sociological theory has ministered to the needs of pure or basic research, rather than those of applied research. Indeed, the casual observer may almost think it is a contradiction in terms to speak of a methodology of applied social sciences. Yet the fact is that the applied social sciences are badly in want of such a methodology. For as a result of this deficiency, the very meaning and character of applied social science remains obscure.... (pp. 5–6)

This book reflects a serious, affirmative attempt to shape an applied social science methodology in the spirit of Gouldner's observation. Gouldner entitled his article, "Explorations in Applied Social Science." The time has arrived when we can go beyond reconnaissance of the terrain and establish a settlement. Its name is social R&D. This volume is not the last word on the subject; it is among the first. Some portions are presented at risk in that they fly in the face of conventional social science wisdom and methodology, and are at the same time in an emergent state of conceptual and technical development. We break with the traditional approaches, keyed mostly to basic research and concentrate on building a bridge between theory and practice. In ten years time everything treated here will be able to be stated better. Hopefully, what is offered here will help bring about such advances by stimulating related work by others. We trust that this endeavor will aid materially in putting the creative energies and earnest efforts of a growing army of social scientists and social practitioners to practical and effective use in confronting the serious social and human problems that plague contemporary society.

BIBLIOGRAPHY

DIVISION OF RESEARCH DEVELOPMENT and ADMINISTRATION, University of Michigan, "The Community Intervention Project," *Research News*, 27, no. 6 (June 1977), 17–22.

ETZIONI, AMITAI, "An Earth-NASA: The Agency for Domestic Policy Development," *Human Behavior*, December 1976.

GOULDNER, ALVIN W., "Explorations in Applied Social Science," in *Applied Sociology*, A. W. Gouldner and S. M. Miller, eds., New York: The Free Press, 1965.

ROTHMAN, JACK, *Planning and Organizing for Social Change: Action Guidelines from Social Science Research*. New York: Columbia University Press, 1974.

ROTHMAN, JACK, JOHN L. ERLICH and JOSEPH G. TERESA, *Promoting Innovation and Change in Organizations and Communities: A Planning Manual*. New York: John Wiley and Sons, 1976.

ROTHMAN, JACK, JOSEPH G. TERESA and JOHN L. ERLICH, *Developing Effective Strategies of Social Intervention: A Research and Development Methodology*. PB–272454 TR-1-RD, National Technical Information Service, Springfield, Virginia, 1977.

ROTHMAN, JACK, JOSEPH G. TERESA and JOHN L. ERLICH, *Fostering Participation and Innovation: Handbook for Human Service Professionals*. Itasca, Illinois: F. E. Peacock Publishers, Inc., 1978. (Formerly *Mastering Systems Intervention Skills*, a publication of the Community Intervention Project, University of Michigan, Ann Arbor, Michigan.)

part one

AN OVERVIEW OF RESEARCH & DEVELOPMENT

2

A Research and Development Model for the Human Services

ENGINEERING—The art and science concerned with the practical application of scientific knowledge, as in the design, construction and operation of roads, bridges . . . communications systems, etc.

Standard College Dictionary

Engineering is the learned profession in which . . . knowledge . . . is applied . . . to utilize economically the materials and forces of nature for the progressive well-being of mankind.

Engineers' Council
for Professional Development

Quoting definitions of engineering as a process and a profession may seem an unusual way of setting out in a book intended for those whose interests lie in the world of human service practice, administration, or academic research; but this is in many ways an unusual book. The chapters and pages that follow enter a new intellectual realm for many readers. In this book we intend to appropriate the methods of research and development associated with the physical sciences and industry for systematic application to the solution of social and human problems.

As you proceed from idea to idea, from illustration to illustration, you will encounter a world relatively unknown to social scientists. It is a world in which the snares and pitfalls are many. Familiar terms will, on occasion, be used in unfamiliar ways. Practitioners and administrators with an indifference toward research, as well as researchers with an indifference toward practice will all be required to suspend their prejudices. In this presentation both groups will be on equal ground: an unfamiliar land that lies between them.

Engineers would be most comfortable with what we will discuss because much of our work has been extrapolated from their professional tradition. This is not, however, a book for engineers. It is for those with a social science perspective. This is a book intended ultimately to benefit those in social professions, be they policy makers, administrators, frontline practitioners, or educators, who normally do not enjoy the luxury of precision available to those working with mathematics, mechanics, and elegant physical laws.

The gap between practice and basic research in the social sciences creates a disquieting tension from which those in the natural sciences and industry are relatively free. That freedom arises not only because the natural sciences are more precise, but also because mechanisms exist in natural science for bridging the research-practice gap. Principal among these mechanisms is the research and development methodology.

The lack of comparable linking mechanisms in the social sciences has served to limit the impact of basic social science research on human service practice. To be sure, an occasional research finding has managed to filter through from the theoretical to the operational realm. For the most part, however, practitioners have not enjoyed the fruits of research to the same degree industry has benefited from research in the physical sciences.

The time has clearly come for building an effective bridge between social research and social practice. The needs of the practitioner and the policy maker have become increasingly obvious. At the same time, we believe, the potential resources of the accumulated body of social science research have become increasingly rich. Some means is needed to join the two.

In this chapter we will assist the reader in developing an R&D perspective and gaining insight into the basic characteristics of the R&D process. We will follow this with a presentation and elaboration of a specific R&D model which we have developed for the human services.

A RESEARCH AND DEVELOPMENT PERSPECTIVE[1]

R&D has, historically, been thought to be the particular tool of the physical sciences. Its applications to industrial product development, aerospace, and military technology are well known. It is safe to say that practically all industries of the world are based to a greater or lesser extent on scientific research and the application of science. R&D in industry is, in fact, essential to continued growth and economic good health. Industries that neglect an R&D effort generally find themselves at a disadvantage in our economic system. Indeed, there appears to be a high correlation between the economic strength of an American company and the amount it spends on R&D efforts. This correlation was demonstrated by Dr. Karl Compton at the time he was president of the Massachusetts Institute of Technology (*The Book of Popular Science*, 1963, p. 88).

There is a lesson in this correlation that should not be lost on those of us in the social sciences. Industry's experience demonstrates that there is value in R&D. The unit-standard of value will be different, of course, for the social sciences. It is our belief, however, that the effectiveness and contribution of human service practitioners will be enhanced through tools derivable through an orderly and testable process from existing social science knowledge.

Some tentative efforts have been made to apply R&D concepts in the field of education (Baker and Schutz, 1971), in the manpower field (National Academy of Sciences, 1974), in vocational rehabilitation (Research Utilization in Rehabilitation, 1975), in health care planning (Flook and Sanazaro, 1973) and in mental health (Urban, 1976). Some related social work applications are discusssed later (p. 30). Yet the broad implementation of this methodology to the human services is still in a primitive state.

Historically, as one National Science Foundation study pointed out nearly a decade ago (National Science Foundation, 1968), only a tiny fraction of the funds set aside by the federal government for R&D work has filtered through to the social sciences. The vast majority has gone to the physical sciences and to industry. Recent NSF data indicate that growth in funding through 1977 has been concentrated primarily in defense and

---

[1]Adopted with permission from an earlier version in Jack Rothman, *Planning and Organizing for Social Change: Action Principles from Social Science Research*, New York: Columbia University Press, 1974, Chapter 11. This also appears in abbreviated form in the CIP technical report, *Developing Effective Strategies for Social Intervention: A Research and Development Methodology*, PB-272/454 TR-1-RD, National Technical Information Service, Springfield, Virginia, Chapter 1.

13

energy (National Science Foundation, 1977). In part this may be explained by tangibility of results. The end result of the physical scientist's work is often a highly concrete product: a bomb, a rocket, a vehicle, a machine. The social scientist is more frequently concerned with bringing about an intangible process: a better form of human interaction, a heightened awareness of something, a change in attitudes.

While the amount of money allocated to research and development work in the social sciences has been small, it is also true that it has been extremely difficult in the past to construct highly persuasive arguments for increasing the social science share of the federal "pie." The body of potentially useful social science knowledge gathered by researchers over the years is vast and rapidly expanding. But since that potential has been poorly and haltingly tapped by human service policy makers and practitioners, practical-minded politicians have not seen any compelling reason to assist in adding to that body of knowledge or to its application. Furthermore, the nature of the responsibilities of human services professionals is such that, as a practical matter, they simply do not have the time or opportunity to search the knowledge pool for that which would be useful to them or to make systematic application of what is there. Swift, easy and efficient access to knowledge in a useable form has heretofore not been available to them.

The basic researcher in social science and the human services professional are separated by a common need: the need for effective utilization of social science knowledge. That separation has not been without its consequences. The practitioner waits impatiently for the researcher to provide information in a practical form. The researcher offers abstract information through journals, monographs, books, scientific papers—written in highly technical language—delivered at conventions, and so forth, and is often puzzled and irritated that the practitioner does not take advantage of what is offered.

Social scientists view practitioners as placing low value on intellectuality and high value on action or change for its own sake. Instead of orderly, systematic examination of issues that requires time and scholarly objectivity, practitioners are seen to come to hasty conclusions and engage in actions not supported by adequate data. Practitioners, in the social scientist's view, are uninterested in self-criticism and offended by outside criticism. They seem to manifest a distrust and fear of research. This is related also to a narrow professionalism, which can result in such intense engagement in the specifics of a given problem situation that generalization on a more abstract basis cannot be carried over from one context to another. Social scientists also resent the smugness of the practitioner who feels that only *he* understands worldly problems or real people because of his direct, everyday engagement. In addition, the social scientists maintain that it is not theirs but the practitioners' responsibility to draw implications for policy and action from research.

Clearly, the social scientist's perception of the practitioner is distorted. There is an equal distortion, however, in the practitioner's view of the social scientist.

Practitioners see social scientists as engaged in studies of low social relevance. The subject matter areas are largely asocial, trivial or esoteric, abstract, and reflect narrow scientism rather than humanistic concern. Quite often, if there is a social value orientation expressed in the social scientist's work, it is one of conservatism. The whole systems theory approach, for example, is indicative in the practitioner's view of this static orientation. Social scientists are seen as avoiding the policy implications of their work, and their failure to relate the outcome of the research efforts to important social issues is perceived by the practitioner as stemming from arrogance or a lack of compassion. There is also a kind of compromised intellectual integrity in the bending of research pursuits to such exigencies of the moment as the availability of federal or foundation grants, or toward subject areas that will yield the largest payoffs in dollars and professional prestige.

The social scientists' preoccupation with methodological "gimmickry" and its attendant overinflated jargon, in the eyes of the practitioner, serve only to alienate those who seriously wish to draw on social science knowledge. Social science writings are viewed as overly vague about conclusions that can be reached. The practitioner is interested in definite answers to specific questions; instead, he believes, he finds inconclusive generalities about broad theoretical matters in the writings of social scientists.

It is obvious that different styles and modes of thinking divide the researcher and practitioner, making communication difficult and the use of each other's contributions and products problematic. The social distance between them—characterized by mistrust, differing outlooks, and ostensibly contrasting goals—is formidable. In the past this has inhibited full communication between the social scientist and the social practitioner.

Perhaps the fundamental difference between the two groups is one of function. The social scientist has the primary function of *comprehending the world:* producing knowledge that permits him and others to understand aspects of it better. The practitioner has the key function of *changing the world* (or, more specifically, parts thereof): producing material effects that permit clients, organizations, or communities to behave more advantageously in terms of specific desired outcomes.

R&D AS A RECONCILIATION AND LINKING PROCESS

The situation may be analyzed through an analogy to a lumbering operation. The social science researchers have gone into the forest of knowledge, felled many a good and sturdy tree, and displayed the fruits of their good work to one another. A few enterprising, application-minded lumberjacks have dragged some logs to the river and shoved them off downstream ("diffusion," they call it). Somewhere downriver the practitioners are manning the construction companies. They manage somehow to piece together a few makeshift buildings with what they can find that has drifted down the stream, but on the whole they are sorely lacking in lumber in the various sizes and forms they need to do their work properly. The problem is that somehow we have forgotten to build the mill to turn the logs into lumber in all its useable forms. The logs continue to pile up at one end of the system while the construction companies continue to make do at the other end.

To carry this analogy one step further, there has been governmental and foundation support for the logging operation. There has also been some support for the construction companies. There has been almost nothing, however, for the planning and running of a mill.

In our view the social science R&D methodology is that mill. Fundamentally, R&D is a systematic process for bridging the gap between research and application. It permits the conversion of scientific principles into particular tools and procedures for dealing with real world problems. Brooks (1965) states the matter simply in the form of a query:

. . . how to use the knowledge which has been gathered primarily for its own sake —fundamental research. How is this knowledge to be considered, summarized, repackaged, and interpreted for use, and how is it to be communicated to those responsible for action—the decision-makers, the technological innovators, the service professionals, and the students? (p. 126)

Schutz (1970) in his succinct definition, concentrates on "the gap between scientific knowledge and user practices" (p. 29).

It has been suggested that in order to bridge the gap a series of organizational structures, linking functions, and professional sub-specialties are required. The experience of the Bell Laboratories, as reported by Guba (1968) illustrates this aspect of the R&D process:

AT&T in its wisdom has interposed a vast organization between the knowledge producers and the ultimate consumers. This system, known as Western Electric, has the unique mission of making the applications and producing the ultimate devices which the various Bell systems will install and use. Western Electric has its own coterie of engineers, who are themselves divided into specialties. Some of their personnel are concerned with developing prototype applications; others with testing these out and debugging them. Still others are concerned with designing these applications in ways that will make their production feasible and economical. And finally, of course, there are productive specialists who actually turn out the devices that will be installed and used by the Bell Telephone companies. (pp. 39–40)

Guba points to the absence of corresponding linkers and conversion mechanisms in the social fields. This results in blockages and inefficiencies in knowledge utilization. But this defect goes unrecognized within the professional structure itself. Instead, personnel tend to "write-off the research-practice gap as stemming from the uncooperativeness of the researchers or the laziness and ignorance of the practitioners, or both" (p. 40). The need for linkage is reinforced by Carter (1968):

In evaluating contemporary problems in education and the social area generally, it seems there is a wide separation between the practitioners in these fields and those engaged in research in our academic institutions. We do not have the middleman who, as in the case of the engineer, is devoted to solving specific problems . . . Such people are lacking in the education and social fields. (p. 17)

Yet another specialist, Boyan (1968), notes that we have failed utterly to notice the absence of R&D mill machinery:

. . . most observers have restricted themselves to an analysis of variability in factors which have been present. Only a few observers have asked whether essential elements have been missing . . . in the total process of converting knowledge into practice. (p. 22)

How may that fully articulated process be described?

THE RESEARCH AND DEVELOPMENT PROCESS

There are literally thousands of organizations, businesses, and governmental agencies that proclaim their association directly or indirectly with research and development. Beginning in the early 1950's, "R&D" like the terms "systems analysis" and "aerospace," took on a special measure of respectability and prestige with industrial, governmental, and scientific agencies and organizations. It was almost as though the integration of such terms into the corporate structure conferred a mystical power on a company that led directly to the federal grant trough. The ranks of quasiscientific and pseudoscientific companies looking for grant money burgeoned. This may have been carried to its logical and absurd conclusion in the play, *Go, Baby, Go!,* wherein Kunkel Tool & Die transformed itself into the Universal Aerospace Systems Research and Development Corporation.

The term "research and development" was carelessly and imprecisely (but profitably) used. This carelessness and imprecision has over the years worked its way into common parlance to the point where today very few members of the lay public fully understand and appreciate the process. This has prompted such specialists as Roberts (1967) to state that too often R&D, even for those engaged professionally in the field, "is based largely on facts and folklore, rather than on principles derived from facts." He deplores "the lack of true understanding of its processes, and a lack of an organized educational base for its managers" (p. 5). Schutz (1970) likewise tells us that individuals in the technical fields that have thus far dominated R&D work have not been predisposed to conceptualize the methodological components of their own activities:

[They] thus have given only modest attention to packaging their macro-strategies in a form readily cognizant to persons within the field or transferable to other fields such as education . . . It is the methodology not the men of aerospace, architecture, business, engineering, and pharmacy that renders these fields ripe for contributing to the development in education [and the human services]. (p. 6)

Schutz urges his readers to identify commonalities in intellectual endeavors across the fields he enumerates. That there are such commonalities is indicated by the fact that it is possible to generalize conceptually basic features of the R&D process, regardless of the particular field in which it is employed.

A useful point of departure in conceptualizing R&D is the set of definitions propounded by the National Science Foundation and employed in its statistical surveys of the field (National Science Foundation, 1966). NSF lays out three relevant areas: *basic research, applied research* (which we shall call conversion/design for the sake of clarity and to reduce overlap with other definitions), and *development.* The definitions are as follows:

Basic Research:

Basic research is primarily motivated by the desire to pursue knowledge for its own sake. Such work is free from the need to meet immediate objectives and is undertaken to increase understanding of natural laws. Wide applications often come from gains in basic knowledge, or scientific concepts are extended or revised with far reaching effects. (p. 11)

Applied Research or Conversion/Design:

. . . is carried out with practical applications in mind and may . . . be concerned with "translating" existing knowledge into such applications . . . It differs from basic research in that it seeks to show or indicate the means in which the first pilot steps may be taken to reduce an abstract idea to a useful purpose. [It] serves to further specific agency missions, frequently as a forerunner to development. (p. 15)

The sense of applied research as *design,* as we will emphasize in this presentation, is brought out by Holt (1975) who defines applied research as follows:

The systematic creation and application of knowledge through the organized effort of people working toward a specific (practical) objective . . . The purpose of (this step) is to find a solution in principle (design concept) for a new or improved product, process, or material. (p. II/61)

This phase attempts essentially to derive goal oriented application concepts from research knowledge. It seeks to convert knowledge from the descriptive to the prescriptive form and to design more specific implementation potentials.

The third of the NSF definitions is:

Development:

In development the findings and understanding derived from research are directed toward the production of useful materials, devices, systems, or methods; such work includes design and improvement of prototypes and processes. Development activities, which are dependent upon research results, usually involve engineering and testing to advance a component, product, or process to the point where it meets a specific functional or economic requirements; . . . development is directed to very specific and generally predictable ends. (p. 19)

The product of development, then, is something that is user-ready. It has a purpose that is well defined, and it functions, ideally, in such a way as to fulfill that purpose in a practical, cost-effective manner.

Havelock (1968), in a major and widely recognized study of the use of social science knowledge, develops a slightly different model in which he designates the *research, development,* and *diffusion* perspective. He thus introduces an additional key element to research and development: namely, *diffusion.* If a new product or tool or process is to be useful, it needs to be disseminated (marketed/promoted) to potential users and put into active operation by them. A product and its diffusion may be directed toward a general population; e.g., consumers, listeners, readers, and so forth. Alternatively, they may be aimed at a specialized, intermediary professional population; e.g., physicians, broadcasting engineers, or human service practitioners, and later directed through them toward broader target systems: clients or constituents, for example. By way of illustration, one visualizes the development of new drug products for direct purchase and use by consumers or for transmission through family doctors in their practice. For the purposes of our own explorations of social R&D, we elected to place emphasis on the development of intervention strategies for use by intermediary professionals as a way of seeking to make practice more effective. The same R&D methods can and should be addressed alternatively to ultimate users; clients or patients.

When Havelock speaks of diffusion, he uses such terms as *dissemination, distribution, installation, adoption,* and target systems *integration.* He also defines two specialized roles in the diffusion: *sender* and *adopter.* He sees the *sender* as engaging in activities such as *promoting, informing-telling,* and *demonstrating-showing.* He views the *adopter* as engaging in collateral activities such as *awareness, evaluation,* and *installation.* (pp. 10:50–54)

Based on Havelock's concepts, then, we now incorporate a fourth definition into the basic formulation of R&D:

Diffusion:

Once knowledge has passed through this development phase, it is ready to be mass produced and diffused to all members of society for whom it might be useful. (p. 2:42)

These, then, may be considered the basic phases of all research and development endeavor:

Basic Research
Conversion/Design (or Applied Research)
Development
Diffusion

Such a four-fold view finds support from other sources. Ames (1951), for example, suggests an analogous model based on an analysis rooted in economics and related to new industrial operations. The suggested *outputs* of each of Ames' *stages* are instructive:

STAGES:	OUTPUTS:
Basic Research	Laboratory results, hypotheses and theories, formulas, research papers
Inventive Work	Working models, sketches, inventions,
[Design]	patents
Development Work	Blueprints, specifications, samples, patents
New-Type Plants and Processes [Diffusion]	Diffusion and establishment of new-type factories

The phases in R&D are not precise, either in definition or with regard to the functions involved. Ansoff (1961) makes this quite clear:

The fact that the *degree* of uncertainty can vary over a wide spectrum gives rise to a major difficulty in defining clear-cut separation between applied research and activities which precede and follow it. At one extreme, it is not uncommon to find applied research proposals whose outcome is so uncertain as to require, in fact, creation of new knowledge and which should, therefore, be recognized as basic research . . .

It is not infrequent to find a product development project mistakenly classified as applied research. As in the previous case, such confusion can result in much misplaced effort and in even further-reaching consequences. (p. 469)

Based on the Bell Laboratory experiences, Kelly (1950) suggests a somewhat broader scheme than our own four-fold formulation. The first two stages are similar to ours: *basic research* and *applied research.* He divides *development,* however, into what might be viewed as two substages: *development* and *design* and *engineering for manufacture.* The distinction between these two substages is based on what people in the field often refer to as *front end* (or "early") development and *back end* (or "advanced") development. The *front end* is the initial phase that overlaps and blends with our notion of *design.* The *back end* is the late phase that may have a close interplay with fabricating and diffusion. Kelly includes in *diffusion* such activities as manufacturing, distribution and installation. He makes the additional point that it may be useful for different stages to have some degree of autonomy. To the degree that this is accomplished, however, he recommends strong cross-linking procedures.

In many ways *development* is the most complex and multidimensional of the stages. For this reason its composition has been described in greater detail by a number of writers. Schutz (1970), for example, talks of *exploratory development, advanced development* and *operating program development.* The staff of the Far West Laboratory for Educational Research and Development drew from a number of their different project experiences to construct what they consider a general pattern for the development process (1973). That general pattern is:

Develop a Preliminary Form of the Product

Do Preliminary Field Testing

Product Revision

Main Field Testing

Operational Product Revision

Operational Field Testing

According to the Far West Laboratory group, these activities are followed by a set of tasks in the diffusion stage, which include preparations for dissemination, completion of a final report on the field test evaluation, and implementation of new products and techniques in widespread target settings. This pattern of recurring cycles of testing-evaluation-development-testing is basic to R&D.

Guba (1968) attempts to convey a sense of development through the use of such terms as *depict, invent, fabricate,* and *test.* These turn out to be handy and useful code words for characterizing developmental tasks.

A RESEARCH UTILIZATION R&D MODEL[1]

Entering the world of social R&D, one feels a bit like Dorothy stepping out of her house and into the Land of Oz. It is a country of considerable interest and excitement, but one that is almost totally unfamiliar. And, like Dorothy, those of us in social R&D are also much in need of a yellow brick road.

As part of our endeavor toward the understanding and application of research and development in the social sciences, we have formulated a working model of what we view as the basic flow of activity in social R&D. It is largely an empirical, inductive formulation. It grew out of the experience of the Community Intervention Project as we attempted to move between existing basic research findings and practical intervention tools. We believe it summarizes and organizes in an effective way the concepts we have been discussing thus far. Whether what we have built is the best yellow brick road remains to be seen. It is, however, one avenue we have found useful.

Our model is composed of six material stages linked by five operational steps. The model is diagrammed in Figure 2-1. At the bottom of the model we have indicated the four basic phases of R&D to demonstrate how the model interfaces with the various concepts and definitions of research and development found in the literature.

The model starts with a social goal or a social problem that is of interest to some group or organization concerned with social welfare or the delivery of human services. The existing body of empirical social science knowledge is examined as a source of possible solutions for the social problem or as a source of possible direction toward achieving the social goal. The model moves along a continuum to wide application by human service professionals in the field. Each of the five operational steps, located within the arrows to indicate their more active function, results in a material stage that is a landmark product. Such products might be experience, data, devices, operational guides, training manuals, etc. Each material stage with its products, represented by the boxes in our model, leads in turn to the next operation and is the basis for that operation. In the rather detailed narrative description of each Material Stage and Operational Step that follows, it will help to refer back to Figure 2-1. In this way you will be able to keep in mind where each of the various components fits in the larger design.

[1]For some of the details within the model I am grateful to Professor Jesse Gordon.

SCHEMATIC MODEL OF RESEARCH UTILIZATION–R & D PROCESS

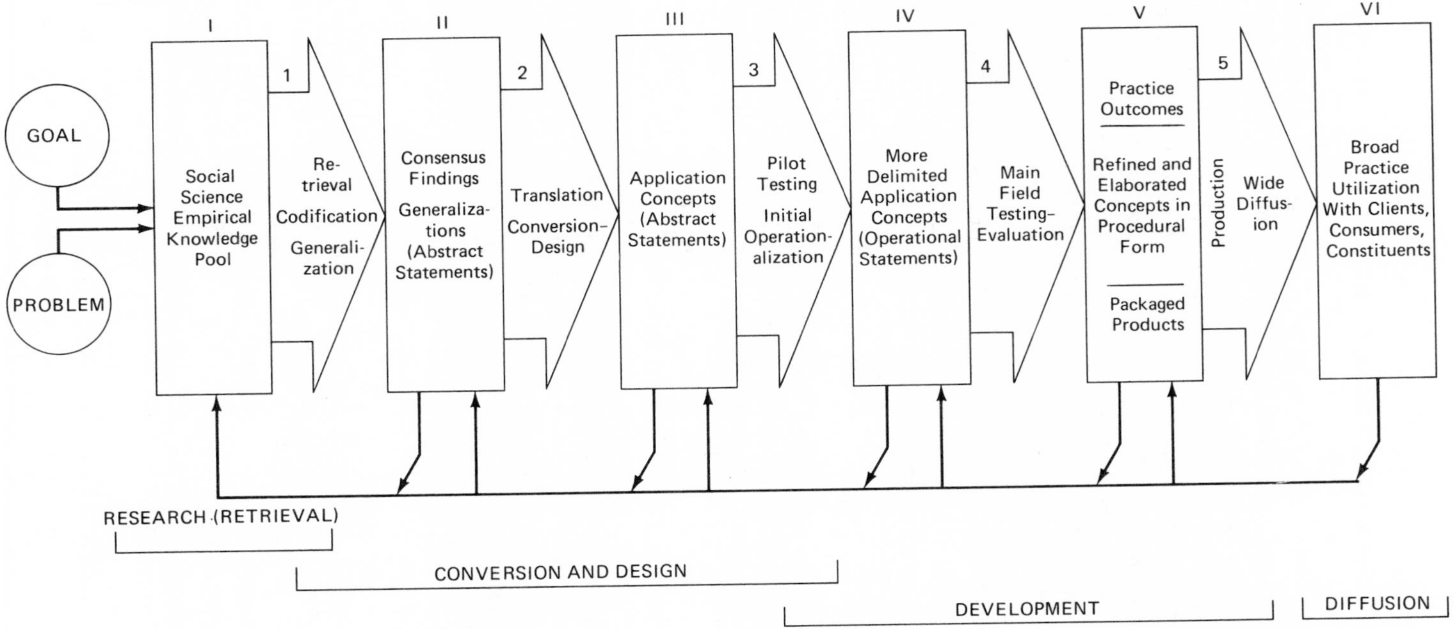

Figure 2–1

Material Stage I: Basic Pool of Social Science Research Knowledge

This is the reservoir of existing empirical research data available in the formal literature of the disciplines and professions. It also includes less formal sources, such as agency reports, dissertations, and project memoranda. Some of this material stands independently. Some is referenced in index books or computerized data banks of various types. Other material is referenced and abstracted in index books or computerized data systems. Which other bodies of literature and data are selected for scrutiny depends on the nature of the social goals and/or problems that are being addressed through the social R&D effort.

Operational Step 1: Retrieval, Codification, Generalization

1. This step requires the location of pertinent research data sources in terms of presenting practice problems or objectives. Both primary and secondary sources can be used, including the use of stored information pools.
2. Those studies bearing on the problem or issue at hand must be selected from the source pool. Here one encounters problems of nomenclature, including the appropriate selection of descriptors. Problems of traversing the disparate taxonomies of knowledge in social science and social practice present themselves. Practice perspectives ordinarily need to be transplanted into typical scientific linguistic analogs in order for scientific sources to be exploited and later reconverted.
3. Data must be assessed for reliability, validity and applicability.
4. Data must be codified into suitable categories of knowledge.
5. Work must be done toward discovering consensus findings or recognized uniformities within the selected data.
6. Work sometimes involves formulating generalizations and propositions from consensus findings.

Material Stage II: Consensus Findings, Generalizations, Propositions

As the previous description of tasks implies, the product here is one or more generalizations based on certain accepted scientific laws or principles, or on the convergence of the findings of a number of disparate research studies. Where numerous studies in varying circumstances, using different subjects and methodologies, are in substantial agreement, one can have a greater degree of confidence in the validity of these generalizations. This is particularly true when there are few, if any, findings with counterconclusions.

The resulting generalizations will likely be abstract as a result of their tendency to synthesize diverse studies and to arrive at uniformities. They will also tend to describe social phenomena rather than prescribe methods of intervention. This is not surprising, since most social science research deals with describing and understanding the social world rather than changing it.

Consensus findings may be descriptive of a simple, empirical regularity, or they may be propositional in describing a constant relationship among two or more variables.

Operational Step 2: Conversion and Design—Formulating Application Concepts

The essential task here is cognitive application.

1. Translations now need to be made from scientific language back to language more suitable to the categories of normal usage in applied situations.

2. Conversion from descriptive to prescriptive formulation may entail making an "inferential leap" across the gap between generalizations and application concepts. A conversion construct entails consideration of the size of the inferential leap and the direction of application (toward achieving organizational stabilization or organizational change, for example).

3. "Reality" dimensions in designing implementation—such as feasibility, or implementability, of a given application, cost, limiting conditions and qualifiers that restrict or channel use—may be weighed at this time.

Material Stage III: Application Concepts

These are the outputs of the translation-conversion-design process. The prescriptive formulations we call application concepts are representative of products in this stage. These prescriptive statements, while now of more immediate relevance to practitioners, are derived from broad consensus generalizations. They tend also to be constituted in rather abstract terms and in cognitive form. At this level, the more concrete implementation of application principles is left to the creative efforts of practitioners unless the utilization process is carried forward into the next stages. In industrial R&D, a fairly tight, mathematically supported design may have been produced. Its workability, impact and economical feasibility remain in question.

Operational Step 3: Initial Operationalization, Pilot Testing

Operationalization involves more finite specification of locations, contexts, materials, resources, and behaviors for implementation. Two examples are the type of agency setting and the types of people to whom the application pertains. All empirical referents of the application concept must be identified and worked with.

Operationalization may be partially a cognitive-perceptual task, but it must include actual experimental implementation, or engineering, including the conducting of a pilot test in the intended implementation setting, or with the materials, processes and actors of that setting. Pilot work is necessary in order to determine whether the application concept will work under real conditions and whether prototypes and models of implementation can be realized. In this step the practitioner functions in a front end social engineering role.

Material Stage IV: Application Concepts in Delimited Form

Initial operationalization results in a much more detailed, narrowed, practical exposition of application concepts. It may involve greater concretization of each of what have been identified as the key elements contained in the application concept. In this form application may be discussed in mental health centers, for example, as compared to city-planning agencies; large cities as compared to small cities; agencies with sizable budgets as compared to those with limited funding; and so on. Specific actors, procedures, or resources may be indicated. Initial working models or prototypes result from this early pilot work in fabricating operational forms of the application concept. Such an operationalized statement of implementation gives a practitioner a great deal more direction and some confidence in the workability of the application formulation.

Operational Step 4: Fuller Implementation—Main Field Testing

1. This step assumes the availability of a preliminary procedural manual, working documents, audio-visual materials, etc. that can be put in the hands of "development engineers." These social engineers are expected to fabricate a detailed and durable operational form of the application concept. An expanded number of experiences and units are studied as compared to the pilot stage.

2. The R&D main field study seeks to modify, expand, and more clearly operationalize the application concept and to assess its effectiveness with respect to intended outcomes with a substantial number of clients, consumers, etc. Performance testing through careful evaluation of outcomes is especially important. Fairly firm specifications of the conditions, constraints, and procedures of application can be delineated. This step incorporates elements of evaluative research but places it in a more product oriented R&D context. This form of reality testing, like that at each stage, may yield feedback that modifies the application concept or even the basic theory that generated it.

3. Field tasks may include selection of sites or users, recruitment and training of a social engineering staff, incentives for use, entry problems, clarification of the role of field practitioners and their relationship to the role of applied researchers, etc.

4. Research tasks include designing a suitable methodology for study and development of instruments; monitoring; adjustment for special problems such as practitioner-engineer resistance or Hawthorne effects; evaluation of effectiveness; and the development of criteria for rejecting, modifying, or authenticating the application concept.

Material Stage V: Practice and Policy Outcomes; Tested, and Refined Application Concepts; Diffusion Media

At this stage several useful products should have been brought into being. In the first place, it is now possible to determine the impact of the application concept when implemented by a cross section of actual ultimate users. This type of assessment may be carried through by means of formal research procedures, or less formal observational-assessment approaches. Ordinarily, the product of main field testing is given an additional operational field test with potential users in order to remove remaining "bugs" and to complete "fine tuning" of the tool, process or product. It also may indicate problems and possibilities to be taken into account in the subsequent diffusion stage.

Finally, based on the field experience, diffusion materials incorporating results of the field work—practitioner manuals and/or handbooks, audiotapes, videotapes, documents, charts, etc.—may be crystallized.

The feedback between Stage V and Stage IV may be heavy and recurrent. There may be a number of cycles of trial, modification, and retrial. The cyclical nature of development is particularly pronounced here.

Operational Step 5: Production and Wide Diffusion

This step includes:

1. The mass reproduction of media incorporating operationalized solution strategies: handbooks, manuals, charts, forms, etc. Production is ordinarily "farmed out" to a printing firm or media house that has the experience and resources to carry out this technical task. It is not a basic social science professional activity. In an expanded version of the R&D model, one might conceive of production as a separate step and stage, as in the area of industrial R&D.

Radnor et al. (1977) discuss this phase as follows: "In the generic sense, the end of the development function is the beginning of the production function—i.e., when a development output is 'user-ready,' it is ready to be produced (it must be noted, of course, that a clear cut separation of development and production does not always exist" (p. 100). These authors indicate that production entails considerations such as absolute costs, available facilities and equipment, cost vs. quality issues, the sequencing of operations and necessary skills to bring forth multiple reproductions of the product.

2. Isolation of a universe of specific practitioners or organizations who are potential target users. This should initially be done at the outset of R&D but needs further specification and reassessment at this time.

3. The determination of the attributes, attitudes, and needs of potential users must be made. This is, essentially, a form of marketing research.

4. Selection of appropriate informational and promotional approaches and further packaging of utilization materials in an attractive, responsive way must be accomplished.

5. Potential users must be reached and motivated. High intensity (personal contact) approaches such as workshops may be used. Alternatively, low intensity (mass communications) approaches such as direct mailings or media advertising may be employed.

6. Functional gatekeepers, opinion leaders, or informal professional networks may be located to use as diffusion channels.

7. Users may need to be provided with initial training and reinforcement.

8. Procedures must be developed for scanning the results of wider application of the product.

Material Stage VI: Broad Practice Use

The end result of the process should be widespread use of the developed application concept in the field. By this time the concept should have withstood testing, and means of effectively communicating its appropriate and detailed implementation to practitioners through operational and procedural guides should have been developed. The eventual beneficiaries are clients, consumers, and constituents in the human service system. Broader experience with clients, involving both method and outcome, should again hypothetically feed back to the entire process, suggesting modifications and refinements for every stage, right back to basic research.

We have, quite understandably, focused this R&D process on the human services practitioner. However, for "practitioner-user" one may read "manager-user," "teacher-user," "politician-user," "labor union organizer-user" or any potential applier of basic social science research converted to an operational form through the social R&D process.

The four basic components of the R&D process synchronize with the R.U. Model in the following way:

Basic research: Stage I, possibly also Step 1 & Stage II.

Conversion & design: (Applied Research) May overlap Step 1 & Stage II. Concentrated in Step 2 & Stage III. May overlap Step 3.

Development: Step 3 through Stage V.

Diffusion: Step 5 & Stage VI.

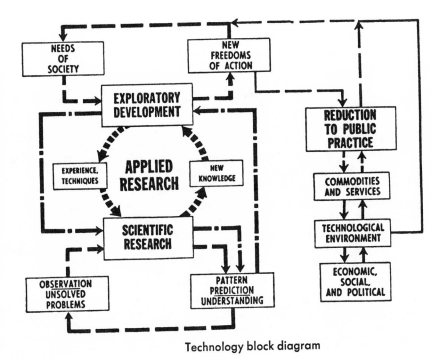

Technology block diagram

Figure 2-2

Reprinted with permission from R. E. Gibson, "A Systems Approach to Research Management," in James R. Bright, ed., *Research, Development and Technological Innovation,* Homewood, Illinois: Richard D. Irwin, Inc., 1964, p. 34.

In the visual presentation of the model (Figure 2-2), we have indicated feedback through the use of the slender arrows among all stages and steps of the research utilization process. The role of feedback in social science research is particularly critical. As Gibson (1964) states:

There are regions of interest in science where it is not possible to make precise observations or accumulate facts under completely controlled conditions. In such cases the system works in a deductive mode through the feedback from "satisfying patterns" to observations ... However, starting from a comprehensive pattern of facts ... it is possible to draw a (reasonable) theoretical picture ... in *sufficient* detail that certain consequences which are susceptible to observation may be deduced. Facts extracted from observations may then be compared with those deduced from theory. The history of the sciences ... shows clearly that as our satisfying patterns grow in depth and breadth, the deductions drawn lead to more and more pertinent and refined observations, and our confidence in them grows accordingly. (pp. 39–40)

Gibson proposes an alternative depiction of the overall R&D process that we present for the purposes of comparison with our own (Figure 2-2).

Gibson's references to the development of working hypotheses from the observation of phenomena and events raises one critical matter in the use of the R&D methodology that may require some clarification lest it lead to some unnecessary confusion later on. The emphasis is on the development, field testing, and diffusion of prescriptive formulations for human service practitioners. This is not hypothesis testing in the traditionally accepted sense of the term. The generalizations upon which application concepts are based have already been established. The process is given over to attempting to achieve a formulation of that concept in an effective operational form if that is possible. Field work involving evaluative performance testing indicates whether and under what circumstances the application concept "works." The main objective is a working operational or procedural guide rather than a scientific truth.

Not all conceptions of R&D take an approach emphasizing stages and components in the type of dynamic formulation represented by our depiction of the R&D process. At least two additional perspectives are to be found. The first views R&D from a systems engineering and scientific management point of view. This perspective emphasizes the bringing to bear of rationality and efficiency in attaining goals within a complex technical task environment (Hall, 1962; Kappel, 1963). Terms such as "organized creative technology" are employed to characterize the approach, and it is seen as achieving improvement in quality, reliability, and uniformity and decreased cost in production operation.

Another posture is that of contributors to the journal *Educational Technology*. Here the stress is on the production of educational media through careful planning and testing with the intended consumer group. The intellectual tradition is that of learning theory or behavior modification and the context is effective, empirically evaluated, instructional design—not necessarily the deliberate conversion of specific substantive scientific knowledge into operational programs and tools. What is carried over and applied in this context is learning theory. Educational R&D follows this format in large measure.

Some readers may question our views about the paucity of existing social R&D activity, suggesting that more along these lines is actually taking place than is being allowed. Part of the difference in perception stems from the very general way in which the term R&D is used, encompassing as it does a wide range of applied social science endeavors, many having an evaluation research character. Few of these evaluation research studies use the full set of integrated steps as is being advocated. Evaluation may or may not involve researchers as integral partners in formulating and carrying out an action program, nor is that action plan necessarily designed explicitly and carefully from past research findings, and it is unlikely to produce a set of field-tested and authenticated operational guides, precisely drawn and use-ready, to aid practitioners in service delivery or practical problem solving. R&D always does all these things because they are its defining criteria. And while R&D incorporates and requires some form of evaluation research, evaluation research by itself does not coincide with or presuppose R&D methodology.

An applied research undertaking that has received considerable attention and is sometimes associated with R&D is the New Jersey Income Maintenance (Negative Income Tax) Experiment. In essence, however, this was a traditional research design carried out in a nontraditional applied field setting. As described by the researchers themselves (Kershaw and Fair, 1976): "It involved the systematic variation of certain economic influences (the 'treatment') on a group of persons as they went about their everyday lives, and a comparison of their resulting behavior with the behavior of another group of persons (the controls) who were similar to the first group in every way except that they did not receive the treatment" (p. 3). The researchers indicate that they were essentially "testing economic hypotheses."

The operational procedures for carrying out the service program, practice techniques and methods, did not become part of the study domain. These were treated as rules within the design that should be handled on a *uniform basis*—"rules had to be standardized to permit the effects of the negative-income-tax treatment to be isolated" (p. 82). In summarizing the study the researchers recognized that these program procedures were an important subject for examination. They state, in recapitulating the experience, "the regulations themselves constitute an important part of the experimental environment, a part that may well interact with the tax rate and guarantee treatments, producing differences in subject response . . ." (p. 94). Without an R&D perspective, the awareness of producing outcomes constituting practice procedures remains by and large a respective insight rather than a basic component of the study plan. This same observation can be made with regard to a host of notable applied studies carried out in recent years: Head Start, Sesame Street and the Electric Company, the Coleman Report on school desegregation, RAND's Experimental Housing Allowance Program, the Urban Institute's study of police patrol methods and VA studies of hospital versus community foster care for psychiatric patients, among others.

Two series of studies reported in the literature geared to yielding practice operational guides are by Fairweather (1967) in the area of community mental health programming and Goldstein (1971) in the area of psychotherapy techniques. Fairweather's "experimental social innovation" approach begins with immersion in a problem situation and the creation of innovative strategies from one's involvement and observations. It does not rely on the retrieval of knowledge from the body of existing research. Its next step employs a set of methods that have many similarities to development, although it leans heavily at the same time on more classic experimental design methods. Goldstein's work follows the retrieval through development phases but omits diffusion. Like Fairweather it is not defined in R&D terms nor does it relate itself to industrial R&D models and methods. Something is lost conceptually and technically in both instances by not taking advantage of a rich body of existing experience in the application of science.

In addition to the studies cited, the field of educational R&D comprises an area, close to the human services field, in which R&D methods have been employed for the purpose of creating new teaching materials. The focus here is specialized and limited relative to general human service practice needs. Of particular interest also are the Research Utilization Laboratories sponsored by the Rehabilitation Services Administration of HEW (Soloff et al., 1975). Recent and emergent practice-oriented research can be found in the work of Thomas (1978, 1979), Briar (1978), and Reid (1978) in the field of social work; none of them, however, use an explicit R&D framework. Thomas' work in "developmental research" coincides materially with the development stage of R&D. A general review of policy and practice-oriented research has been presented by Tripodi (1974), a reading of which generally substantiates our view that R&D is an innovative initiative.

The cynic may discount or set aside an innovative concept; on the contrary, there is an insidious pitfall awaiting the incautious investigator who gets hold of a novel scientific notion. He must be ever on his guard not to become so dazzled by the novelty of an idea that he fails to assess fully its utility. We believe that the application of R&D methodology to problem solving in the human services is, without question, a novel idea. We believe, however, that we have exercised due caution, and we are strongly inclined to concur with Coser (1975):

No doubt, modern methods of research have immeasurably advanced sociological inquiry. Only sociological Luddites would argue that computers be smashed and path diagrams outlawed. What I am concerned with is not the uses but rather the abuses of these instruments of research. They serve us well in certain areas of inquiry, but they can become Frankenstein monsters when they are applied indiscriminately. (p. 692)

But, just as scientific iconoclasm ill becomes sincere seekers after truth, so does adopting the posture of the scientific pharisee, eschewing all that is new simply because it is new. Meaningful contributions to research and practice in the social sciences and the human services come as carefully measured steps forward, tentatively probing the unknown both with proven tools and with some devices less familiar. It is a matter of progressive, forward-leaning balance. We believe our R&D concept reflects such a balance as the conceptual scheme underlying our investigations has shown, and as our elaboration of the context and implications of the R&D method will further demonstrate.

The skeptic may also be troubled by the use of the term "social engineering"—a term we will rely upon heavily in this book. For many in the social sciences, social engineering is an emotionally loaded concept engendering the image of a callous, technocratic approach to areas of social concern. Let it be clear from the start that this is not what we hope to bring about. Our value stance in undertaking this work has been open and specific, as set forth by the project director in the first formal project publication (Rothman, 1974):

I have come to my subject with certain points of view (read biases) that ought perhaps to be made explicit at the outset . . . My social perspective involves a commitment to the elimination of social injustices and economic inequities. This implies working toward a social structure where concepts of the common good or the collective fate of the community are brought into better balance with a professed preoccupation with "individualism." In other words, the public welfare broadly viewed is of higher moment on the scale of human values than is private profit. (pp. 2–3)

We will be using the term social engineering in a deliberate, precise, and consistent manner, rather than in the global way it is often employed. Our usage is conveyed in a common dictionary definition of *engineering:*

The art and science concerned with the practical application of scientific knowledge, as in the design, construction, and operation of roads, bridges . . . communication systems, etc. (*Standard College Dictionary,* Harcourt, Brace and World, 1966).

This accents the idea of converting basic scientific knowledge into a form which can serve useful purposes, which is the core engineering concept and the function undergirding this book. We believe that *social engineering* is identical in this connection to physical engineering, and we look upon it in paraphrase form as:

The art and science concerned with the practical application of social science knowledge, as in the design, construction, and operation of programs, techniques, agency structures, etc.

We further believe that this volume will amplify and illustrate this contention. It is obvious that there is some peril in the use of the term social engineering. It has been used in the past in an extremely loose and varied way. This may tend to contaminate the concrete and delimited meaning we attach to it here.

The purposes of social engineering, as we envision them, are the solution of social problems and the enhancement of the less powerful or less advantaged members of society. It is our hope that social R&D will promote the providing of services to members of the community in a more effective and humane manner. Tools to assist people directly or indirectly toward these ends are viable outgrowths of social R&D.

At the same time, it is true that any new technology (nuclear energy, aerospace flight, new drugs) is, in itself, value-neutral and can be employed by human users for multiple purposes—evil or beneficial, destructive or elevating of human worth. Social technology is no different from physical technology in this respect. Scientists or engineers who invent a new technological method cannot control the way in which it is ultimately carried forward. They can only communicate their intentions and hopes regarding their technology's eventual impact. There is a chance that conveying a philosophical perspective may in some way direct the way the technology is put to work.

Engineering, for some, goes beyond mechanistic neutrality to decidedly negative connotations. Indeed, the dictionary carries this popularly held view of engineering: "to put through or manage by contrivance: to engineer a scheme . . . maneuvering."

There exists the danger that social R&D techniques can be employed in this cynical way, but this need not be inevitable. We have been able to avoid this pitfall in our own program over a decade of work. The chapters that follow will illustrate that in both our goals and our operating procedures, humanistic rather than Machiavellian considerations guided method and relationships. Some specific social results brought about by our social engineering field staff will be indicated in subsequent pages. This should suffice to demonstrate that the method can produce positive social goals when used by professionals with the conviction, discipline, and good sense to proceed in that manner. Indeed, the development of the methods was predicated on the assumption that they would bring about such beneficial outcomes in a more powerful way than existing methods are able to accomplish.

BIBLIOGRAPHY

AMES, EDWARD, "Communications: Research, Invention, Development and Innovation," *American Economic Review*, 51 (June 1951), 370–381.

ANSOFF, H. I., "Evaluation of Applied Research in a Business Firm," *Technological Planning on the Corporate Level,* Proceedings of a conference sponsored by the Associates of the Harvard Business School, September 8–9, 1961, ed. James R. Bright. Cambridge, Mass.: 1961, pp. 208–224.

BAKER, ROBERT L., and RICHARD E. SCHUTZ, *Instructional Product Development.* New York: Von Nostrand Reinhold Co., 1971.

The Book of Popular Science. Vol. 1, New York City: Grolier Press, 1963.

BORG, WALTER R., "The Balance Between Educational Research and Development: A Question of Strategy," *Educational Technology,* 5, no. 7 (July 1969), 5–11.

BOYAN, NORMAN J., "Problems and Issues of Knowledge Production and Utilization," *Knowledge Production and Utilization,* Terry L. Eiddell and Joanne M. Kitchel, eds., University Council for Educational Administration (Columbus, Ohio) and Center for the Advanced Study of Educational Administration (University of Oregon), 2 (1968), 21–37.

BRIAR, SCOTT, "Toward the Integration of Practice and Research," Paper delivered at the National Conference on The Future of Social Work Research, Sponsored by the National Association of Social Workers, San Antonio, Texas, October 15–18, 1978.

BROOKS, HARVEY, "Scientific Concepts and Cultural Change," *Daedalus,* 94, (Winter 1965), 66–83.

CARTER, LAUNOR F., "Knowledge Production and Utilization in Contemporary Organizations," *Knowledge Production and Utilization,* Terry L. Eiddell and Joanne M. Kitchel, eds., University Council for Educational Administration (Columbus, Ohio) and Center for the Advanced Study of Educational Administration (University of Oregon), 1 (1968), 1–20.

COSER, LEWIS, A., "Presidential Address: Two Methods in Search of a Substance," *American Sociological Review,* 40, no. 6 (December 1975), 691–700.

FAIRWEATHER, GEORGE W., *Methods for Experimental Social Innovation.* New York: John Wiley and Sons, 1967.

Far West Laboratory for Educational Research and Development, *A Training Program in Educational Development, Dissemination and Evaluation,* Berkeley, Calif.: Far West Laboratory for Educational Research and Development, March, 1973.

FLOOK, E. EVELYN, and PAUL SANAZARO, *Health Services Research and R&D,* Health Administration Press, 1973.

GIBSON, R. E., "A Systems Approach to Research Management," *Research, Development, and Technological Innovation: An Introduction,* ed. James R. Bright, pp. 34–57. Homewood, Ill.: Richard D. Irwin, Inc., 1964.

GOLDSTEIN, ARNOLD P., *Psychotherapeutic Attraction.* New York: Pergamon Press, 1971.

GUBA, EGON G., "Development, Diffusion and Evaluation," *Knowledge Production and Utilization,* Terry L. Eiddell and Joanne M. Kitchel, eds., University Council for Educational Administration (Columbus, Ohio) and Center for Advanced Study of Educational Administration (University of Oregon), 2 (1968), 37–63.

HALL, ARTHUR D., *A Methodology for Systems Engineering.* New York: D. Von Nostrand Co., Inc., 1962.

HAVELOCK, RONALD G., "Dissemination and Translation Roles," *Knowledge Production and Utilization,* Terry L. Eiddell and Joanne M. Kitchel, eds., University Council for Educational Administration (Columbus, Ohio) and Center for Advanced Study of Educational Administration (University of Oregon), 4 (1968), 64–119.

HOLT, KNUT, *Product Innovation.* Trondheim: The University of Trondheim, The Norwegian Institute of Technology, 1975.

KAPPEL, FREDERICK R., "The Systems Approach in Science-Based Industry," Based on an address at the 13th International Management Congress, New York City, September 16, 1963.

KELLY, MERVIN J., "The Bell Telephone Laboratories—An Example of an Institute of Creative Technology," Proceedings of the Royal Society, Series A, *Mathematical and Physical Sciences,* 203, no. 1074 (October 1950).

KERSHAW, DAVID, and JERILYN FAIR, *The New Jersey Income-Maintenance Experiment, Volume 1: Operations, Surveys and Administration.* New York: Academic Press, 1976.

National Academy of Sciences, National Research Council, "The Experimental Manpower Laboratory as an R&D Capability," Washington, D.C., February, 1974.

National Science Foundation, *Federal Funds for Research, Development and Other Scientific Activities, Fiscal Years 1966, 1967, 1968,* Vol. 15, 1966.

National Science Foundation, "Defense and Energy Spur Federal R&D Growth from FY 1974 to FY 1978," *Science Resources Studies Highlights,* (NSF 77-320), Washington, D.C., 1977.

RADNOR, MICHAEL, et al., "Comparative Research, Development and Innovation: With Implications for Education," Center for the Interdisciplinary Study of Sciences and Technology, Northwestern University, Evanston, Illinois, April 1977.

REID, WILLIAM J., *The Task Centered System,* New York: Columbia University Press, 1978.

"Research Utilization in Rehabilitation," Special Issue of *Rehabilitation Counseling Bulletin, Journal of the American Rehabilitation Counseling Association,* 19, no. 2 (December 1975).

ROBERTS, EDWARD B., "Facts and Folklore in Research and Development Management," *Industrial Management Review*, 8, no. 2 (Spring 1967), 5–18.

ROTHMAN, JACK, *Planning and Organizing for Social Change: Action Principles from Social Research*. New York: Columbia University Press, 1974.

SCHUTZ, RICHARD E., "The Nature of Educational Development," *Journal of Research and Development in Education*, University of Georgia (Winter 1970), 39–64.

SOLOFF, ASHER, et al., "Running a Research Utilization Laboratory," *Rehabilitation Counseling Bulletin*, 19, no. 2 (December 1975), 416–424.

THOMAS, EDWIN J., "Generating Innovation in Social Work: The Paradigm of Developmental Research," *Journal of Social Service Research*, 2, no. 1 (Fall 1978).

THOMAS, EDWIN J., "Beyond Knowledge Utilization in Generating Human Service Technology," Paper prepared for the National Conference on the Future of Social Work Research, sponsored by the National Association of Social Workers, San Antonio, Texas, October 15–18, 1978.

THORPE, MERLE, "Industry on the March," *The Book of Popular Science*, Vol. I, pp. 87–97. New York: Grolier, 1963.

TRIPODI, TONY, *Uses and Abuses of Social Research in Social Work*. New York: Columbia University Press, 1974.

URBAN, HUGH B., "Systems Methodology in the Design of Treatment Strategies for Depressive States," Draft of paper prepared for symposium, "Current Developments in the Psychotherapy of Depression," Eastern Psychological Association Meeting, New York, April 1976.

3

Context and Environment of Research and Development

Probably it ought to be noted somewhere for the record just how damned difficult it is for us to keep in touch with our folks in the field. This morning, for example, between 9:10 and 9:35 A.M., I attempted to reach seven of our field practitioners. Not a single one was in. In three instances, I either had to leave a message for a "telephone recorder" or was asked to call back because there was no one available to take a message.

Somewhere in our final report it ought to be pointed out very clearly how much time is involved in maintaining contact with people in the field.

Memo from CIP Field Operations Director
to CIP Project Director, February 26, 1973

Someone once described the process of flying an airplane as "hours of boredom punctuated by moments of extreme panic." The process of conducting social R&D—and perhaps R&D in any context—might be viewed conversely as hours of anxiety, frustration, triumph, and disappointment punctuated by moments of deep reflection or placid routine. From this one can infer, quite properly, that the environment of research and development—particularly that in which development takes place—is one of turbulence. An appreciation of the place and character of research in R&D will provide some insight into why this is so. In this chapter we will discuss this point, and we will indicate how knowledge is built through development. We will examine the development environment itself in some detail and then set forth some of the methodological implications of such a turbulent environment.

THE PLACE AND CHARACTER OF RESEARCH IN THE R&D PROCESS

Let us begin by delineating the place of research and its particular character in the research and development process. There is a great deal of confusion, uncertainty, and contradiction in the writings on the subject. We will deal with two aspects in particular in this discussion. The first treats the subject of how *basic research* is involved and used in R&D work. The second concerns the interplay of research and development during the development stages.

Basic Research: Production or Retrieval-Conversion

It is clear that basic research is a type of scientific, knowledge-building endeavor that occurs and can be conceptualized independently of any R&D process. It becomes connected with this process only when it is drawn upon in the deliberate formation of its practical derivations. Not all basic research is used for R&D, and exceedingly little basic research (partly by definition) is conducted for a specific R&D purpose. Basic research constitutes essentially a pool of existing knowledge to feed given developmental objectives.

This orientation is supported by a number of observers who have been involved in different aspects of R&D and observed it from different vantage points. As R&D specialists in the industrial sphere have the longer established R&D tradition, let us examine some of their representative views.

Frederick R. Kappel (1963), who had general responsibility for overseeing the widely respected Bell Laboratories program, offers this observation:

I venture to say that no business has more consistently sought new knowledge than the Bell System, or has been on the whole more successful in producing and using it. Yet . . . I would say that the prime need in modern technology is for wiser, smarter thought and action about what we have, rather than reliance on a headlong hunt for miracle solutions, or brute force, extravagant effort to find what we do not have. (p. 6)

Howard Reiss (1969), director of the Science Center at North American Aviation, directs his attention to the integrative functions in the R&D

process. He believes that both applied science and engineering development laboratories can be set up for the purpose of inducing specific technological events. He sees such laboratories succeeding only to the extent that they feed upon pre-existing knowledge, and he emphasizes that "the novel act in both engineering development and applied science is creative 'synthesis' " (p. 108).

Drawing upon "Project Hindsight," a systematic, extensive study of federal research and development defense programs, Carter (1968) asserts that major impacts may be anticipated, "not so much through the recent, random scraps of new knowledge, as it is through the organized 'packed-down' thoroughly understood and carefully taught *old* science" (p. 5, emphasis in the original).

These same conclusions are reached by that rare new breed, the R&D professionals in social fields. Borg (1969), for example, lists two alternative strategies for a development program geared to improving teacher skills. These were projected by the staff of the Far West Laboratory for Educational Research and Development and weighted one against the other:

Conduct a major research program leading to the discovery and description of those teaching skills and behavior patterns that proved to be important in the teaching-learning process—

OR

On the basis of . . . whatever evidence is available, identify and define those teaching skills that have a high probability of fitting into any system of teacher training that may evolve. (pp. 7–8)

Borg's colleagues at the Far West Laboratory rejected the first in favor of the second. We have summarized their reasoning as follows:

1. the basic research program called for in the first approach is outside the R&D concept;
2. that approach would require a concentration of research talent and funds beyond the resources of the laboratory; and,
3. even if resources were available, the time frame required for such a sequence would prohibit the making available of usable products for too long a number of years.

This same orientation is advocated by a study committee that evaluated the R&D program of the Department of Labor (National Academy of Science, 1974). This committee pointed to a lack of sophistication in problem solving by R&D labs as a result of a lack of attention to previously published work and available research data in certain areas. The possibility exists that the poor showing over the past decade or so by heavily funded educational laboratories and regional centers hinged on this issue. Many staff members, coming from a basic social science orientation, failed to function with a developmental mindset. Since the social sciences generally are devoid of a systematic applied orientation and do not provide articulated training in social engineering methodologies, staff members automatically gravitated to basic research projects. They viewed these as the only natural, legitimate, and professionally prestigious (and financially rewarding) form of activity open to them.

It is inconceivable to think of R&D without thinking of the body of basic research that fuels the process. At the same time it is erroneous to think of R&D as the activity that creates that basic knowledge. Most people in R&D work will tell you that they have quite enough to do without placing upon them that additional onerous burden.

KNOWLEDGE BUILDING THROUGH DEVELOPMENT

The counterpart of a tendency to put too much emphasis on basic research in the R&D research phase is an equally mistaken tendency to underplay important research aspects of the development phase. Often a dichotomous distinction is made between dealing with knowledge at one end of the continuum and practical matters at the other. Such a dichotomy inevitably leads to confusion, a confusion compounded by what O'Brien (1961) refers to as an "inflation of terms." A term such as "drafting" develops into "design." "Design" then becomes "development," while "development" translates into "research." O'Brien clearly deplores such inflation: "When a product can be identified as the outcome of experimentation, I would refer to the process as development and not research" (p. 93).

Ansoff (1961) takes this same position, maintaining that development has the distinct purpose of offering a product to potential users; it is "*never* justifiable unless it holds promise of making a profit for the company" (p. 211). In other words, development must have practical value in terms of its utilization purpose and content. *Ipso facto,* Ansoff implies that development is not research.

The trouble with this perspective is that it places too much emphasis on purpose and not enough on the empirical reality of what occurs in the process. It is true that the *primary* purpose of development is the creation of practical tools and products. It is also true that the concomitant accumulation of knowledge concerning how things work is difficult to divorce from research. Many of the methods of careful observation, evaluation, and experimentation necessary for development are identical to those employed in research. O'Brien (1961) concedes:

Once the development objective has been established and the key technical problems identified, one can plan experiments; from these experiments one can plan the design and manufacture of test equipment, and so on. (p. 92)

Ansoff (1961) is more explicit in indicating that applied research activities and development activities "are very similar (involving usually construction of a working device)" (p. 211).

It was our experience in the Community Intervention Project that much of a research nature accompanied and grew out of our work in the development phase. It was essential that evaluation tools and procedures be constructed and carefully applied. In this effort we were able to obtain information concerning variables that were associated with successful implementation of specific social intervention strategies. Further, by examining data across a range of considerably different types of interventions, we were able to reach tentative conclusions concerning variables that may generally be associated with successful systems of intervention. These findings, as with most research in the social sciences, are tentative and suggestive of possible avenues of further, fruitful investigation.

Several writers in the industrial field concur in this understanding about the development phase. Morton (1969) talks of this issue in the Bell Labs situation:

Back in the early days of transistors, after we had learned how to grow single-crystal germanium and silicon, Bill Pfann had a sweet idea on zone refining. Bill is one of our most creative metallurgists and had developed his idea to the point where he could grow a single crystal . . . Well, it turned out Bill Pfann was right . . . Being a metallurgist [he] was thinking of its relevance to materials problems —not just transistor materials, but on a broader scale. In the area of materials research, his judgement of relevance was [superior] (p. 222).

A discovery in the metallurgy field, in this example, was a byproduct of examining how transistors might best be mass manufactured.

Ames (1951) observes that "bugs" in development operations may stimulate knowledge. For example, pitchblende spoiled photographic plates; this observation led to the discovery of radioactivity. Another Bell scientist, Kelly (1950) makes the observation that the pattern of scientists engaged in early level development work stimulating further research is one that repeats itself again and again.

Experienced professionals in educational development make similar assertions. Baker and Schutz (1971) indicate that, while the research components and the development components can be distinguished as separate activities, "clearly the two enterprises are related. Indeed, every phase of development can serve as a highly heuristic source of expanding the limits of elegant and sophisticated educational research" (p. xv).

Why, then, has the knowledge-building aspect of development been denied or confused by those involved in R&D? Perhaps, in the harried, turbulent, task- and product-oriented atmosphere of development, there is not the time to capitalize on discoveries. The pressure is on to use newly gained knowledge for product completion purposes rather than to refine and diffuse it as knowledge itself. As O'Brien (1961) observes:

The development man gets his data and goes on. The research man gets intrigued with the subject and wants to round it out and write a paper on this general phenomenon. That, of course, is a good thing if you're a scientist; but for the development project it's financial murder. (p. 99)

Thus, it is contextual and personal factors, temperamental inclinations and reward systems—and the keeping of discoveries as industrial secrets—rather than any inherent qualities of the process that have led to too wide a conceptual wedge between what is considered *research* and what is defined as *development.*

Our own work at the Community Intervention Project was, likewise, not free from the impact of this conceptual wedge, though our awareness of its existence mitigated its effects to a considerable extent. The critical concern is not *whether* there is research in the development stage, but rather, what should be the *relative emphasis* given to the research components during development work. The following procedural questions are typical of those which arise in development work:

–to what degree do instruments need to be fully refined before being used in field testing?

–how many field trials should be completed before one can be reasonably satisfied with a product from both scientific and practical points of view?

–how much additional surrounding data (contingent variables, intervening variables) should be collected and analyzed during the course of using a product in the field?

–to what degree does testing of a preliminary version of a procedure or manual contaminate "naturalistic" application and data collection?

Though the history of educational research and development has been relatively brief, the educational developer Borg (1969) believes that one question of strategy emerges above all others: "What should be the relative balance in an R&D program between research and evaluation on one hand and development on the other?" (p. 5). He goes on to point out that such a balance is critical if products are to be developed that can assist in educational improvement. The application of resources to product development to a degree that excludes research and evaluation yields products that are unproven in the scientific sense. We might think that such products are better than those they replace, but we have no "real" (i.e., scientific) way of proving it.

In Borg's view, the problem is less critical when excess attention is given to research and evaluation, slighting the development effort. Such a slight usually means that a great deal of research, much of which may add valuable knowledge to the field, is carried out in the process of manipulating and evaluating a poorly developed product. (p. 6)

A preoccupation with research in its own right can result in no R&D product at all. Potential theoretical contributions of development are given cogent analysis by Butman and Fletcher (1974). They believe the best way to see development is as a fluid, rapidly changing process, calling for intuition, a sense of how well something is working and what might make it work better, and simultaneous development of a sense of the theoretical basis for the work. Butman and Fletcher see the conceptual and operational organization of development work as proceeding in an ongoing series of efforts to conceptualize the problem "with each new try holding only for a short while until, with further work, a redefined problem and some next steps become clear" (pp. 47–48). Furthermore, all this happens within a broad political setting that calls for a variety of accommodations and exchanges between the "ideal" and the "practical." They indicate that feedback, if effectively used, will not only serve to alter the product, but may actually alter the conceptual foundation from which the product emerged—and that this, quite properly, can take place during a well conducted development stage.

The staff at Borg's regional laboratory evolved a useful rule of thumb on the research-development issue embracing the notion that the research and evaluation phase of educational product development should be carried to the point where "hard" evaluation data reveals the degree to which the product meets its objectives. The evaluation process cannot stop until this point. "Our current policy calls for testing at least one or two important research hypotheses during the development of each mini-course" (Borg, 1969, p. 11). Especially development conducted under university auspices or government sponsorship (such as by the National Science Foundation) can afford and should strive to balance practical outcomes with scientific ones.

The National Research Council of the National Academy of Sciences (1974) offers some practical advice for maintaining the balance between the development and research components of an educational R&D laboratory. The Council points out that there are mutually reinforcing aspects to the work of the research staff and that of the service personnel who generate data for research. While each group makes a separate contribution to the lab, these contributions are interrelated and interdependent. If this interdependence is constantly stressed, each will derive reinforcement from the other. The research staff will be rewarded by the excellence of the services offered, while dividends will accrue to the service staff through the success of the research effort. "Such a contingency is not easy to construct, but in its absence the research or the service will fail to become operational" (pp. 59–60).

It is possible for development to take place without the creation of scientific contributions, or at least without the recognition and explication of the scientific side of development. That it can take place in this way is no justification for making it an ideal or even acceptable notion of what development is about.

THE ENVIRONMENT OF R&D: TURBULENCE, UNCERTAINTY, MULTIPLICITY

Take a biology lab at the Rockefeller Institute. Add on to it part of the assembly line at Ford. Tie in the marketing department of Squibb. Put the whole thing under the management of a systems specialist at RAND. This begins to give the flavor of the environment in which development takes place. An understanding and appreciation for the precincts of R&D are essential if one is to comprehend and to assess development work—and this book. There are correlate constraints and requirements placed on this particular methodology of applied research—applied research that is product oriented and that takes place in the user environment. The milieu of development is substantially different from that of traditional basic or laboratory research. The criteria for judgement of investigatory and evaluatory methods, therefore, must be correspondingly different and unique. A different critical perspective is demanded and this we shall now attempt to provide.

R&D typically takes place within an organizational structure. A group effort is involved where specific, practical products are expected to be brought into being at a given cost within a limited time period. A variety of interests are usually engaged in the effort—political, organizational, economic, intellectual—among actors representing somewhat different goals, professional disciplines, and personal commitments. In developing a handbook for community practitioners, for example, we required a staff with competency in the theoretical and research literature. We needed practitioners or people intimately connected with the intended social agency application setting and the skills of practice. A specialist with methodological capacities in evaluation and data processing was a necessity. Administrative and management people were needed to keep the flow of materials and tasks timely and appropriate. We required people with editorial or writing skills to compose the handbook. Technicians of various kinds were required for field collection of data and data processing. The people in each of these categories had differing points of view.

The complex, fluid character of this process is brought out by a pair of educational R&D specialists, Butman and Fletcher (1974) who have given special attention to the institutions within which R&D takes place, the funding agencies, and the political process within which both are embedded. They see these as having a profound effect on what actually happens in any R&D effort and the results obtained by that effort:

> The developer/evaluator is constantly faced with trade-off decisions between reality pressures and the logic of development. Timelines, available funds, administrative decisions concerning allocation of resources, perceived institutional reputation, prestige, service and survival needs, all can potentially influence such critical decisions as to whether to make a "best guess" about the effect of a given teaching variable on a set of outcome variables and hold that variable constant at some assumed optimal point, or to test the relationship empirically before making such a choice. (p. 45)

External pressures, therefore, often influence decisions, and these may affect the internal consistency of the system and the interpretability of data. These authors neither ignore nor decry these conditions. Rather, their view is: "that decisions and demands are politically as well as empirically derived is both inevitable and appropriate" (p. 45).

A number of specific components of this turbulent development environment may be identified. For one, uncertainty. Schutz (1970) pointedly reflects on the unpredictability of the outcome of an R&D program. "Attempts to develop an object that represents a marked advance in the state-of-the-art are subject to great uncertainty" (p. 167). Baker and Schutz (1971) see uncertainty as a key characteristic in their definition of applied research and its outcomes. One is, after all, generally dealing with a problem that has not been solved before and for which existing knowledge can be used to produce a solution. Sometimes the outcome is so uncertain that it requires the creation of new knowledge, a process that requires linkage with basic research efforts. Scott and Shore (1974) observed that "modern development programs have life histories filled with unanticipated crises, unpredicted barriers and impediments" (p. 31).

The element of risk in R&D undertakings is underlined in discussions by both O'Brien (1961) and Roberts (1964). In industrial R&D the risk of failure is exacerbated by competitive workings of the market. A competing firm may achieve a finished product quicker or at a lower cost or in a form that is more attractive to consumers. The overall cost of the development process may make a product ultimately unprofitable for a company—as Lockheed can testify. In social R&D, competition is likely to play a lesser part. But because of the early stage of the art, products may be ineffective, at least in the short run. That is to say, there will be slippage in the conversion of scientific knowledge into reliable programs and practices which will have an impact. The trial and error aspects of development during this experimental period may result in the cutting off of funding with no tangible products materializing.

Nevertheless, realizing the natural time lag between the discovery of scientific principles and their innovative use for practical purposes, R&D must be viewed as a significant, though far from foolproof, method of accelerating this process. "The risks were great," O'Brien acknowledges, "but the gains were correspondingly high when the work was successful" (p. 86).

The risk element is joined by *pressures for successful and prompt completion* brought about by demands of funding sources, competition from other organizations or institutions, and so forth. Shepard (1963) points to the frustration and stress that are apt to affect the staff of an R&D laboratory, especially when a company does not enjoy a large "cushion of monopoly" and yet must meet immediate competitive threats with limited resources.

Development work reduces profits on an immediate basis for the prospect of sustained profits in the future, "but there can be no certainty that these hoped-for profits will materialize" (O'Brien, 1961, p. 75). The principal dilemma, and also the principal decision for a technical business, centers strongly on the problem of the extent to which immediate profits can and should be used to support fairly risky development work. The practical businessman must be ever mindful of two questions: will the potential product be profitable, and can the organization achieve the desired results at an acceptable cost in time to exploit the potential market? In the human services one need only substitute the phrase, "improved or more efficient services," for the business term, "profit."

Because of the adverse forces at work, it is necessary to harmonize and synthesize divergent tendencies. Decisions in R&D projects, thus, are a *compromise in the blending of contending requirements.* Such a blending may optimize the unique advantages embedded in this rich environment, if skillfully managed. On this, Schutz (undated) provides food for thought:

The complex intermeshing of scientific needs, engineering requirements, budgetary limitations, organizational constraints, and personal goals and values almost ensures that project decisions will involve a complex of trade-offs among many different gains and a variety of losses. Experienced and knowledgeable participants cannot eliminate the need for trade-offs, but they can approach the bargaining with a realistic evaluation of the possible outcomes. (p. 35)

Under these circumstances risks are multiple and diverse. Bright (1964) categorizes the various risks and their unsettling effects on R&D in the industrial context. He defines six categories of risk: technical, marketing, interference, timing, obsolescence and personal.

Technical risks include such subcategories of risk as scientific, engineering, and production. Scientific risks are those where uncertainties arise out of a lack of complete theory or knowledge of needed scientific principles. Engineering risks are those associated with the inability (including excessive delays) to translate known scientific principles into practical developments. Production risks are those that arise out of an inability to translate a working model into a fullscale production operation.

Risks in the marketing area, according to Bright, are characterized by special emphasis on certain adoption problems. They are due often to the novelty of the device or concept.

Interference risks arise when forces external to the supplier-customer sequence seek to delay the innovation through interference tactics. This is seen particularly when the innovation is viewed as radical. Among those who may generate resistance, Bright lists competitors, labor, government agencies, professional institutions, trade associations, religious organizations, special pressure groups, or individuals who are financially or emotionally involved. In the human services interference may be generated from a number of sources including clients, funders, managers of other agencies, and board members.

Timing risks are those where the "sound innovation may fail because it is launched in an inauspicious time" (p. 462). Obsolescence risks come from "uncertainties arising from technological or style changes, or changes in the technical means of accomplishing a portion of the task" (p. 462).

Personal risks arise from the human element in the equation—the individuals who appraise, plan, and execute the R&D effort. However perfect the innovation might be, however sound the technical environment for development, managers involved in risk situations influence both the decision and the outcome of action by their human qualities. All of these risk elements have close analogies in social R&D.

Clearly, then, wherever one encounters a multitude of risks, where objectives of the many components of a system may be in conflict with one another—may even be diametrically opposed to one another—where the probability of failure is high, yet the potential of success and pressures to produce are equally high, *turbulence may be expected*. Indeed, anxiety and frustration are no strangers to those who would undertake research and development.

In addition to these other attributes, *power* is clearly an element of R&D. It takes a considerable concentration of power to mobilize the sizable resources—money, manpower, technical and professional expertise, equipment and materials—necessary for the implementation of R&D. Power is intertwined with values and purposes around which the R&D enterprise is organized. The policies guiding R&D endeavors clearly emanate from those individuals and institutions which are capable of controlling key decisions and manipulating large scale resources. The question of the exercise of power in R&D is worthy of extensive treatment in its own right. Here we acknowledge it, but choose to concentrate instead at this stage on the conceptual and technical aspects of social R&D. We view this intellectual task as a vital prelude to the emergence of social R&D. Some concomitant organizational and resource requisites are discussed in the concluding chapter.

RESEARCH METHOD IMPLICATIONS
OF A TURBULENT ENVIRONMENT

Our sympathies must go out to the methodological purist who, in reaction to this description of the typical R&D environment, must be sorely tempted to throw up his hands in despair and walk away. Still, this would leave this means of applying social science research to real world problems abandoned—a situation already too prevalent in the social sciences. Another way to approach the matter is to work toward developing and refining a methodology *geared* to dealing with *multiple, interactive variables.* Some encouraging efforts along these lines have been underway, particularly in recent years in the field of evaluation research (which will be discussed specifically in Chapter 7).

Wold (1970), for example, discusses a movement away from an experimental technology that manipulates a variable of interest while seeking to isolate all others. He indicates a trend, that he favors, toward a more comprehensive mode of analysis based on a more complex model. The attempt is to assess the effects, both direct and interactive, of a multiplicity of variables assured to be operating in a given situation. In such complex processes as community action or organizational change, such a procedure seems particularly advantageous. First, there are so many variables at work that an experimental study of each of them in isolation would require an inordinate amount of time to accomplish. Second, a study of any given variable in isolation might provide only highly limited or misleading intelligence.

Several additional application-minded social scientists support such a view. Schutz (undated) is concerned with the difficulties experienced from more traditional sources, particularly theoretically oriented academicians who are "more impressed by *pro forma* bows to methodological convention than by highly generalizable but conceptually simple technological gains" (p. 60). He is especially distressed when they "insist that some of the sacred cows of educational research be visible in every development effort, in a misguided attempt to provide professional respectability" (p. 60).

Scott and Shore (1974) mildly lament their difficulties in doing policy research in the New Jersey-Pennsylvania Negative Income Tax Experiment. The social science literature, they report, did not provide much direct help in dealing with the policy problems they had to deal with in their research. They were required to develop a coherent framework for their research based on the policy-relevance criterion they decided upon:

Academic criteria are not very helpful since the underlying criteria for assessment differ essentially from those of policy analysis. While the former are based on notions of validity and reliability in the abstract, they are also founded on ability to predict outcomes accurately or ability to account for significant proportions of variance in dependent variables without reference to the problem of deliberate control. On the other hand, policy criteria revolve around programmatic and utilitarian considerations. (p. 57)

Ben-David (1973), a respected scholar in the sociology of science, goes further. He suggests and urges this type of engineering methodology become the *dominant mode of investigation* among social scientists. He is persuaded that social scientists have done a disservice to their own work by trying to mold it according to the model of basic natural science. He recommends that social scientists organize their work according to models that suit their own purposes. He finds this preferable to distorting their work to fit the requirements of some ideal (or idealized) model. The most logical models for sc‌ial science, he suggests, are those of clinical medicine, engineering, geology, and genetics, whereas those of physics are inappropriate. This means that in those cases where the social scientist is actually a social clinician or engineer, he will have to face this fact more consciously than he ever has before. The social science profession has grown to the point where it can no longer be concerned only with the conception of ideas. It must now also be concerned with putting them into practice:

Not only does the social scientist's lack of concern with the practical applications of his research expose him to blame for the failures of others, but it also deprives him of the benefit of learning from his own mistakes. (pp. 48–49)

Guba (1968), in a methodologically penetrating examination discusses four characteristics of conventional research that are dysfunctional for applied research in natural field settings. These characteristics include:

Terminal Availability of Data: Usually data is produced upon completion of the evaluation period rather than during the process. It does not tell what is taking place during the process, which may be of great importance to the applied scientist. *Retrospective View:* Along the same lines, one has only a retrospective view of the results and implications of an applied treatment. The researcher or intervener does not have an opportunity to obtain information that might improve the treatment.

Restrictive Constraints: There can be no variation in the treatment or context of the treatment once the evaluation is underway. This mitigates against experimenting with improving the treatment or the context of treatment based on what is learned during the term of evaluation.

Limited Generalizability: These kinds of constraints establish a laboratory type condition within which the treatment is tested. The many variations existing in the real world are excluded from having an effect on the outcome. Thus, the evaluation describes what occurs under laboratory circumstances and not under typical operating circumstances. For research which is intended to contribute practical applications to typical circumstances, the generalizability of such findings to these circumstances is highly questionable.

Guba goes on to recommend an alternative strategy geared to the peculiar assumptions and demands of applied research. These include:

Level of Control: Typical experimental controls must be eliminated. The evaluator must be concerned with how things occur in the field rather than in the laboratory. Hence, the kind of control that we have been accustomed to in laboratory experimentation will be sharply different, perhaps nonexistent—data collection must be carried on without disturbing either the context or the subjects.

Continuity of Data Collection: Data are not collected simply at pre- and post-experimental periods (or at some particular check points) but continuously throughout the evaluation. The baseline of data must be dynamic rather than static.

Treatments: Treatments cannot be regarded as invariant but should be seen as susceptible to continuous change (improvement). Context conditions must also be alterable.

Scope: Attention must be given not only to particular variables which have been identified and operationalized beforehand, but to any emergent variables which appear to be of concern. (pp. 61, 62)

Guba concludes that evaluation in a dynamic applied context must conform to the realities of that research task and environment. It cannot simply be a forced carry-over of traditional methodological canons and assumptions (though those of us in social R&D have, on occasion, felt that something akin to a cannon is used to force compliance with tradition). This conforming to reality requires an open approach and creative work that social scientists, including evaluation researchers, have only begun to undertake in substantial numbers. It also requires attention to the assumptions and methods of engineering rather than to those of "pure" science.

Mackie (1974) has shed some particularly useful light on the subject. He reviewed a number of research studies and categorized them as *high* or *low* in *Application Potential* (A/P). From his analysis we can isolate some of the key differences between the two sets of studies as follows:

Mackie found that in low A/P studies the response repertoire is often very limited and may have no significance outside the experimental con-

studies with low a/p		studies with high a/p
	Objective	
to understand something		to change something
	Task	
selected or contrived		actual or simulated
	Stimulus	
simple, convenient		complex, natural
	Response	
limited meanings, highly structured		operationally meaningful; may be unstructured
	Motivation	
imposed by experimenter		often intrinsic
	Time	
usually compressed		less compressed, may be real
	Environment	
artificial, meaningless		natural or simulated

text. In high A/P studies, the response alternatives are typically quite meaningful in relation to some operational criterion. In addition, there may be many response options and not all of these may be fully specified in advance by the experimenter.

He also found that in studies having low A/P, the stimulus tends to be simple, experimentally convenient, and to reflect the interest of good experimental control. The subject's response tends to have meaning only in relation to the experimental task (i.e., "if stimulus A is presented, press the lever marked X as quickly as possible"). In high A/P studies the stimulus is often inherent in the experimental task; i.e., the stimulus condition is not contrived by the experimenter but is presented in some natural context. The experimenter may have little control of the exact character of the stimulus, although he may program it according to some orderly pl . In fact, determining the precise nature of the stimulus in many high A/P studies may, in and of itself, be a significant part of the investigation.

A final difference between low and high A/P studies is the difference in the experimental environment itself. In the typical low A/P case, the experimental environment is sterile and deliberately shielded from the influence of variables that are not the focus of the investigator's attention. In the typical high A/P case, the experimental environment is often much more like the operational one or a careful simulation of it. In high A/P studies, therefore, many more uncontrolled variables are likely to influence the results, and the effects of independent variables are likely to be evident only if they are highly influential.

Mackie's general perspective on the methodological issues are quite consistent with our own. There is much less experimenter control in high A/P studies. There is a risk in such studies that comes from possible unanswered questions about the roles of various variables in behavioral outcome. While the control possible in low A/P studies may eliminate this risk and make possible a clear understanding of laboratory phenomena, it may be difficult if not impossible to relate the findings to the real world.

The solution to the dilemma may lie in training investigators to design studies with a higher level of A/P than is traditionally found in the laboratory, but at not so high a level as to sacrifice totally the kind of experimental control associated with rigorous scientific inquiry. This approach requires establishing in the social sciences an engineering outlook and methodological slant. The early stages of movement in that direction may not be entirely satisfying to either advocates or critics. But progress based on experimental work seems inevitable. Historical precedents from the physical and natural sciences and the possibility of technological borrowing from them justify a hopeful assessment.

Kurt Lewin was an outstanding pioneer in action-research social science endeavors. In his genius, Lewin (1968) early on underlined the importance of research for social engineering or social management. He recognized that it had a different research logic and posed unique requirements. At the same time, this does not imply, he states, "the research needed is in any respect less scientific or 'lower' than would be required for pure science in the field of social events" (p. 443). While conveying the different characteristics of applied research, Lewin also pointed out *elements of unity or continuity* between basic and applied methodologies:

[Field] experiment, as opposed to a more descriptive analysis, tried to study the effect of conditions by some way of measuring or bringing about certain changes under sufficiently controlled conditions. The objective is to understand the laws which govern the nature of the phenomena under study, in our case the nature of group life . . . A diagnosis of the before and after situation permits us to define the change or effect; studying the happening should be designed to characterize the factors which brought about this change. (p. 443)

Thus, the effort to discriminate and define a social engineering methodology, while needing distinct, specialized attention, need not be fully divorced from common goals and ways of work among social scientists in general. (In the same way that engineering is not in conflict with the methods of the physical sciences.) We view the R&D conception as a direct and logical extension of Lewin's pioneer work geared toward constructing an action-research outlook and methodology. The social engineering methodology inherent in this R&D formulation is a useful and perhaps inevitable way of applying social science knowledge in an action context.

Its precise application will be demonstrated in Part II where we will examine, in turn, and in detail, each of the steps in R&D.

BIBLIOGRAPHY

AMES, EDWARD, "Communications: Research, Invention, Development and Innovation," *American Economic Review*, 51 (June 1951), 370–381.

ANSOFF, H. I., "Evaluation of Applied Research in a Business Firm," *Technological Planning on the Corporate Level*, Proceedings of a conference sponsored by the Associates of the Harvard Business School, September 8–9, 1961, ed. James R. Bright. Cambridge, Mass.: 1961, pp. 208–224.

BAKER, ROBERT L., and RICHARD E. SCHUTZ, *Instructional Product Development*. New York: Von Nostrand Reinhold Co., 1971.

BEN-DAVID, JOSEPH, "The Search for Knowledge," *Daedalus*, 102, no. 2 (Spring 1973), 39–51.

BORG, WALTER R., "The Balance Between Educational Research and Development: A Question of Strategy," *Educational Technology*, 5, no. 7 (July 1969), 5–11.

BRIGHT, JAMES R., ed., *Research, Development and Technological Innovation: An Introduction*. Homewood, Ill.: Richard D. Irwin, Inc., 1964.

BUTMAN, JEAN W., and JERRY L. FLETCHER, "The Role of Evaluator and Developer in Educational Research and Development," *Evaluating Educational Programs and Products*, ed. Gary D. Borich. Englewood Cliffs, N.J.: Educational Technology Products, 1974.

CARTER, LAUNOR F., "Knowledge Production and Utilization in Contemporary Organizations," *Knowledge Production and Utilization*, Terry L. Eiddell and Joanne M. Kitchel, eds., University Council for Educational Administration (Columbus, Ohio) and Center for the Advanced Study of Educational Administration (University of Oregon), 1 (1968), 1–20.

GUBA, EGON, "Development, Diffusion and Evaluation," *Knowledge Production and Utilization*, Terry L. Eiddell and Joanne M. Kitchel, eds., University Council for Educational Administration (Columbus, Ohio) and Center for Advanced Study of Educational Administration (University of Oregon), 2 (1968), 37–63.

KAPPEL, FREDERICK R., "The Systems Approach in Science-Based Industry," Based on an address at the 13th International Management Congress, New York City, September 16, 1963.

KELLY, MERVIN J., "The Bell Telephone Laboratories—An Example of an Institute of Creative Technology," Proceedings of the Royal Society, Series A, *Mathematical and Physical Sciences*, 203, no. 1074, (October 1950), 287–301.

LEWIN, KURT, "Feedback Problems of Social Diagnosis and Action," *Modern Systems Research for the Behavioral Scientist*, ed. Walter Buckley, pp. 441–444. Chicago: Aldine Publishing Co., 1968.

MACKIE, ROBERT R., "Chuckholes in the Bumpy Road from Research to Application," Paper presented at the American Psychological Association Meetings, New Orleans, August, 1974.

MORTON, JACK A., "From Research to Technology," *The R&D Game—Technical Management and Research Productivity*, ed. David Allison, pp. 213–235. Cambridge, Mass.: The M. I. T. Press, 1969.

NATIONAL ACADEMY OF SCIENCES, National Research Council, "The Experimental Manpower Laboratory as an R&D Capability," Washington, D.C., February, 1974.

O'BRIEN, M. P., "Technological Planning and Misplanning," *Technological Planning on the Corporate Level*, Proceedings of a conference sponsored by the Associates of the Harvard Business School, September 8–9, 1961, ed. James R. Bright. Cambrid_e, Mass.: 1961, pp. 72–99.

REISS, HOWARD, "Human Factors at the Science-Technology Interface," *Factors in the Transfer of Technology*, William H. Gruber and Donald G. Marquis, eds., pp. 105–113. Cambridge, Mass.: The M.I.T. Press, 1969.

ROBERTS, EDWARD B., *The Dynamics of Research and Development*. New York: Harper & Row Publishers, 1964.

SCHUTZ, RICHARD E., "The Nature of Educational Development," *Journal of Research and Development in Education*, University of Georgia, (Winter 1970), pp. 39–64.

SCHUTZ, RICHARD E., "The Conduct of Development in Education," Unpublished internal report of Southwest Regional Laboratory for Educational Research and Development, (undated).

SCOTT, ROBERT A., and ARNOLD SHORE, "Sociology and Policy Analysis," *The American Sociologist*, 9, no. 2 (May 1974), 51–59.

SHEPARD, HERBERT A., "Nine Dilemmas in Industrial Research," *The Sociology of Science*, Bernard Barber and Walter Hirsch, eds., pp. 344–355. The Free Press of Glencoe, 1963.

Technological Planning on the Corporate Level, Proceedings of a conference sponsored by the Associates of the Harvard Business School, September 8–9, 1961, ed. James R. Bright. Cambridge, Mass.: 1961.

WOLD, HERMAN, "Causal Inference from Observational Data," *The Evaluation of Instruction*, Wittrock and Wiley, eds. New York: Holt, Rinehart and Winston, 1970.

part two

STEPS IN THE RESEARCH AND DEVELOPMENT PROCESS

4

Retrieving Knowledge: Codification and Generalization

Social Scientists . . . study reasons for social and psychological action, or individual or collective motivation, and they outline, in varying degrees of gracefulness, elegance and wit, the evolution of cultures, traditions, peoples, single minds. When the assessment and searching are completed, we receive the results. And in the social sciences they come at us in tons, megatons even, of hard and soft data, dry and damp data. Where, I wonder, is the end of it? . . . How have we reached this point?

Thomas J. Cottle
The New Republic, December 31, 1977

RETRIEVAL OF EXISTING SOCIAL RESEARCH KNOWLEDGE

Before the advent of modern scientific technology—before massive governmental research programs, before national tax structures gave significant motivation for private research foundations—knowledge was ordinarily generated on an individualistic, "as needed" basis. One began with a personal interest, found out in a venturesome way what was already known, and conducted research to discover what was not known in order to satisfy that interest. Before the advent of rapid and relatively inexpensive printing methods, audio and visual recording techniques, computers and data banks, the storage of information was simply not practical. That which was not useful within a relatively short time was forgotten, requiring rediscovery at a later time when it would be useful. Because the total scientific output was relatively modest, this procedure was workable.

The nineteenth century scientist was starved for information—the twentieth century scientist is overwhelmed. As late as twenty-five years ago, a conscientious specialist could read all the important research relevant to his field. For most specialists that is now impossible. In part, the reason is that about 90 percent of all scientists who ever lived are alive today. Available modern technology has them working and publishing at a frenzied pace. The proliferation of scientific and technical journals has made it necessary to find new ways to store information and to facilitate the flow of information among investigators, increasing the possibility that the information will be read and utilized sooner than might otherwise occur. For the last half-century we have gone beyond preserving information, and created methods for inventorying such knowledge for future applications.

We have not, however, maintained effective control of our knowledge inventory. Science has been far too fertile in generating new knowledge. The resources we have brought to bear in research during the past half century have been enormous, and the growth of our scientific data base has been awesome. Our knowledge warehouses are bulging at the seams, and new ones must be constructed all the time.

Industry, with its entrepreneurial emphasis on delivering goods and services, while garnering profits, has had an acquisitive affinity for the information of the natural and physical sciences. It has developed reasonably effective techniques for rummaging through the information warehouses to acquire that knowledge useful to its ends. The processes of industrial R&D have demanded a certain facility in "tapping" the knowledge base. Indeed, if one views industrial R&D as a "black box," then knowledge is fed in one end and products and innovations come out the other. Because the physical sciences have a long history and tradition of knowledge accumulation and preservation, this information has proved to be a valuable industrial fuel.

The knowledge of the social sciences has been a somewhat more esoteric—or exotic—fuel for those engaged in human problem solving. Though our own scientific knowledge base is also vast—though our own knowledge warehouses, too, are brimming over, especially those built since World War II—we have only begun to scratch the surface of its problem-solving potential.

We have expressed the view that a viable means of mining the riches that are available to us lies in the application of the R&D process to the social sciences. The task of retrieving relevant information from the body of existing knowledge, indeed, constitutes the very first step in initiating the R&D process.

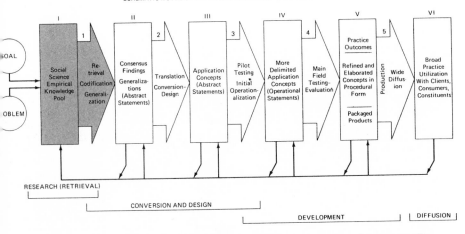

SCHEMATIC MODEL OF RESEARCH UTILIZATION—R & D PROCESS

When those engaged in R&D have a problem to solve, they go to the warehouse—the existing body of knowledge that may contain relevant and useful information. They take with them a "shopping list" of categories of information they seek. The assumption is that possible solutions may be contained in the pool of scientific knowledge, and that some systematic, sustained search of this knowledge will uncover them. In all probability what will be found are parts of relevant knowledge scattered here and there throughout the inventory, the contours of which are both shadowy and irregular. Therefore some coherent strategy of data seeking must be applied. Much social science knowledge is in a highly disorganized state, requiring a greater degree of reconstructing and codifying of isolated strands of knowledge than is the case in the physical sciences with their longer tradition of communicating and consolidating knowledge. For these reasons a systematic, well-thought-out retrieval plan is essential.

ELEMENTS OF A RETRIEVAL PROGRAM

Although the retrieval of information for social R&D purposes is far from a well-established technology, a series of typical sequential tasks can be identified. Based on the extensive retrieval program conducted in the Community Intervention Project, and other published accounts, the following retrieval steps may be outlined:

1. Defining the problem/goal to be dealt with
2. Identifying general knowledge relevant to the problem/goal
3. Identifying specific knowledge and data sources
4. Determining appropriate descriptors for the search
5. Establishing parameters of a retrieval search program

6. Establishing search procedures, including the recording of information
7. Establishing procedures for aggregating and codifying information
8. Pilot testing the retrieval design
9. Reformulating and implementing the retrieval program

In his book on industrial design, Jones (1970) lays out a similar list of steps in industrial R&D. His are designated as follows:

1. Identify the purposes for which published information is being sought.
2. Identify the kinds of publications that are likely to contain information that can be relied upon for these purposes.
3. Select the most relevant of the standard methods of beginning a literature search.
4. Minimize the search cost by allowing for retrieval delays and continuously evaluating both the choice of sources and the applicability of data collected.
5. Keep accurate and complete references to documents that are found to be usable. (pp. 202–205)

The two lists, although produced independently from different social R&D and industrial R&D experiences, overlap considerably. This again suggests common attributes of R&D in the social and physical fields. Some of the Jones' observations will be woven into this discussion, both because of their instructive utility in their own right, and to bring attention to similar features of social and physical R&D.

Defining the Problem/Goal

In the normal sequence of R&D a fairly delimited, practical problem or goal is designated at the outset. Problem and goal are, ordinarily, opposite sides of the same coin, stated one way or the other for reasons of preference. In industry, for example, the *problem* for a particular company might be that the cost of a special kind of transistor is too high. This prevents that company from producing a particular appliance that is attractive and affordable to the public. The *goal* would be the development of a lower-cost transistor that is efficient at the level of current operational standards. In the human services context, the problem may be stated as client reluctance to use a given agency service and the goal may be a method to stimulate a greater degree of service utilization. The R&D objective is more clearly pinpointed when the goal formulation is employed. In recent association with colleagues and students the author has observed the following retrieval objectives:

To develop methods for reducing the sense of dependency experienced by elderly clients in receiving social services;

To develop methods for speeding up social cohesion among group members during the early stages of forming a new group;

To develop methods for broadening and sustaining member participation in a graduate training assistants union in college;

To develop effective group treatment methods for released mental patients living in a halfway house residence in order to enhance their reintegration into the community;

To provide community based human service workers with better tools of persuasion and opinion change for their intervention activities.

In each case a specific objective is indicated; ordinarily in the form of a procedure, technique or method which will aid in fulfilling human service professional goals.

Jones indicates it is helpful to draft a written statement of purposes in order to formalize and delimit the effort. He also suggests that in an established, ongoing R&D organization retrieval efforts may involve generally keeping up with the state of the art in an area of concern, let us say mental retardation or day care. In this way, when more specific searches are necessary for particular development undertakings, a pool of generally relevant information is already available and close at hand.

Identifying General Knowledge Areas Relevant to the Problem/Goal

At first blush the identification of knowledge areas pertinent to a given development undertaking may seem simple and obvious. Experience shows that this is not the case. For example, with regard to the problem of reducing dependency of elderly clients, multiple knowledge sources were drawn upon, including the fields of medicine, gerontology, psychology, social work, nursing, rehabilitation and several others. For particular problems, the potential number of knowledge areas may be so numerous as to prohibit exploration of them all. Judgement ordinarily needs to be exerted to allow a sweep which covers enough knowledge areas to make the search productive and meaningful, without being so broad as to rule out the feasibility of the search and manageability of the data that is collected. This type of judgement requires consideration of the most pertinent knowledge areas as well as their appropriate number and blend, relative to the task at hand and the resources available to execute it. Jones highlights the need for discerning scope of inquiry: "Inefficient searches can tie up expensive people for months and can involve costly delays at the start of a project" (p. 208).

Thomas (1967) has written cogently on the matter of selecting knowledge from the social sciences for practice use. He lists a number of substantive areas of sociology ordered by objects of analysis in social work. For example, information about "client," the terminological referent in social work, may be found in sociology under such categories as social stratification, race and ethnic relations, personality and social structure, social disorganization and deviant behavior, sociology of mental illness and criminology. Data about agencies and service organizations may be discovered in areas such as organizations, institutions, social systems theory and political sociology. He states:

> It is clear that there are substantive domains of sociology relevant to all of the specific analytic areas of social work, that some substantive domains are either uniquely or most particularly associated with certain social work areas and not others, and that altogether a large portion of the knowledge of sociology bears upon one or another aspect of social work. (p. 11)

Both the pertinence and the complexity of connecting up knowledge domains with applied objectives are revealed in that statement.

In selecting knowledge areas it is important to keep in mind that the ends being sought are applied in nature, therefore it is appropriate to have a mix of basic and applied research sources. It is neither necessary nor desirable to confine the search to pure science fields, as the practice of clinical fields may offer some beginning intelligence about the working through of more fundamental principles. This balance of perspectives should optimally be represented, resources permitting, in a retrieval staff itself (researchers, researcher-practitioners, empirically oriented practitioners), as well as in the research literature explored. Thus, if the area under development pertains to an agency management issue both the *Administrative Science Quarterly* and *Public Administration Review* could likely be included among the sources; if it deals with group treatment methods both *Sociometry* and the *International Journal of Group Psychotherapy* would be valid candidates for inclusion.

Identifying Specific Knowledge and Data Sources

The delineation of knowledge areas to be exploited is a necessary but hardly sufficient step in the conduct of a retrieval program. Knowledge is reported and stored in a variety of different forms and sources. Jones puts it this way:

> It is worth remembering that the quantity of *knowledge* in a library is less than the vast number of *documents* would suggest. Most publications, academic or otherwise are merely repetitions, or small extensions, of fundamental discoveries that are themselves quite rare. The knowledge in most books and papers, like the knowledge in this one, appears in many different publications. *The main difficulty is that of knowing where to look.* [emphasis added] (p. 202)

Selecting the most relevant method of beginning the literature search, Jones continues, requires that one be aware of what methods are available. These include consulting various reference works as a guide to reputable experts and their publications, consulting with librarians, information staffs, or professional consultants, consulting individuals who, by the nature of their work are likely to have had to find a portion of the information sought, using any of various mechanized or automated key word indexes, consulting abstracting journals, and consulting periodicals.

A useful way to review knowledge sources is to examine four particular forms: Computerized Data Banks, Indexes, Review Services, Synthesized Works.

COMPUTERIZED DATA BANKS   One of the major advances in the storage and inventorying of information, we have stated, has been the use of computer-assisted information systems. A considerable number of such systems already exist, and additional ones are being established all the time. Some of the more prominent ones which have reference to the social and behavioral sciences are the following:

Data Users Services Division, Bureau of the Census

Education Resources Information Center (ERIC)

Institute for Science Information (ISI)

Lockheed Information Retrieval Service

Medical Literature Analysis and Retrieval System (MEDLARS)

National Center for Voluntary Action Clearing House (NCVA)

National Clearinghouse for Mental Health Information (NCMHI)

National Clearinghouse for Smoking and Health

National Criminal Justice Reference Service (NCJRS)

National Institute on Drug Abuse

National Reference Center, Science and Technology

National Technical Information Service

Psychological Abstracts Information Services (PAIS)

Smithsonian Science Information Exchange (SSIE)

(Full information on these and other sources can be found in *Information Sources and How to Use Them,* Human Interactor Research Institute in Collaboration with the National Institute of Mental Health, Rockville, Maryland, 1975.)

Some of these data banks are broad in scope (such as the Lockheed and Smithsonian) some are more narrow (such as the mental health, education and criminal justice banks). They vary in terms of cost and the form in which information is provided. The complexity of format for employing key words and descriptors varies considerably from system to system.

Some, such as the Lockheed have a rapid response capability, employing on-line interactive search procedures.

Because of the sophistication of the technology brought to bear and the prodigious amount of information in the data pools, one can mistakenly have a beguiling sense of confidence about the utility of these services. In the Community Intervention Project we investigated a half-dozen systems and found all of them lacking with regard to our purposes.

Various problems quickly became evident: 1) the systems were often too cumbersome, complex, or expensive to use; 2) information was simply in reference form, suggesting which articles to examine on various subjects in another step rather than providing abstracts that could be used directly; 3) if abstracts were provided, they sometimes gave so little data about findings or methods that they were virtually unusable except as a reference to the original studies; 4) the systems generally did not yield research data exclusively—we had to plod through an incredibly massive gallimaufry of theoretical, speculative, conceptual and experiential reports to extract the occasional research-based materials; 5) some of the systems primarily gave information on studies or projects in progress rather than the findings of completed studies.

Other researchers and developers have experienced similar difficulties. This subject will be discussed further later in the chapter when the requisites of a more ideal user-responsive data system are presented.

INDEXES TO PERIODICALS   Indexes are a well-known and much-used resource for students and others engaged in library research. It is the rare student who is not familiar with the *Readers' Guide to Periodical Literature* as a comprehensive inventory of popular and social science references. Many are also acquainted with *Social Sciences and Humanities Index* (formerly the *International Index*) for a wide range of specifically social and behavioral science materials. Both of these sources index but do not abstract published articles. Another general source with much utility is *The Social Sciences Citation Index,* which gives complete coverage of over 1,000 social science journals and selective coverage of another 2,000, presenting information under a source index, a citation index and the Perlmuter subject index. This program is an outgrowth of the previously established *Science Citation Index,* managed by the Institute for Scientific Information of Philadelphia.

Two other services that are well known, and quite broad in their scope, are *Psychological Abstracts* and *Sociological Abstracts.* While maintaining a definite discipline focus, much surrounding and related literature is included. For example, the sociological publication has good coverage of social work materials and the psychological one of education and business writings. Both present brief summaries of articles that are indexed.

Beyond these somewhat general sources, there are a variety of more specialized information sources related to particular subjects and fields. For example, in medicine the searcher is able to rely on the *Bibliography of Medical Review*, the *Cumulative Index to Nursing Literature, Excerpta Medica*, the *Hospital Literature Index*, and *Index Medicus*. Some of these include abstracts, others do not, and the subject cataloging procedures vary considerably. Other indexes by specialties include the following:

Child Development Abstracts and Bibliography

Coordinate Index Reference Guide to Community Mental Health

Mental Retardation Abstracts

Poverty and Human Resources Abstracts

Psychopharmacological Abstracts/Quarterly Journal of Studies on Alcohol

Rehabilitation Literature

Social Work Research & Abstracts

Knowing of the availability of a specialized source can add immeasurably to the efficiency of a search program. These publications and others are described in detail in the previously mentioned *Information Sources and How to Use Them*. A limitation of almost all these sources is that a sparse amount of information is provided for any entry, enough to indicate ordinarily whether particular reports or studies are likely to be pertinent for a given development purpose. In almost all instances a further trip to the original publication will be necessary.

REVIEW SERVICES Many organizations provide the service of reviewing and summarizing literature related to various kinds of problems or fields of study. This carries the indexing concept one step further. An ambitious example of this is the Project Share program of HEW's Office of Intergovernmental Systems. The service is aimed primarily at managers of human service organizations with the intention of aiding them in carrying out their administrative functions. In addition to routinely abstracting literature in the field, Project Share issues various annotated bibliographies on selected subjects considered to be of interest to agency administrators. Two recent reviews were on the topics of "Providing Human Services to the Elderly" and "Trends in Mental Health Services Coordination." The Project also issues ten-page, comprehensive Executive Summaries of selected documents in their collection upon request. An additional service is a series of Project Share *Monographs*, state of the knowledge summaries in selected topical areas written by recognized experts familiar with the particular area.

There has been a growth of these special knowledge consolidation programs concomitant with the expansion of accumulated knowledge. A few additional illustrative examples may be of interest:

Alcohol and Health Notes (National Institute on Alcohol Abuse and Alcoholism)

Crime and Delinquency Literature (National Council on Crime and Delinquency)

Digest of Neurology and Psychiatry (Institute of Living, Hartford)

Evaluation (National Institute of Mental Health)

Innovation Information and Analysis Project News (George Washington University Policy Studies)

JSAS Catalog of Selected Documents in Psychology (Journal Supplement, Abstract Service, American Psychological Association)

Mental Health Digest (Government Printing Office)

Schizophrenia Bulletin (National Institute of Mental Health)

Smoking and Health Bulletin (Center for Disease Control, HEW)

SSIE Science Newsletter (Smithsonian Science Information Exchange)

An exhaustive listing of such sources is obviously beyond what can reasonably be undertaken here. Those given are suggestive of what might be found in other areas of interest. The trick is to locate the appropriate source for a particular R&D venture.

SYNTHESIZED WORKS   A number of scholars have prepared academic books that seek to consolidate or synthesize research literature in their fields of endeavor. These works, sometimes referred to as propositional inventories, concentrate on conveying to the reader in a comprehensive fashion the current level of scientifically validated knowledge in a given field or discipline. While most such inventories are fairly narrow and highly focused, Berelson and Steiner's *Human Behavior: An Inventory of Scientific Findings* (1964) was an early (and highly recognized) attempt to codify all available social science knowledge concerning individual and social behavior.

Another excellent example is to be found in the work of Goldstein, Heller, and Sechrest (1966). Here, research findings in psychotherapy have been compiled to provide guidelines to the clinician in a variety of matters. Included are such areas as interpersonal attraction in the therapy relationship, resistance to behavior change, transfer of therapeutic learning, and composition of psychotherapy groups. A similar compendium was completed by Fischer (1978) for social case work.

Decision making in small groups is the focus of still another inventory compiled by Collins and Guetzkow (1964). The generalizations concern such issues as direct and indirect sources of power in decision-making groups, obstacles to effective interpersonal relations, participant satisfaction, and leadership traits and roles.

The 101 propositions derived in Robin Williams' *The Reduction of Intergroup Tensions* (1974) represent an early landmark work in retrieval of information dealing with the techniques and procedures for improving relations among various racial and ethnic groups. Williams' collation of research on programs conducted by human relations agencies allowed him to provide background research information on such matters as the origins of hostility, types of conflict, and reactions of minority groups. He was able to suggest programmatic initiatives based on the effects of information and education, of contact and collaboration among contending groups, of legislation and law enforcement, and of different social arrangements among groups.

Some additional related studies in fairly specific subareas include Rogers (1962, 1971), having to do with the diffusion of innovations, Price (1968), on organizational management, Deutsch (1973), on the resolution of conflict, and Erlich (1973), on prejudice.

A less extensive variant is the *Annual Review* books that present summaries of research on several different selected subjects. *The Annual Review of Sociology,* for example, has included chapters on topics such as political participation, health care delivery systems, community power, and voluntary action groups. *The Annual Review of Psychology* has covered the effects of the mass media, personality and social development, gaming, and organizational development. (These are published by Annual Reviews, Inc., Palo Alto, California. The JAT Press of Greenwich, Connecticut, also runs an *Annual Series* summarizing advances in various areas of social science.)

Rather than turning to these organized secondary sources, the searcher can go directly to original sources for information. For example, a specific set of relevant journals can be singled out for study and scanned systematically for pertinent subject matter. Or the card catalogs in the library can be examined for books that will likely have content that is appropriate. There are advantages to direct engagement with such sources. The searcher is close to the original data and can readily appraise its usefulness and quality. If the journals or books are strategically selected, the time saved from a two step arrangement can be put to efficient use. Some specialists, such as Rogers, have moved in progression from a manual, original source approach to a computerized approach. His first book in 1962 on diffusion of innovations relied entirely on manual treatment of individually collected original sources. His second book with Shoemaker (1971) employing the categories developed earlier, was computer assisted.

DETERMINING APPROPRIATE DESCRIPTORS FOR THE SEARCH   In sociology "functional autonomy" implies a sub-system of a larger organization that operates autonomously. In social psychology the same term means the continuance of an individual's behavior after the condition that originally stimulated it has been removed. The lack of common terminology among social science disciplines, and even within them, creates severe burdens upon systems for the storage and communication of information. Even more severe is the absence of shared language between social scientists and practitioners. This is an important component of the gap between research and its application that was discussed in an earlier chapter.

This absence of a shared language handicaps the efforts of potential applied users who wish to dip into social scientific literature for information and guidelines. As Jones observes, the same condition prevails in industry and the physical sciences:

The underlying difficulty of literature searching is not the magnitude of information explosion but poverty of the "intermediate language" of library classifications and indexes that separate the richness of publications from richness of the problems to which they could be applied. Far too little of either the contents of a published document, or of the complexity of a specific problem, can be represented by the category titles, code numbers or key words that are meant to transmit information from document to seeker. Therefore one can expect to retrieve lots of irrelevant documents before finding one that is useful. (p. 207)

The difficulty is compounded because different data systems require different descriptors for the same information. Referring again to the inquiry into dependency by the elderly, the variations in descriptors for several different sources is indicated:

Index Medicus	Personality
Excerpta Medica	Psychology, Nursing, Rehabilitation, Social Welfare, Psychiatry
Psychological Abstracts	Self-esteem, Dependency
Journal of Gerontology	Medical Care and Diagnosis, Geriatrics, Psychological Processes

The best way to become adept in using given sources or systems is through experience. Such acquaintance with their workings, special requirements and peculiarities permits the user to exploit their benefits expeditiously. R&D programs of long standing or with concentrated effort in certain problem areas have such experienced people on staff. Fortunately, the novice and neophyte can draw on a variety of experienced functionaries to speed up their facility in using resources: librarians, information specialists, information scientists, retrieval staff from other organizations, professional consultants and the like. Jones points out a trap to avoid in employing such consultation:

It can be equally difficult to convey the objectives of an information search to librarians, or to subject experts of whom one may seek guidance. When faced with this difficulty, one might resort to describing one's interests very broadly for fear that one's guide will miss a vital point of the enquiry. This, however, is a bad tactic as it will cause the retrieval of a large mass of documents, most of which will be irrelevant or already familiar. (p. 204)

An intermediate level of subject matter conceptualization seems desirable. Another aid to choice of descriptors, although the point pertains to the R&D retrieval process generally, is to operate at the level of middle range theory. Broad, vague, diffuse theoretical concepts and terms such as *id, anomie, social system, collective unconscious,* and *historical determinism,* will probably be of little use to the practical purposes of the R&D enterprise. Rogers in his retrieval work on innovations specifically eschewed "grand theory" primarily on the basis that it is not subject to empirical testing. For general knowledge development purposes of the social science disciplines, grand theory has an honored place and a vital purpose. For R&D, however, the level of abstraction aimed for should be "middle-range" or moderate empirical generalization. The effort is directed at describing regularities in the way specific social processes occur. This retrieval product will be subjected to empirical testing and variable manipulation in the development stage. A leaning toward concrete pragmatic theory rather than very broad or loose theory is a bias inherent in the R&D process.

ESTABLISHING PARAMETERS OF A RETRIEVAL SEARCH PROGRAM   Because the body of literature that potentially can be examined is so vast it is necessary to place boundaries around the pool of information that will be searched. Otherwise the task may become overwhelming and chaotic. Unless one has reasonable control of the literature search, it is entirely possible to wind up that search with much *information* and little *intelligence:*

This can happen when too much time is spent in identifying, retrieving and reading documents and when too little time is spent in evaluating their relevance to the problem in hand. (Jones, 1970)

There are basically three factors to include in structuring parameters. One is the *range number of sources,* a second is the set of *descriptors* to be employed and a third is the *time frame.* With regard to *range of sources,* it was pointed out earlier that a balance is necessary between scope and feasibility. Nothing is gained by attempting to cover all existing knowledge. Given the rudimentary state of information retrieval technology in the social sciences, that would be an impossible aspiration. One can aim to encompass a "satisfactory" rather than a universal knowledge base. Parsimony and good sense must be applied in order to make the task manageable; balance is provided by venturesomeness in order to give sufficient breadth. On this latter point Bright (1961) suggests that many times sources of information have been found in "unlikely" places and provides the following examples:

CONCEPT	"LOGICAL" CONCEPT SOURCE	ACTUAL SOURCE
Synthetic fiber (nylon)	Textile industry	Chemical industry
Diesel locomotive	Railroad equipment industry	Automobile industry
Ballpoint pen	Fountain pen industry	Hungarian sculptor and chemist (Biro brothers)

No rules are available to program for scope and manageability while allowing venturesomeness. One is left only with an orienting frame of reference as a guide.

The second factor, selection of appropriate *descriptors* has already been discussed. These descriptors serve as a compass for guiding the searcher through an often disordered and confusing terrain of information. The more finely tuned the descriptors are relative to the knowledge source, the easier and more effective is the search.

The *time frame* encompassing the sought after literature is the third factor. Is relevant research likely to have been produced only very recently because of rapidly changing research technology or social trends? Is it likely to have been produced in small increments over a very long period of time? Has it developed bimodally, first in an early period and again very recently?

There are probably situations—R&D problems—where a time frame may be easily and clearly defined. More likely, the time frame will be selected somewhat arbitrarily, with the results of a pilot review indicating whether it is adequate, too large, or too narrow.

The parameters of a search program can be depicted from an example in the Community Intervention Project. Thirty journals were selected as original sources for review, based on a high percentage of social and social psychological content, many empirical reports and an applied orientation. These journals were surveyed for a period of publication time covering six years, 1964 to 1970. Among descriptors for selecting and coding articles were included the following: participation, diffusion of innovations, political and legislative behavior, change agent roles and organizational behavior. The parameters of the search may be visualized as below:

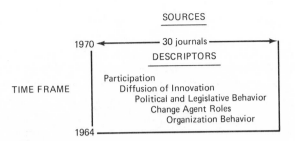

The boundaries and content of the search are clearly defined. This type of boundary setting permits one to explore in the expansive world of social science knowledge without becoming lost in the underbrush.

ESTABLISHING SEARCH PROCEDURES, INCLUDING THE RECORDING OF INFORMATION A comprehensive search can yield an unwieldy, entangling morass of information. For this reason it is important to keep accurate and complete reference data. Formalized and agreed upon procedures and forms are essential.

Probably the most critical element of a properly conducted search is a recording form for setting down information in a standard, complete and goal-directed way. From our experience, we can detail certain basic features of such a form. First of all, basic identification of the document or study being entered—title, author, original source, subject matter or main themes addressed. Such information might also include such factors as key variables, social context, types of subjects, study design and methodology, instruments used. This beginning section might also provide a mechanism for screening the document into or out of the data pool—is it an empirically based study, does it explicitly include one of the set of variables defining the domain of the search, does it lend itself to some type of applied formulation?

At the core of the report is a summary or abstract of the retrieved document. This should include: elaboration on the theoretical perspective or problem investigated, including conceptual framework or hypotheses; a reasonably well-developed description of the methodology; and a statement of the major findings. Reviewers should "stay close to the data"; i.e., report in mainly quantitative form what the findings of the study are, rather than accepting as primary data the conclusions, implications, or conjectures of the author that are elaborations of basic data. When this is accomplished, the study may be coded into relevant variables of the search. This may simply be the descriptors themselves or rubrics which cut across and organize sets of descriptors.

In addition, the reviewers may have an open-ended section in which to make general comments and notes. Here, for example, they might reflect on the importance or quality of the study, its relationship to other studies reviewed, limitations of the study, and so forth. A sample recording form is shown on page 75.

It may be advisable to create a separate file for each major search variable. Typically, we found that a study may be coded in anywhere from one to five of these areas. A copy of the study should be placed in as many separate files as the number of separate variables into which it had been coded with proper cross referencing. A study on behavior modification treatment may also have something to say concerning the climate of the service delivery structure and/or desirable qualifications and traits of treatment personnel. The same study may give equally valid and important information on each of these variables. Adequate orientation and systematic monitoring of staff is essential in this phase.

ESTABLISHING PROCEDURES FOR AGGREGATING AND CODIFYING INFORMATION   This task is on the one hand extremely tedious and on the other, highly imaginative. It may be necessary to sift through sometimes hundreds of studies in order to group similar elements, and visualize connections among distinct languages, concepts, and findings from diverse disciplines and contexts. Clusters of data comprising a consensus of findings must be constructed, and appropriate statements constituting generalizations be composed.

The importance of such codification in all R&D must not be overlooked. Gibson (1964) conceives knowledge development in R&D in terms of both experimental research and theoretical research. This latter, in Gibson's terms, is roughly equivalent to codification and is defined as the "ordering of knowledge." Gibson's comments regarding the "theoretical research" block of activity are instructive:

The input to this [theoretical research] block is new and old knowledge, and the function of this block is to arrange the new facts and the old knowledge in consistent and satisfying patterns which we call theories. Its outputs are new or extended consistent patterns of knowledge—increased understanding that comes when the new and strange are logically related to the old and familiar and the power of predicting new facts by extrapolation from well-established theories. In other words, the primary function of this block is to reduce the myriad facts emerging from experimental research to systematic and manageable form. (pp. 37–38)

The culmination of the retrieval effort is embodied in this codification exercise, as available bits of knowledge become "condensed, summarized, repackaged." Two important technical problems relating to this task deserve mention, one dealing with the validity or power of truth statements, the other with the treatment of conflicts or contradictions among them. Neither of these problems are amenable to a quick or easy solution, but some approaches to dealing with them exist.

STUDY REPORT FORM

Reporter _____

Journal _____ Vol. _____ Issue _____

Date _____ Pages _____

Author(s) _____

Title _____

I. *Basic checklist*

   a) Variables related to CO practice   Yes _____

      Major variables or themes _____

      _____

   b) Empirical _____ Other _____

   c) Study Design: Exploratory _____

               Quantitative-Descriptive _____

               Experimental _____ Other _____

   d) Study Methods Survey _____ Case study _____

               Part. Obser. _____

               Doc. _____ Demograph date _____

                             Other _____

   e) Any major defects (sample size or representativeness, logical inconsistencies, major statistical problems, etc.) _____

      _____

      _____

   f) Context: U.S.: South-Urban _____   Foreign: Developing Urban _____

                    Rural _____   Rural _____

                    Other-Urban _____   Developed Urban _____

                    Rural _____   Rural _____

                    National _____

                    Institutional _____

                        total institutions _____

                        mental hospitals, etc.

II. *Abstract:* 1) *General area of inquiry and conceptual framework* (hypothesis if any) 2) *Methodology,* 3) *Findings*—you may copy abstract of article if given.

III. Practice Issue Areas:

    1. Communication _____

    2. Decision Making _____

    3. Diffusion and Adoption _____

    4. Legislative-Political-Governmental Process _____

    5. Movement of Populations _____

    6. Participation _____

    7. Planning Process _____

    8. Power _____

    9. Practitioner Roles _____

    10. Resistance to Change _____

    11. Service Structure and Delivery _____

    12. Social Influence _____

    13. Strategy _____

        a. Conflict _____

        b. Consensus _____

        c. Bargaining _____

        d. Other _____

For each item checked, indicate *major findings* from abstract and *practice implications.* Emphasize and develop implications. *Name below* those *issue areas* relevant to a given set of findings-implications. General guidelines—stay close to the *actual data;* push ahead from findings to practice implications. Be specific about directives suggested to the practitioner. What does this finding tell the C.O. practitioner about what he should *do.*

IV. *Comments* (other findings, significance of study, relationship to other studies, important references and their implications or findings, etc.):

Methods for assessing research for use have been proposed by various writers (Tripodi, et al.; 1969; Thomas, 1967; Zetterberg, 1965). Criteria for adequate assessment essentially parallel the criteria for good research. These include matters of validity, reliability, representativeness of the sample, logic of the design, comparability of comparison groups, and the match between the form of data and statistical techniques used. Tripodi has singled out five major criteria of assessment: measurement accuracy, empirical generation, internal control, hypothesis researchability and concept translatability. The assessor, then, should be sophisticated in methodology for production of social research, and then apply his or her technical acumen carefully in evaluating the output of other researchers.

In conducting retrieval programs certain difficulties in follow-through along these lines quickly become apparent. The staff is dealing ordinarily with large numbers of studies. The studies may be reported in journals and periodicals of varied sorts. We discovered that in many instances the journal report did not give full details of the methodology because of space restrictions. Most journal articles, after being located, still required tracing back to a primary source if one wished full methodological documentation. Sometimes this is a book or monograph, occasionally already written, often still in preparation. The original larger study may be in fugitive form and not readily available for general access, i.e., an in-house technical report of a study, a document of a governmental bureau, a report to the funding sponsor of the study, etc. Sometimes the journal-sized version is the only formally written report of the study. Such obstacles to obtaining the full technical detail are a serious handicap to meticulous assessment.

Assuming technical details are available, one then quickly has an encounter with the reality of the burgeoning technical advancements and innovative methodological approaches in the social sciences. Nowadays the variety and complexity of statistical techniques, mathematical models, computer treatments and design intricacies are staggering. Often only specialists in a single technique are fully able to decipher and appraise work related to that technique. At the same time, new methodological forms and variations are constantly being reported. It is unlikely that any retrieval programs can include the varied staff capability necessary to appraise technically a substantial portion of the full range of social science research output. Mullen (1978) relates many of these same problems which he encountered in his retrieval program.

These problems suggest two broad approaches to the assessment question; one may be termed the "elegance" approach, the other the "bulk" approach. The former employs a procedure wherein one seeks only a small number of studies related to a given R&D problem, but these studies are to be the very best. The design and methodology of acceptable retrieved studies should be above reproach: meticulous, sophisticated, and definitive. Since only a small number of studies are sought for the total data pool, much time can be spent in seeking out the original report, scrutinizing the methodology, consulting with technical experts if necessary concerning the fine points of the study, and so on.

The bulk approach uses the opposite procedure. It assumes that at the current state of the art few definitive studies exist in the social sciences. One should therefore aim for aggregated intelligence rather than the rare breakthrough. Assessment here entails screening out the overtly faulty and dubious studies based on the available information. The remaining majority of studies are included in the data pool. When large numbers of these studies converge in their findings, despite use of different methodologies, subjects, contexts, assumptions and disciplines, this is considered the mark of a strong generalization. Bulk, with diversity of context and consistency of results—rather than elegance with methodological distinction—characterizes this approach. It is too early to say which of these approaches holds the most promise for social R&D. Perhaps their relative efficacies may vary depending on the technical circumstances surrounding a particular R&D undertaking. Also new developments in information sciences may offer still other fruitful alternatives.

A useful guide to the evaluation of individual studies has been formulated by Tripodi and his associates (1969) in *The Assessment of Social Research*. A three part assessment frame is suggested. The frame and some factors to be considered under each part are as follows:

Problem Formulation

Use of existing literature in conceptualizing the problem under study.

Definition of major concepts conceptually and operationally.

Explication of hypotheses and of independent and dependent variables.

Assumptions made by the investigator regarding the selection of variables for study.

Research Design and Data Collection

Maximizing the internal validity of the experiment through the design.

Sampling and experimental control.

Reliability and validity of methods.

Control of the effects of measurement.

Minimizing potential bias including effects of relevant variables which are not controlled.

Data Analysis and Conclusions

Do the data provide evidence for testing the hypotheses or issues under investigation?

Appropriateness of statistical tests for the problem and the design.

Consistency of findings with the data.

Consistency of conclusions with the findings.

Extent to which the researcher accomplished the purposes set forth for the study.

In the view of the authors, somewhat different emphases need to be given to different types of studies in applying this scheme. For example, in experimental studies control of variables is a highly important factor to review; in quantitative-descriptive studies one should look to see if statistical cross tabulations were made in order to take into account potentially influential variables; in more qualitative exploratory studies, sources of conclusions (the literature, findings of the study or initial biases of the authors) have to be given special attention. While scrutiny of individual research reports is necessary, the authors point out the importance of the pattern of multiple research reports. "Scientific knowledge is based on cumulative, replicative studies, and in the social sciences and social work, it is highly unlikely that any one study will resolve all pertinent questions about a single phenomenon" (p. 67).

The second major problem associated with codification pertains to potential contradictions in findings. Those engaged in large scale codification projects have handled this in different ways. Rogers and Shoemaker (1971) explicitly list all studies supporting or contradicting a given generalization. Collins and Guetzkow (1964) assert the generalization and then include information about inconsistent findings in their general discussion. Rothman (1974) uses a four point rating scheme which indicates the strength of literature support, including uniformity or variation among findings.

Based on our work in this area we have come to conclude that the problem of inconsistency is not as large as is often claimed. If a reviewer focuses upon differences and inconsistencies he will find them. If he leans in the direction of synthesis and reconciliation among studies, the potential in that direction is great. As will be elaborated in the next chapter, it is possible to bring an intellectual stance of demolition or of salvage into the cluttered warehouse of social science knowledge.

Two techniques were found by our staff to assist in the task of synthesis: raising the level of abstraction one notch higher, and finding an intervening variable that explained and reconciled differing conclusions. An example of each will be provided. With regard to level of abstraction, we often found it possible to group different findings under a concept that embraced them all. A simple illustration will suffice. Under the subject of participation, some studies found that participation rates were highest among subjects with higher levels of education, others concluded that participation was associated with greater income, still other studies found that participation was elevated for those of higher social status. The issue was easily resolved by indicating that participation varies with socioeconomic status. Sometimes the generalization may merely express the existence of differences as the most useful empirical description of a phenomenon. For example, some studies indicate that practitioners engage in a narrow band of role activities, others have found a wide spectrum of practice roles. The issue was resolved in the following set of generalizations:

Some practitioners utilize a limited role set, others utilize an extended role set encompassing a range of subroles.

Multiple role performance is associated with a clientele that is distant or distrustful of the practitioner's sponsoring organization.

Decentralized organizational structures foster broader role sets than do centralized structures. (Rothman, 1974, pp. 61–64)

Each generalization and sub-generalization is based on specific studies, and in the original presentation detailed references were given.

The last sub-generalization demonstrates also the notion of locating an intervening variable that explains differences. A yet more pointed illustration can be taken from the area of diffusion of innovations. Some studies have found that higher diffusion rates are associated with small organizations, other studies conclude that higher rates correlate with larger organizational size.

In inspecting this set of studies a variable termed "organizational slack" emerged. This term refers to the amount of excess or unused resources available in an organization which can be applied in a venturesome way to innovative activities. A set of generalizations and sub-generalizations conveying this understanding was presented as follows:

The size of an organization does not appear to have a consistent relationship with its innovativeness.

Large organizations tend to have more organizational slack (uncommitted resources), which can be applied to innovative programs. When organizational size is associated with organizational slack, large organizations will be more innovative on the whole than small organizations.

Large organizations can afford to employ more and higher level professionals, who may serve as an innovative force. When organizational size is related to the number of professionals employed, an organization will be more innovative.

Smaller organizations devote their resources to fewer and smaller innovative programs, but implement them more intensively and comprehensively than do larger organizations. (Rothman, pp. 468–470)

In many, many areas, however, it was our experience that large numbers of studies had findings which were essentially consensual and required neither of these reconciling techniques.

As Gibson stated above and our own work verified and reflected, codification is not a mechanistic, routine chore. Instead it is a demanding intellectual task of "theoretical research" requiring highly developed skills of creative synthesis.

Glass (1976, 1977) has termed this methodological area "meta-analysis of research" and has been exploring technical issues and approaches. Other scholars such as Feldman (1971) and Light and Smith (1971) have also been grappling with the problem. The National Science Foundation decided to sponsor a study of the state of the art of knowledge synthesis in sociological, psychological and educational research in an effort to stimulate technical advances (Jackson, 1978).

The distinctive and qualified function of this theoretical knowledge in R&D again should be clarified. The codified output is not construed to constitute scientific principles or truths which are to be communicated to the scientific community, or disseminated in professional journals as validated knowledge. Rather it has a more internal and instrumental purpose, to provide the development staff with ideas that can be transformed into problem solving concepts. Thus the output of the retrieval stage is an always tentative creation which must be further processed, programmed and tested in empirical contexts. These tests provide verification of the authenticity or power of what the retrieval effort has brought into being in solving social problems and meeting human needs.

PILOT TESTING THE RETRIEVAL DESIGN   Once a retrieval plan has been designed which incorporates the elements that have been discussed, it is wise to engage in a small-scale, time-limited experimental implementation. Such a pilot test will reveal whether these procedures and approaches are workable and what modifications need to be made in order to obtain the necessary information. The principle of pilot testing is incorporated into the general conceptualization of R&D, and it applies as well within this particular phase. Defects discovered in small-dose samples are easier to handle and correct than those manifested in massive accumulations of materials. In addition to bearing out the operational validity of the reporting forms, filing arrangements and coding procedures, the pilot test can signal whether the descriptors are connecting up with the information that fits, as well as whether certain types of sought-after information are not being acquired. The importance of this early trial run cannot be overstated.

REFORMULATING AND IMPLEMENTING THE RETRIEVAL PROGRAM   When defects have been identified and "bugs" in the procedures worked through, the basic retrieval program can begin. The time allotted for this activity should be clearly noted, with an eye to the time requirements for the overall R&D undertaking. Conformity to the time frame needs to be carefully watched. Appropriate staff should be engaged, oriented, supported and monitored. In some R&D programs this may be full-time, ongoing, specialized personnel, in others it may be temporary, untrained staff. Responsibility for overall coordination and management should be established.

User-Oriented Information Systems

The difficulties and exasperations we described in our attempted use of data banks are by no means unique to our experience. Wilner (1977) and his associates, who have been engaged over several years in developing a specialized information system of reports on evaluative research, list some of the main problems they have encountered:

The information-hungry users of data-banks and clearing-houses do not yet have completely clear sailing. Experience of users is not uniformly satisfactory and users at several levels of sophistication—experienced as well as naive—find that access is sometimes frustrating or inhibiting and that the output is insufficiently informative. (p. 12)

Wilner then goes on to catalog the limitations of such systems:

1. Bibliographic databanks require learning a dictionary of key words. Like most dictionaries, organization is often unstructured (except for alphabetical position) and appears vague; key words have several meanings (e.g., "evaluation"). Search logic sometimes results in overkill, a dumping of wheat plus plenty of chaff.

2. Many bibliographic databanks cover too vast an array of topics. It is hard to find a single set of key words to cover all topics properly; it is easy to distinguish the category "depression" from the category "cancer screening" but fine tuning in either category is not easy.

3. Output does not tell enough. Some databanks consist only of citations or of abstracts that are "indicative" rather than "informative," which necessitates acquisition of an actual copy of the reference before the aptness of the search or the data required can be determined. Current research services tend not to require a standardized format for abstracts and consequently there is no guarantee that any particular bit of information will be included in an abstract . . .

4. There is failure to integrate data analysis with search capability. It is no easy job to grasp the import of a batch of 50–100 printouts resulting from a computer search. Normally, an analytic task of some dimension is needed to analyze the yield, necessitating extensive staff time. (p. 12)

The problem of using data banks, as we discovered, reduces itself simply to the fact that such data banks are not sufficiently user-oriented at this stage in their development. It was far more efficient and effective for us, for the present, to go directly to the documents (the journal articles) and to perform the information search.

What is required, of course, for future social R&D work, is an information system that will be increasingly responsive to specific development objectives. That is to say, they should be user-oriented in design and operation. It is certainly within the realm of our present understanding and capabilities to develop such a system, and guidance is readily available (Kochen, 1974).

There have been, of course, some attempts made to develop on-going information systems in the human services area. A number of these were described earlier. One whose work is of interest because of its applied thrust is the Technical Information Service located in the Center for Social Work Research at the University of Texas, Austin. This center serves the Continuing Education Program and the Resource Center on Child Abuse and Neglect. According to Marta Wolfe (1976), Director of Information Services for TIS:

The Technical Information Service of the Center for Social Work Research was developed to assemble, organize and provide access to technical materials in several areas, not available through existing indexes or regular library channels. These areas include professional continuing education programs; the design, operation and evaluation of social service programs; child abuse and neglect; human services; management; systems design; health care delivery; and services to older persons. (p. 8)

TIS attempts to alert researchers to materials pertaining to their fields of interest by keeping abreast of what is currently available. In addition, TIS performs an information coordination and information searching function through the use of formal and informal networks of other information specialists. TIS also carries on a vigorous acquisitions program, especially for those materials deemed useful but not easily available from other sources. As Wolfe points out, "information services of this sort are relatively new and untested" (p. 9). They do, however, represent an important and necessary beginning if social R&D is to become an important linking mechanism between research and application.

In *The Impact of the Social Sciences,* Boulding (1966) speaks of the potential role of information collecting institutions such as this, drawing analogies also to lessons to be learned from the physical sciences. He points to such things as an embarrassingly imperfect sampling system and the lack of centralized information and processing as reasons why he believes it may be as much as a century before the full impact of the social sciences will be felt:

We operate by bits and pieces, by lights and flashes, and there is up to now no steady process of cumulation, prediction and feedback in the sociosphere as a whole. I have argued, for instance, that if we were going to take the social sciences seriously we should at least establish a world network of social data stations, analogous to weather stations . . . As a matter of fact we have not even established a global system of information about the atmosphere as yet, so that the global information system about the sociosphere is still presumably at least a generation away. (p. 21)

From Retrieval to Design

In R&D knowledge retrieval has a particular utilitarian goal. Unless retrieval is carefully dovetailed with the next step of conversion and design, that goal is likely to be missed. To guard against this there must be integration of function—and probably personnel—between retrieval and design. McCrory et al. (1961) bring this out based on their work at the Battelle Institute:

Unfortunately, the lines of communication between information producing researchers and designers remain nebulous. The justifiable complaint is often heard that the researcher and the designer do not care to, or are not able to, speak the same language. To bridge this gap, the designer must take the initiative and approach the researcher because it is the designer who is directly responsible for utilizing advanced technology . . .
It must be recognized that state of the art, wherever generated or however communicated, has the singular ultimate purpose of supporting the design function. The extent to which the designer taps into this resource will largely determine the value of his design concepts. (p. 58)

Having acquired information from the knowledge base, it is now necessary to manipulate that information in some meaningful fashion, to convert it to a form that will yield workable design concepts. Such conversion and design perspectives and capabilities have been lacking in the social sciences. This problem will be the focus of attention in the next chapter.

BIBLIOGRAPHY

BERELSON, BERNARD, and GARY A. STEINER, *Human Behavior: An Inventory of Scientific Findings.* New York: Harcourt, Brace and World, 1964.

BOULDING, KENNETH E., *The Impact of the Social Sciences.* New Brunswick, N.J.,: Rutgers University Press, 1966.

COLLINS, BARRY E., and HAROLD GUETZKOW, *A Social Psychology of Group Process for Decision Making.* New York: John Wiley & Sons, 1964.

DEUTSCH, MORTON, *The Resolution of Conflict: Constructive and Destructive Process.* New Haven: Yale University Press, 1973.

EHRLICH, HOWARD J., *The Social Psychology of Prejudice: A Systematic Theo-*

retic Review and Propositional Inventory of the American Psychological Study of Prejudice. New York: John Wiley & Sons, 1973.

FELDMAN, K. A., "Using the Work of Others: Some Observations on Reviewing and Integrating." *Sociology of Education*, 44, 1 (1971): 86–102.

FISCHER, JOEL, *Effective Casework Practice: An Eclectic Approach.* New York: McGraw-Hill, 1978.

GIBSON, R. E., "A Systems Approach to Research Management," *Research, Development, and Technological Innovation: An Introduction,* ed. James R. Bright, pp. 34–57. Homewood, Ill.: Richard D. Irwin, Inc., 1964.

GLASS, G. V., "Integrating Findings: The Meta-analysis of Research." *Review of Research in Education* 5, F. E. Peacock Publishers Inc. Itasca, Ill. (1977), 351–79.

GLASS, G. V., "Primary, Secondary, and Meta-analysis of Research." *Educational Researcher* 5, 10 November (1976), 3–8.

GOLDSTEIN, ARNOLD, KENNETH HELLER, and LEE B. SECHREST, *Psychotherapy and the Psychology of Behavior Change.* New York: John Wiley & Sons, 1966.

Information Sources and How to Use Them, Human Interaction Research Institute in collaboration with the National Institute of Mental Health, Rockville, Md., 1975.

JACKSON, G. B., *Methods for Reviewing and Integrating Research in the Social Sciences.* Final report to the National Science Foundation, April 1978.

JONES, J. CHRISTOPHER, *Design Methods: Seeds of Human Futures.* New York: John Wiley & Sons, 1970.

KOCHEN, MANFRED, *Principles of Information Retrieval,* Wiley-Becker and Hayes Series, Los Angeles: Melville Publishing Co., 1974.

LIGHT, R. J. and P. V. SMITH, "Accumulating Evidence: Procedures for Resolving Contradictions among Different Research Studies." *Harvard Educational Review* 41, 4 (1971), 429–71.

McCRORY, R. J., W. H. WILKINSON, and D. W. FRANK, "Synthesis of Concepts in the Design Method," *Technological Planning on the Corporate Level,* Proceedings of a conference sponsored by the Associates of the Harvard Business School, September 8–9, 1961, ed. James R. Bright. Cambridge, Mass.: 1961.

MULLEN, EDWARD J., "The Construction of Personal Models for Effective Practice: A Method for Utilizing Research Findings to Guide Social Interventions," *Journal of Social Service Research* 2, 1, 1978, 45–63.

PRICE, JAMES L., *Organizational Effectiveness: An Inventory of Research.* Homewood, Ill.: Dorsey Press, 1968.

ROGERS, EVERETT, *The Diffusion of Innovations.* New York: The Free Press, 1962.

ROGERS, EVERETT M., and F. FLOYD SHOEMAKER, *The Communication of Innovations.* New York: The Free Press, 1971.

ROTHMAN, JACK, *Planning and Organizing for Social Change: Action Principles from Social Science Research.* New York: Columbia University Press, 1974.

Technological Planning on the Corporate Level, Proceedings of a conference sponsored by the Associates of the Harvard Business School, September 8–9, 1961, ed. James R. Bright. Cambridge, Mass.: 1961.

THOMAS, E. J., "Types of Contributions Behavioral Science Makes to Social Work," *Behavioral Science for Social Workers.* New York: The Free Press, 1967.

TRIPODI, TONY, *Uses and Abuses of Social Research in Social Work.* New York: Columbia University Press, 1974.

TRIPODI, TONY, et al., *The Assessment of Social Research.* Itasca, Ill.: F. E. Peacock Publishers, Inc., 1969.

VILLERS, RAYMOND, *Research and Development: Planning and Control.* New York: Financial Executives Research Foundation, 1974.

WILLIAMS, ROBIN M., *The Reduction of Intergroup Tensions: A Survey of Research on Ethnic, Racial and Religious Group Relations.* New York: Social Science Council, 1947.

WILNER, D. M., et al., "The Custom Research Databank in the Analysis and Transfer of Information," *Evaluation,* 3, no. 1–2 (1977), 11–12.

WOLFE, MARTA, "Concept of Information Services—Old and New," *Contact,* 2, no. 1–2, (Spring–Summer, 1976), 8–9.

ZETTERBERG, HANS L., *On Theory and Verification in Sociology.* (3rd rev. ed.), Totowa, N. J.: Bedminister Press, 1965.

5

Formulating
Application
Concepts

Design is:

The imaginative leap from present facts to future possibilities.

J. K. Page

It involves bringing into being something new and useful that has not existed previously.

J. B. Reswick

CONVERSION AND DESIGN

The leap from research findings to tangible concepts about their practical application seems in the social sciences to constitute a feat of Olympic proportions. In part this may be so because we have neglected to conceptualize what is involved in taking this step or to develop a methodology to power the thrust. Nor do there exist trained specialists with capacities to perform such knowledge transfer roles. We typically give the name "implications" to the output of this conceptual activity. It remains a largely neglected intellectual area in the social sciences and social professions, reminiscent of the intuitive way in which "environmental manipulation," for example, has been treated in the past in clinical practice. It is, however, the next step in our R&D model.[1]

SCHEMATIC MODEL OF RESEARCH UTILIZATION–R & D PROCESS

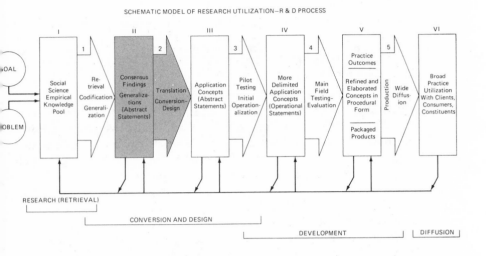

In order to illuminate the issue and offer suggestive avenues of approach, it is useful to look at the experience in research and development in the physical sciences and industrial field. There, the R&D activities involved in converting a scientific generalization into a practical application concept are typically referred to as design, a function afforded recognition and prominence. By bringing into view the place of design in the industrial context, we may obtain clues concerning its utility to the social sciences and human services. From time to time, therefore, connections to industrial R&D will be made.

Let us begin by observing how design has been defined in industrial R&D. Fielden (1963) views design in a manner consistent with our own concept:

Engineering design is the use of scientific principles, technical information and imagination in the definition of a [device or procedure] to perform prespecified functions with the maximum economy and efficiency. (p. 3)

In support, Van Doren (1954) states:

The engineer who *conceives a new machine or appliance,* [and] builds an experimental model . . . is certainly the designer of that machine. (p. 17)

[1]Portions of this discussion appear in Jack Rothman, "Conversion and Design in The Research Utilization Process," *Journal of Social Service Research* 2, 1 (1978). pp. 117–131.

Ansoff (1961) gives a similar perspective and clarifies that this process can materialize in either a hardware or software product. The process involves:

> ... the application of knowledge to the solution of previously unsolved (usually generic) problems. It can either be device-oriented, such as a breadboard which demonstrates that optical diffractive properties of matter (knowledge) can be used to compress electromagnetic pulses (problem), or it can be technique-oriented, such as a procedure for growing semiconductor crystals. (p. 210)

Basically, the utilization of research in this way requires the conversion of "findings" or "generalizations" from descriptive to prescriptive form, from a statement about a relationship between two variables to a statement about how the manipulation of one of the variables might result in particular changes in the other variable. A cognitive leap is made involving the exercise of inference, conjecture and imagination. Thereby, the relationship statement "X is associated with Y" is converted to the application concept "if you wish to bring about X, then do Y."

We know that changing an associational relationship to a causal one is a complex and precarious exercise of reasoning. Some of the following possibilities may be implicated: X causes Y; Y causes X; X causes Y in the presence of A; both X and Y are caused by B; X is caused by C but this relationship is obscure. In developing an application concept inferences about the causal relationship should take into account other theoretical research bearing on the relationship, applied or practiced research illuminating the question, and relevant practice experience. In other words, the application is made in a broadly informed rather than a narrowly mechanistic way.

Formation of hypotheses is on the same basis in traditional experimental research; i.e., they involve hunches and speculations that are rooted in relevant theories and observations. Hypotheses regarding practice theory may perhaps be informed by wider and more varied sources. Thomas (1978) suggests that the following range of knowledge sources are pertinent for forming application concepts in social work: basic research; applied research; values, norms, and laws; allied technology; applied practice procedures; allied administration and policy and practice experience. A research utilization perspective on enhancement of human service practice draws primarily on the first two of the listed sources, supplemented by the others. Thomas indicates that any of the sources may be a primary stimulus for application concepts. Havelock (1969) also advocates diverse sources in retrieval.

It may be useful to think of a two-step process in forming application concepts, the first of which can be referred to as *conversion* and the second as *design*. Conversion implies cognitive attention to the area between existing research knowledge and its reformation as a basic action construct. Design suggests the intellectual work involved in the more detailed articulation of the action construct with reference to the specific application environment—as reflected in anticipated structural, interpersonal, ethical, and administrative problems and considerations. Design is more detailed in its implemental ramifications, but it remains a cognitive expression. This particularized notion of design is distinctly different from its more usual meaning—the design of a study. The design concept here denotes a cognitive formulation suggesting aspects of an action approach or strategy. This may be highly detailed or quite broad, depending on the amount of knowledge available in the area of concern and the exactness of that knowledge.

Several social scientists have used the term conversion to describe the entire linkage area between existing research and its application by a user. For Lundberg (1966) the best way of "specifying conversion roles is to specify a continuum along which roles are ordered" (p. 12). The continuum described by Lundberg extends the full range of research utilization from "science" to "practice." In Lundberg's scheme conversion has a very broad rather than a delimited connotation. Guetzkow's (1959) view is similar. In industry, the word design ordinarily is used as a general term to cover *both* conversion and design.

In the formulation advanced here, conversion and design are specifically attached to the contemplative realm. They designate a mental process involving the translation and synthesis of ideas: arm chair conjecture, consultation with informed professionals and technicians, drawing board work and mathematical modeling.

The workability or effectiveness of a resulting application concept in real world contexts is not established at this stage. Additional empirical investigation and development work are necessary in order to confirm the feasibility and reliability of the application concept and to determine the specific procedural operations needed to implement it. Here one shifts to engagement with people, materials, interrelations, etc., *in situ,* as necessary to test the concept and to begin fabrication of working models of implementation. In other words, even though based in the first instance on scientific evidence, the converted concept essentially represents a hypothesis about intended and hoped for effects and requires subsequent systematic investigation.

This conceptualization may become more clear through a diagrammatic depiction and an application example. The concepts, their relationships, and the time sequence involved are shown in Figure 5-1:

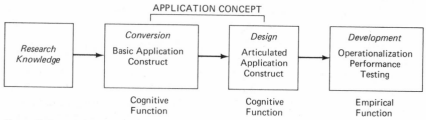

Figure 5–1

Two points of further clarification are necessary. First, while the diagram shows existing research as the basic and initiating source of knowledge for application concepts, in keeping with an R&D perspective, it was indicated earlier that this is supplemented by other sources of knowledge in shaping both conversion and design ideas. Second, including design as a step and the extent of articulation refinements are dependent on the state of the art. In other words, in some less developed areas of knowledge or practice it may be wise to simply frame the basic conversion construct and allow the articulation to evolve from field tests by practitioners in the application environment. When knowledge and practice are more advanced, initial design considerations may be shaped in greater specificity. These two design variations are manifested as well in industrial R&D Kline and Mechling, 1958; Low, 1961.

I will illustrate conversion and design by drawing from an example in a previous work (Rothman, 1974). A generalization stated approximately as below was offered:

Organizations that operate under conditions of a high degree of environmental certainty tend to be characterized by centralization in decision making. Further, this relationship is associated with efficiency of operation.

This knowledge statement was derived from studies by Simpson and Galley (1962), Hage and Aiken (1969), and Kaufman (1960) and several others. Lawrence and Lorsch's (1967 a,b) study of organizations in three types of environments is of particular interest here. They found that effective organizations in the plastic industry, an industry characterized as new, emergent, and rapidly changing (high degrees of uncertainty), were generally highly decentralized in their decision making. Effective organizations in the box manufacturing industry, however, a long-established and routinized field (high degrees of certainty), were highly centralized. There were still different levels of centralization and decentralization in industrial organizations intermediate to these two. (The research also indicates that high degrees of uncertainty are associated with decentralization.)

When events are recurrent and predictable, organizational technology that is fairly routine seems to be efficient. Also, top leadership can be up to date and knowledgeable about these recurring events and plan work activities in a controlled and structured way.

In reformulating this as a conversion construct the following is proposed:

Practitioners in organizations functioning in a context of relatively high degrees of certainty should consider a centralized structure in order to increase efficiency of operation. (This statement puts the generalization in an active, prescriptive form while remaining close to the original content and spirit of the findings codified in the generalization.)

More detailed design considerations emerge from contingent factors that might be assumed to be implicated in such a practice initiative. Some contingencies fall in the following areas:

Structural Factors
It is not necessarily assumed that *extreme* centralization is associated with effectiveness. There needs to be judgement exercised concerning degree of centralization. Most social welfare agencies probably operate optimally under a degree of centralization in the middle range. They may move toward one or another end of this range in order to increase task effectiveness. Income maintenance agencies, for example, can probably tolerate a greater degree of centralization than can settlement houses or grass-roots social action organizations.

Administrative Factors
Managerial and planning-oriented leadership is necessary for a centralized structure. Increasing centralization may require technical equipment, forms, routines, etc., that take a good deal of planning and of administrative know-how. Attention must be paid to the latest and most effective equipment, successful forms and procedures used elsewhere, etc. Monitoring and feedback procedures may be important.

Interpersonal Factors
A negative consequence of centralization in a rather routinized formal organization may be the lowering of employee feelings of satisfaction, identity, or solidarity. For example, studies of industrial workers doing highly routinized jobs show low morale. Other data suggest that a way of minimizing the morale problems associated with high centralization and routinization may be to maximize interpersonal relationships and satisfactions associated with the job. Painting and fix-up projects turned into social events, and the stuffing and mailing tasks of political campaigns treated as parties, are examples of maximizing interpersonal satisfactions to offset the unpleasantness of routine tasks.

Ethical Factors
A highly centralized organizational structure may evolve charges of "dictatorship" or "oppression," particularly in human service contexts. This again suggests a moderate or "soft" style of centralized leadership.

In applying the basic conversion construct the following design considerations might be taken into account:

Centralization should not be at an extreme level; administration staff with well-developed bureaucratic skills should be employed; socio-emotional needs of staff should be attended to by encouraging interpersonal events and relationships; the administrative style should be "soft" in order to avoid the aura of harsh authoritarianism.

The overall application concept (still an action hypothesis) includes the italicized passages comprising the conversion construct and design articulations.

In light of this illustration, it should be apparent that design considerations are governed by the implementation setting. The focus in the case of the Community Intervention Project was on the problem of enhancing human service practice. It could as easily have been upon increasing a manager's effectiveness in a large corporation, or upon increasing the effectiveness of a precinct worker in a political party. In all cases, the core action principle derived from the research literature remains the same. The applied statement will vary slightly, however, as it is directed at particular application settings. Both conditions of certainty and uncertainty are considered in the following examples:

Automobile Manufacturer A plant manager faced with the task of departmental reorganization should consider a centralized, formalized structure to promote effectiveness where that department is to function in a context of relatively high degrees of certainty. (The product has been produced in fairly suitable numbers and using similar materials and methods over a period of years.) A decentralized, low structural arrangement should be considered where the department must function in a context of relatively high degrees of economic uncertainty, technical change, and consumer vacillation. Within the organization the assembly line should operate under greater centralization than the sales department.

Political Campaign Manager In organizing the efforts of campaign workers in a politically "safe" precinct (one in which the outcome of the electoral process is relatively certain because individuals there vote fairly regularly for the desired ticket), the Campaign Manager should consider a precinct organization with a centralized, formal structure. In a politically "dangerous" precinct (one in which the electoral outcome is relatively uncertain because the position of the voters is unknown or shifts from campaign to campaign) the Campaign Manager might wish to consider a precinct organization with a less formalized structure (one which permits flexible, intensive, and independent action by precinct workers).

The possible permutations and combinations of applied statements that may be derived from a given generalization (itself derived from a consensus of the research literature) appears to be limited only by the possible varied application settings. A design concept must be carefully examined for feasibility and fit in relating a generalized principle to a particular implementation setting.

SOCIAL POLICY AS AN APPLICATION CONCEPT

In the social sciences a design concept may form the basis of a social policy or a practice procedure. Often policy statements are action derivations of research findings that make possible broad strategy tendencies. Most often such policy derivations remain untested and unoperationalized before being brought to the point of widespread implementation. The development phase is almost universally overlooked and bypassed.

A few examples of our work illustrate how social policy may emerge as a design concept. For each of the following we will first present a consensus generalization derived from the body of social science research. We will then discuss application implications for policy makers suggested by that generalization. Finally, we will also show application directives for practitioners:

Generalization The rate of adoption of an innovation is related to the geographical accessibility of the innovation to the target system. Innovations that are highly accessible to the target system will have a higher adoption rate than innovations that are not.

Policy Implication This suggests a policy of decentralization in delivering new services, for example, in neighborhoods and natural settings in order to increase accessibility of those services. This may be especially important in "poor" neighborhoods where people may not be informed of new programs or may not have the economic means of time flexibility in using them.

Practice Implication The practitioner should be aware that innovations must be made accessible to the target systems for which they are designed, or they may not be used. One method of at least communicating the existence of an innovative service is to approach the target group in the social environment (work place, church, voluntary association) in which it functions. Thus, the information or service can be brought directly to the target group rather than waiting for the group to discover the innovation on its own. Public health nurses who visit people in their homes to offer health education services or store front crisis clinics offering guidance are examples.

Generalization: The response of other groups, especially elites and gatekeepers, to social-movement initiatives is an important factor influencing the likelihood that a particular social-action protest will result in collective violence. The research indicates that protestors often use violent means only after they have attempted other nonviolent means of seeking redress for their grievances. Furthermore, abrupt or arbitrary actions by officials are a prime cause of violence.

Policy Implication: For organizational administrators this suggests a policy of reacting in such a way as to minimize or reduce the level of conflict—keeping communication open and discussion fluid. For conflict-oriented social-action groups, it suggests a policy of attempting to elevate the level of conflict by provoking an arbitrary and ill-considered response.

Practice Implication The practitioner can influence the likelihood that a particular social protest will result in violence. First, the practitioner must try to assess the response "authorities" will make to that protest. If a protest has been preceded by an unsuccessful period of intergroup communications, there is a greater likelihood that the protest will become violent. One strategy for avoiding violence in such a situation is to persuade a third party to intervene and to act as a mediator in the conflict. By making administrative and political authorities aware of the possibility of violence, the practitioner may increase the possibility for peaceful resolution of grievances.

The practice implications bring out more detailed, design-related factors. While our examples have involved social aggregates, the R&D techniques that are being discussed apply as well to work with individuals and small groups. Mullen (1978) has been engaged in retrieving and converting research findings for purposes of assisting clinical practice in casework. It is interesting and instructive to examine a set of generalizations he developed regarding interpersonal empathy, and a set of derived intervention guidelines for use by practitioners.

Generalizations An intervenor's sensitivity to the moment-to-moment feelings of the client and the intervenor's verbal facility to communicate this understanding in a language attuned to the client's current feelings (as measured by the Accurate Empathy Scale, Truax, 1961a) are positively associated with the client's depth of self-exploration (as measured by the Self-Exploration Scale, Truax & Carkhuff, 1967) and are frequently associated with attitudinal, cognitive, and behavioral improvements in clients. A low level of empathic responses (as defined above) is associated with low levels of client self-exploration and is frequently associated with deterioration in attitudinal, cognitive, and behavioral areas. Although associated with intervention outcome, this quality does not appear to be either a necessary or sufficient condition, nor does it appear to be among a set of necessary and sufficient conditions for successful outcomes. Empathy accounts for a relatively small amount of variance in intervention outcomes, yet this amount is often statistically significant. (pp. 57–58)

Action Guidelines
1. In practice situations where client self-exploration is desirable, intervenor responses that reflect accurate empathy should be used to facilitate client self-exploration.
2. Expression of low levels of accurate empathy should be avoided, especially with more fragile and vulnerable clients, to avoid harming clients.
3. Since expression of accurate empathy appears to a large extent to be reciprocal, intervenors should be aware of how they are empathically relating to their clients and should exert control over their expression of empathy.
4. Since accurate empathy at best appears to account for only a small portion of variance in intervention effects, other intervention qualities should be used to enhance effectiveness.
5. Since research evidence supporting the efficacy of accurate empathy is of questionable validity, intervenors should closely monitor and evaluate the effective-

ness of this response when applied in practice and should use this feedback to rethink the substantive generalization. Similarly, new research findings should be monitored and utilized to rethink the substantive hypothesis. (p. 59)

Another interesting example of using a design formulation in the clinical area is provided by Urban (1976). In his work he was interested in developing a set of procedures that might alleviate symptoms of persons experiencing depressive states. A search of the literature revealed two theories that characterized the ingredients of the condition with sufficient coherence to suggest intervention strategies: Beck's cognitive theory and Lewinsohn's interpersonal behavior theory. Beck's theory postulates that depressives perceive and evaluate their experiences with others in negative terms. Lewinsohn assumes the existence of deficient interpersonal skills leading to low rates of positive reinforcement from others.

Specific approaches to treatment were devised from this knowledge concerning the etiology of depression. The cognitive approach suggested a set of group experiences in which clients would be led to realize that their states were essentially of their own making and that alternative ways of construing their relations with other people were possible. In addition, in the interpersonal behavior approach, there would be structured coaching and supervised practice in the exercise of interpersonal skills so that objective deficiencies in this area could be overcome. In this particular study, an effort was made to determine which of the two design concepts that had been devised was more effective in bringing about an improvement in depressive conditions.

SOME CHARACTERISTICS
OF THE CONVERSION/DESIGN PROCESS

Although one is hard pressed to present a precise methodology for formulating application concepts, some key characteristics of the process can be discerned. Again, the industrial experience will be a point of reference.

Conversion/Design as Utilitarian and Goal Oriented

Various writers in the R&D field have agreed on the importance of focusing on specific purposes and outcomes. Conversion/design implies using knowledge to solve problems rather than building on knowledge to acquire additional, more refined or more valid knowledge. Jones (1970) maintains that "the stating of objectives is undoubtedly one of the most important and difficult parts of designing" (p. 199). McCrory (1961) relates objectives to needs as a precondition of design.

Unlike fundamental scientific research, design is motivated by need rather than by curiosity. Therefore, in addition to acquiring knowledge of the state of the technical art, the design method requires recognition of a need which warrants an investment of effort and funds. . . . When the designer can arrange technical art into useful combinations forming a system satisfying need, he has a design concept. (pp. 61, 62–63)

McCrory points out that need satisfaction can be guided either by technological advances or by social conditions:

Matching can originate from either the need or the art. Given a defined need, the designer can search the art for the inputs which can be synthesized to satisfy the need. Conversely, there are many concepts which are originated largely on the basis of known art, and the concept stage is attained by finding a need which can be fulfilled. (p. 63)

While McCrory's interest is focused on industry, conversion/design in the social area is equally motivated by need rather than by curiosity, and each of the conditions related to the development of a design concept in industry is equally present in the human services. For example, innovative practice arts that catch on, such as behavior modification or demonstration projects, generate their diffusion momentum while matching techniques and strategies to needs.

Conversion/Design as a Synthetic Function

Because design requires a blending of knowledge of science and of practice, and other related technical areas as well, a design person must possess knowledge, experience, and skill in a variety of pertinent areas and the capacity to integrate them in appropriate ways. It calls for the synthesis of ideas and methods that are different, segmented, or in apparent contradiction. Jones (1970) holds that design is a hybrid activity, involving science and mathematics. Van Doren (1954) speaks of combining the skills of the artist, engineer, mechanic, model-maker, statistician, analyst, and merchandiser. The type of skills in social R&D will be different, but the range will be as great and the task of synthesis similar.

McCrory (1961) summarizes the synthesis function well:

The responsibility of the design engineer is to use the maximum powers of creativity, judgment, technical perception, economic awareness, and analytical logic to devise uniquely useful systems, devices, and processes. (p. 59)

Diverse substantive knowledge and skills in interrelating may inhere in one person or, alternatively, in an organization with sufficient resources. These competencies may be achieved by composing a group of individuals with different backgrounds (the synectics approach). The possibilities—and some difficulties—that might be encountered have been suggested by Jones (1970):

The team will have to represent interests and professions that have not hitherto been obligated to collaborate. Such tensions are not unproductive in R&D, but procedures need to be used to encourage communication and collaborative work. (p. 37)

Diverse knowledge inputs suggested by Thomas may derive from a composite design team, even when it relied primarily on the research source.

Conversion/Design as an Art

Design involves an intricate blending of science and art. The discovery of untried, useful, new uses of scientific constructs requires imagination and inventiveness of a somewhat different sort than that which goes into the accumulation of knowledge *per se.*

McCrory (1961) states the position as follows:

The designer could be considered somewhat similar to the artist. The artist does not create new colors and forms. He combines colors and forms into new creations; and the results are, at times, masterpieces. (p. 59)

McCrory goes on to place the artistic aspect in context:

But imposed upon technological design is a crucial requirement which has no counterpart in classic art. Design must adhere to a plan which has objectives involving cost, performance, effort for attainment, probability of success, and even aesthetics. (p. 59)

There is no formal counterpart to this kind of structured role in the social sciences. Frequently, the concept of an artful reshaping of a scientific principle for practice purposes, is viewed by social scientists as suspect or even tarnished, especially among those with strong "empirical" or "methodological" leanings. Still, as Robert Nisbet (1976) argues in his *Sociology as an Art Form,* the element of artistic creativity has been prominently present in the theoretical works of the sociological greats such as Weber,

Durkheim, Marx, and Simmel. Such creativity and intellectual power, if concentrated on pragmatic application of theory, could have profound utility in aiding social amelioration and change.

Conversion/Design as Tentative and Exploratory

As stated earlier, the fact that application concepts are systematically extrapolated from research findings may give them an appearance of authenticity or finality that, in reality, they do not possess. Their scientific character stems from the method used in deriving and further testing them rather than their intrinsic nature. Application concepts have neither the status of empirical validation nor that of wide professional approval. For this reason they must be viewed as preliminary and provisional—emergent practice principles and procedures—in process and on their way to subsequent validation of an empirical and/or consensual nature.

FACTORS RELATED TO MAKING
CONVERSION/DESIGN DECISIONS

It is possible to go a step beyond describing the process and to move toward manipulating it. This can be aided by examining factors that enter into conversion/design decisions.

In this connection previous writings by Thomas (1967) are a useful point of departure. Thomas concerned himself with the question of selecting knowledge from behavioral science. Three main criteria are indicated: content relevance, knowledge power, and referent features. Content relevance refers to the suitability or applicability of given items of knowledge for a practice or policy goal. Knowledge power connotes the level of confidence one can have in the knowledge source—its validity and potency as a predictive variable. Referent features pertain to the real world operational connection of the knowledge. The first two criteria are largely related to the conversion task, the last criterion, largely to the design task. In other words, content relevance turns one's attention to broad knowledge questions, and knowledge power relates to the assessment one makes of the intrinsic soundness of the knowledge. There remains the question of its more specific applicability to a given problem, goal, or situation. This is where design considerations are salient.

Drawing on discussions by Thomas (1967), and Tripodi (1974) and other social researchers, a series of decisional factors may be formulated. We will list them on a continuum as follows: the more abstract, general, and conversion-related; an intermediate level; and the more concrete, specific, and design-related.

More Abstract: Conversion-Related Factors

Empirical Accessibility: Can the practitioner gain access to associated variables—can they be approached, touched, addressed?

Identifiability for Selection: Are knowledge variables observable and in operation in most practice situations?

Situational Potency: Will the variables have influence or impact if injected into most practice situations?

Quantifiability: Can the variables be described in concrete, measurable terms, such as number of people, number of times, rate of speed, percentage increase, etc.? This has implications for the feasibility of development work, in particular evaluation and performance testing.

Intermediate Level: May Relate to Conversion or Design

Organizational Feasibility: What are typical organizational constraints and resources related to execution of the intervention?

Ethical Suitability: Will the concept be viewed as ethical from the standpoint of typical, relevant actors: the practitioner, the profession, clients, agency, the community?

Frequency: Is this concept likely to be used with reasonable frequency by a typical practitioner during a typical year?

Commonality: Will the concept be used by a range of practitioners in various settings rather than only by specialized practitioners in esoteric or irrelevant settings?

Temporality: Is there sufficient time to execute the intervention within the time perspective of a typical agency and practitioner?

Most Concrete: Design-Related Factors

Manipulation Cost: What amount of funds are necessary, and are finances available to implement the intervention?

Manipulability or Engineerability: Does the typical practitioner have sufficient resources and skills to execute the intervention?

Rewards for Use: Are there sufficient incentives and supports within the application setting to reasonably assure that the concept will be utilized by practitioners? Can such incentives be added or enhanced?

Implementation Control: Does the practitioner have decision making power necessary either to introduce the concept into the application situation or to carry it through to execution, once introduced?

Risks and Side Effects: Are effects sufficiently predictable that anticipated damages to clients or to the organization will be of reasonably low scope or impact?

These categories are approximate and meant to be suggestive rather than definitive. They do give some indication of decisional ingredients and points where these may fall in the process of formulating application concepts.

It is interesting to observe that while these elements of design were brought together from social science sources, they are consistent with those that have emerged from industrial R&D. Several additional considerations that may usefully be taken into account are also suggested in R&D. Jones (1970), for example, projects a set of questions to be asked by a design team:

Questions about Product	*Sources of Answers*
Does it make the best use of available materials and components? [Personnel]	Suppliers [Professional Associations]
Can it be made cheaply enough with available resources? [Including Personnel]	Producers [Sponsoring institutions, United Way foundations]
Can it be distributed through available channels?	Distributors [Agencies]
What appearance, performance, reliability, etc., is required?	Consumers and sales organizations [Clients]
To what extent are its effects and side-effects acceptable to all concerned?	Political institutions and pressure groups [Board members, citizen groups]

Matters of diffusion and resource utilization are given accent in this listing.

In addition, Ansoff (1961) suggests the following analytic factors as pertinent design criteria. Human services considerations have been added in brackets by this author.

1. *Application Analysis,* which is concerned with the translation of customer needs into product performance specifications, as well as studies of economic justification of the product from the point of view of the customer. [What will be the economic or social costs to clients?]

2. *Market Research,* which analyzes the demand, the competitive factors, and the pricing structure as well as the marketing costs. [Does client need exist?]

3. *Applications Research* (sometimes called preliminary design), which translates the performance specification into a specific technical design and an estimate of the development and manufacturing costs. [What will be the cost of the development phase?]

4. *Business Analysis,* which consolidates all the preceding factors into an analysis of profit potential, risks, and strategic fit.   [How does this project relate to an organization's overall policy and service configuration?]

He then goes on to place technical and practical considerations in context:

Applied research merely tells us that a particular type of device can be built or a fabrication technique used to produce a particular type of product. Missing at this point are the following essential pieces of information: Does a demand exist for this type of device [or product]?
What *specific* performance characteristics are desired. [Client outcomes.]
How does performance relate to the price the customers are willing to pay? [Like traveling downtown to request services.] How is performance related to our costs to make the device? [What types of staffing and facilities and equipment are necessary?]
What competing devices are already available? [Like similar services and programs.] How does our device compare with them? What will it cost us to put the product on the market? [Start up costs, administrative costs, staff and client recruitment.]

It is obvious that in industrial R&D cost and profit criteria rank very high. In human services R&D cost is also an important consideration. Nevertheless, social benefits and economic costs need to be addressed and balanced against one another in a responsible way as an aspect of the design process.

In our R&D model, concern with need is a fundamental original factor which precedes both the retrieval and design phases.

PROCEDURAL AIDS FOR CONVERSION AND DESIGN

The conducting of design tasks is more difficult than would appear on the surface. In directing a team of graduate students who were involved in both the retrieval of knowledge and its systematic conversion, a number of these problems quickly became apparent. The students, serving as project staff members, came from a variety of different academic disciplines (sociology, psychology, political science, and anthropology) and professional fields (social work, education, community mental health, and public administration). It became evident early on that without exception they were unprepared to perform design functions. Their training had not only failed to equip them with the requisite skills, it had indeed resulted in a built-in incapacity for design. Social research courses and related social science work in these fields are based overwhelmingly on a "pure" research approach. An engineering outlook, required for the design function, is almost totally absent.

We can depict the problem with an analogy to a demolition firm and a salvage firm. In the social sciences students are systematically trained to engage in demolition with regard to existing social research. They are taught to have a critical eye, to be skeptical, to look for weaknesses and defects in studies they read. They are provided with skills to scrutinize and dissect studies in order to find out what is wrong with them. This is highly functional for knowledge-building roles. There it is important to discover deficiencies in existing knowledge in order to be able to plan investigations that will correct, refine and expand the knowledge base. This is the expected and legitimate role of the man or woman of science.

In the physical science field, however, a complimentary salvage role also is institutionalized through the profession of engineering. The engineer is trained to conserve and use existing scientific knowledge rather than to discard it. In order to build bridges, design aircraft or improve telephone communication, those promising bits of knowledge in the available science pool are carefully selected and painstakingly tested for use. The social sciences and social professions lack an area given over to formal preparation for salvage. Consequently, they provide all students exclusively with proficiency in demolition, using the scientific knowledge building model as the sole intellectual posture. We need to equip some students to ask, "Given the current low level of development of the social sciences, what, nevertheless, are the more firm and favorable bits and areas of knowledge that systematically can be put to purposeful use?" It would be foolhardy to impose this specialized outlook on all students in the social fields; it is equally unwise to withhold it from all of them.

Our staff group was initially seriously handicapped in moving from a simple finding to a logical action concept. Some individuals could only stare at a finding and reaffirm it as a truth. Others found new words to restate the same idea. Those who tilted in the direction of conversion often devised statements that were so global, abstract, or diffuse that they failed to offer any meaningful behavioral initiatives for intervention.

Often such prescriptions involved an inferential leap from the original data of such distance that it left that data behind and forgotten. These became conjectures or ideas independent of the original source. Reviewers had to be cautioned to hold speculation within reasonable bounds—to make inferential statements grounded solidly in the data.

It was necessary to provide formal reporting forms and written rules which could structure staff effort in the direction of appropriate application functions. The language used indicates the kind of support that is needed:

"Stay close to the actual data."
"Push ahead from findings to practice implications."
"Be specific about directives suggested to the practitioner."
"What does this finding tell the practitioner about what he should *do*!"

In addition to such supportive devices, close training and supervision is necessary. Continuing conferences involving mutual exchange between reviewers and supervisors were helpful in our situation. Supervisors reviewed all design reports and helped to expand on the range of potential application possibilities. This dual personnel arrangement often involved mixtures of individuals with different backgrounds. Such mixtures were useful for the synthesis function.

Some additional procedural aids are available from industrial R&D. Jones (1970) discusses four techniques used commonly to facilitate the creative function. These include *synectics, brainstorming, morphological graphs,* and *removing mental blocks.* Some of these are familiar to those in the social fields. Others are new or offer a new twist.

Synectics is defined as a means of directing the spontaneous activity of the brain and nervous system toward exploratory and transformational activity. It involves the formation of a selected, generally diverse, group of individuals with high potential. The group is given a great deal of practice in the use of analogies to foster facility in a particular type of mental operation. Subsequently, the group is presented with specific application problems to work on, with allowance of substantial amounts of time to find solutions.

A more common technique is *brainstorming.* Here the aim is to stimulate a group of people to produce many ideas quickly. The norm is established that all ideas are welcome, quantity of output is desired, and the rule is that no idea is to be criticized or discouraged. A multiplier effect is sought through urging participants to build upon, amplify, and combine the ideas of others. All ideas are recorded and evaluated at a later time.

Morphological charts seek to widen the area of search for application possibilities. This technique starts by defining a multiplicity of functions that an acceptable application concept must be able to perform. A chart is used to list a wide range of sub-solutions or means of performing each function. In this way one can work back to determine if existing research supports one or another solution, or if a given focal research generalization or set of generalizations applies. In this sense, the application concept is shaped quasi-independently of the generalization, and linked back in an *ex post facto* fashion. The effect is to free up the designer from constraints imposed by the usual directionality of application.

The approach designated *removing mental blocks* is employed in particular when the usual application effort has yielded no acceptable solution. Based on creativity literature, three unfreezing approaches are used: coaching people in transformation rules geared to discovering new cognitive relationships; establishing new connections between parts of a current unsatisfactory solution; reassessing and redefining the application situation. As an example of this approach, a staff member can be asked to experiment in an ordered manner with the following transformational rules: magnify, substitute, combine, reverse, rearrange, adapt, minify, modify. These are defined and illustrated as a way of systematically drawing forth new solutions.

The work of Guilford (1967) on creativity is another potential source of support for fruitful conversion. According to Guilford "divergent" thinking is a mode of productive thought, typical of the creative person, which tends toward the novel or unknown. This is in contrast with "convergent" thinking which is oriented toward a known or authorized solution. Divergent thinking has some of the following characteristics:

fluency–producing a large number of ideas

flexibility–taking a variety of different approaches or using many different categories of ideas

originality–shifting meanings or uses in unusual or off-the-beaten-track directions

elaboration–rounding out or developing ideas, seeking a variety of implications.

In Guilford's view it is possible to educate people toward greater creativity through giving them training in the development of the capacities indicated above. A conversion training program could readily be formulated to combine the ideas of Guilford with the techniques of Jones.

Whether these types of application activities relate to the human services area, or more specifically, how they relate, is a matter to be determined through experience. They do, however, offer an increment beyond the rather vacuous current state of affairs.

BIBLIOGRAPHY

ANSOFF, H. I., "Evaluation of Applied Research in a Business Firm," *Technological Planning on the Corporate Level*, Proceedings of a conference sponsored by the Associates of the Harvard Business School, September 8–9, 1961, ed. James R. Bright. Cambridge, Mass.: 1961, pp. 208–224.

FIELDEN, B. B. R., *Engineering Design*. London: Her Majesty's Stationery Office, 1963.

GUETZKOW, H., "Conversion Barriers in Using the Social Sciences," Administrative Science Quarterly, 4 (1959), 68–81

GUILFORD, J. P., *The Nature of Human Intelligence*. New York: McGraw-Hill, 1967.

HAGE, J., and M. AIKEN, *Social Change in Complex Organizations*. New York: Random House, 1969.

HAVELOCK, RONALD G., "Translating Theory into Practice," *Rehabilitation Record*, November–December, 1969, 24–27.

JONES, J. C., *Design Methods: Seeds of Human Futures*. New York: John Wiley & Sons, 1970.

KAUFMAN, H., *The Forest Ranger*. Baltimore: Johns Hopkins Press, 1960.

KLATZKY, S. R., *Organizational Size, Complexity, and Coordination: Alternatives Hypotheses*, Paper presented at the American Sociological Association Meetings, San Francisco, 1969.

KLINE, B., and W. MECHLING, "Applications of Operations Research to Development Decisions," *Operations Research*, 6 (1959), 352–363.

LAWRENCE, P. R., and J. W. LORSCH, *Organization and Environments*. Cambridge: Harvard University Press, 1967.

LAWRENCE, P. R., and J. W. LORSCH, "Differentiation and Integration for Complex Organizations," *Administrative Science Quarterly*, 12 (1967), 1–47.

LOW, W. C., "Identifying and Evaluating the Barrier Problems in Technology," *Technological Planning at the Corporate Level*, Proceedings of a conference sponsored by the Associates of the Harvard Business School, September 8–9, 1961, ed. James R. Bright. Cambridge. Mass.: 1961, pp. 194–213.

LUNDBERG, C. C., "Middlemen in Science Utilization: Some Notes Toward Clarifying Conversion Roles," *American Behavioral Scientist*, 10 (1966), 11–14.

MCCRORY, R. J., "The Design Method—A Scientific Approach to Valid Design," *Technological Planning at the Corporate Level*, Proceedings of a conference sponsored by the Associates of the Harvard Business School, September 8–9, 1961, ed. James R. Bright. Cambridge, Mass.: 1961, pp. 59–67.

MULLEN, EDWARD J., "The Construction of Personal Models for Effective Practice: A Method for Utilizing Research Findings to Guide Social Interventions," *Journal of Social Service Research*, 2, 1 (1978), 45–63.

NISBET, R., *Sociology as an Art Form*. New York: Columbia University Press, 1976.

ROTHMAN, J., *Planning and Organizing for Social Change: Action Principles from Social Science Research*. New York: Columbia University Press, 1974.

SIMPSON, R. L., and W. H. GALLEY, "Goals, Environmental Pressures and Organizational Characteristics," *American Sociological Review*, 27 (1962), 344–351.

THOMAS, E. J., "Selecting Knowledge from Behavioral Science," *Behavioral Science for Social Workers*. New York: The Free Press, 1967.

THOMAS, EDWIN J., "Beyond Knowledge Utilization in Generating Human Service Technology," Paper prepared for the National Conference on the Future of Social Work Research, sponsored by the National Association of Social Workers, San Antonio, Texas, October 15–18, 1978.

THOMAS, E. J., "Generating Innovation in Social Work: The Paradigm of Developmental Research," *Journal of Social Service Research*, 2, 1 (1978), pp. 95–115.

TRIPODI, T., *Uses and Abuses of Social Research in Social Work*. New York: Columbia University Press, 1974.

URBAN, HUGH B., "Systems Methodology in the Design of Treatment Strategies for Depressive States," Draft of paper prepared for symposium: *Current Developments in the Psychotherapy of Depression*, Eastern Psychological Association Meeting, New York, April 1976.

VAN DOREN, H., *Industrial Design: A Practical Guide to Product Design and Development*. New York: McGraw-Hill, 1954.

6

Initial Operationalization— Pilot Testing

It is not enough to know in our minds that a thing is true; we must also put that thing into practice, for man progresses only to the extent that his truths take practical form.

Attributed to Alfred North Whitehead

DEVELOPMENT

The Function of Pilot Work

When we move into pilot testing in social R&D, we enter into an experiential vacuum—a vacuum that we hope to fill by establishing the reality of whether a thing can or cannot be done. Yet, it is an unfortunate fact that this type of pilot testing is only sporadically employed in the human services. In R&D, pilot testing provides the first elements of substantiation and reality contact for the application concept. As such, it is an extremely important step in moving from theory to practice. Many human service professionals in positions of leadership or influence make policy statements or suggest broad programs of action. Then, however, instead of authenticating such statements by subjecting them to concrete empirical testing, they jump directly to what is analogous to the diffusion step of the

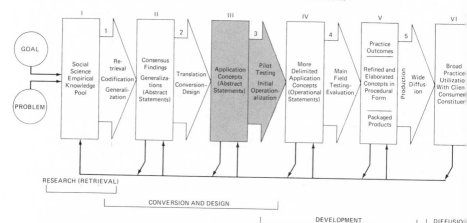

R&D process. Many important programs in the health, education and welfare fields are put into widespread and instant operation across the country. OEO, Title XX, and Head-Start are all examples of such an approach. Ideology, enthusiasm, professional "one-upmanship," and political maneuvering substitute for a logical progression of action. While timing and political vagaries are important factors in decisions regarding establishing new programs, sometimes the pilot-test phase is overlooked, not for these reasons, but merely for lack of recognition of its place and utility. The result, too frequently, is an inappropriate or ineffective outcome because of application concepts that lack demonstrated efficacy. Yet, the social R&D process provides a systematic method for confirming or denying the soundness of the application concept, if we elect to follow that course.

The application concept, as we earlier demonstrated, should inherently incorporate a strong likelihood of being feasible. It requires, however, an empirical verification of this assumption. McCrory (1961) expresses this as follows:

At the design concept stage, the concept need not be described completely. Rather, it may be expressed in terms of functional requirements or "black boxes." The key criterion is that, in the judgement of the designer, the concept has sufficient potential to justify further effort in designing the individual elements of the system. (p. 63)

In McCrory's view a number of failures can occur: insufficient definition of need (or objective), not enough attention to synthesis, bypassing the feasibility stage. In his listing of steps in design, he includes feasibility considerations that actually overlap into early development work or pilot testing. These include: "critical experimentation to test specific questionable aspects of the design concept; [and] operation of experimental prototypes to confirm adequate functioning of the total system or subsystems" (p. 57).

McCrory adds that:

The feasibility stage must be approached coldly to avoid over optimism in presenting feasibility and to insure realistic estimating of the effort required to reach the next stage of production and marketing success. (p. 66)

Basically, then, pilot work involves *initial operationalization of an application concept* in the sense of bringing about a working model or demonstration. It requires early engagement with the real world empirical referents of the application concept.

Gibson (1964), who terms pilot work "exploratory development" and main field testing as "Reduction to Public Practice," gives us a clear picture of where pilot work fits in the R&D process:

Although the techniques and methods employed in exploratory development [i.e., pilot work] are often similar to those employed in scientific research, and there has always been a close connection and interchange of results between the two, their objectives are quite different. Scientific research seeks new and uncontaminated knowledge from which to make patterns of facts and ideas that lead to a deeper understanding of man and his environment. The exploratory developer, sensing the need for a new freedom of choice and action, uses all knowledge he can glean from any source whatever and exerts his ingenuity to put it together to give a new device, commodity, technique, or service that supplies the need. (p. 41)

Gibson depicts exploratory development/pilot work and the relationship to reduction to public practice/main field testing in Figure 6–1.

CONCEPTUALIZING THE METHODOLOGY OF DEVELOPMENT AND THE PILOTING TASK[1]

Typically in social R&D, one begins with a practical problem or objective rather than a theoretical issue. The objective will involve the formulation of effective strategies and techniques to be used by human service practitioners or "change agents" in their work.

[1]Portions of this discussion appear in the CIP technical report, Jack Rothman, Joseph G. Teresa and John Erlich, *Developing Effective Strategies for Social Intervention: A Research and Development Methodology*, PB-272/454 TR-1-RD, National Technical Information Service, Springfield, Virginia, 1977, with special reference to chapters 2 and 3.

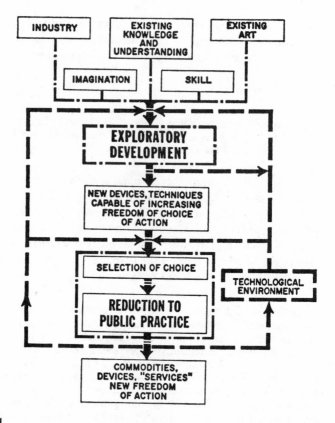

Figure 6–1

Reprinted with permission from R. E. Gibson, "A Systems Approach to Research Management," in James R. Bright, ed., *Research, Development and Technological Innovation,* Homewood, Illinois: Richard D. Irwin, Inc., 1964, p. 42.

The developmental research task can usefully be posed in terms of the relationship between an intervention, *X* and an outcome, *Y:*

Some examples of this relationship include:

Promoting acceptance   -through-   Using a limited portion
of an innovation (Y)   of target system (X) initially

Changing organizational   -through-   Shifting the structure
goals (Y)   of influence within an
                                                  organization (X)

| Increasing participation in community organizations (Y) | -through- | Providing appropriate benefits (X) |
| Increasing effectiveness in practitioner role performance (Y) | -through- | Achieving role clarity and consensus among appropriate superordinates (X) |

The purpose of development is not hypothesis testing in the traditionally accepted sense of the term. Application concepts gleaned from existing research are not taken as hypotheses whose validity is to be tested. Rather, they are conceived as having already been given sufficient support in the literature to warrant further testing for application. In the previous chapter we indicated some problems of causal reasoning that may be involved. The objective is to determine the ways by which these concepts or guidelines may be put into practice, or operationalized, assessing carefully what happens in different contexts and under different kinds of conditions when guidelines are implemented. The natural settings of practice are the field sites for the study. Evaluation, or performance testing, is conducted in order to determine whether outcome goals are adequately achieved. Unlike traditional social science undertakings, there is no intent to establish proof or validation in the sense of a scientific truth. There is, however, an attempt to demonstrate feasibility and workability of an application concept, not necessarily in comparison with an alternative theoretical or conceptual approach. Effectiveness in attaining an objective at a given rate may suffice for development purpose. A pragmatic end is sought, and pragmatic methods are used. Thus, control groups and the full complement of techniques of customary scientific experimental design may not be standard requirements. Rather, the newer methods of single-case study and quasi-experimental design are pertinent (Campbell and Stanley, 1966; Hersen and Barlow, 1976; Howe, 1974).

A key intent is to determine those factors involved in treatment X that are associated with its optimal implementation; that is, with successful attainment of outcome goals. This is inherent in the logic of the research and development process. There is an overriding interest in the production of some operational guide to enable human service practitioners to replicate effective intervention techniques through manipulation of salient variables.

In this formulation, outcome Y is the independent variable; intervention X is the dependent variable. We may refer to the Xs as process variables—a constellation of operative variables associated with the intervention. There are also antecedent variables. These may be viewed as comprising a predisposing, initial setting, defining the baseline situation and influencing the process of implementation.

Conceptually, four social-psychological factors may be identified as hypothetically operative in terms of articulating with the process X. These may be enumerated as follows:

Personal: personal attributes and attitudes of the practitioner

Organizational: the organizational or agency structure employing the practitioner and in which he or she functions

Client: the nature of the client system or target group with which the practitioner is engaged

Community: the structural aspects of the community in which the intervention takes place.

The variables may be conceptualized in terms of what Rosenberg (1968) has referred to as *conjoint* or *concomitant* variables in a given theoretical relationship. Further, these process variables may have a facilitating and/or limiting effect on outcome. R&D effort is directed toward determining which process variables, in implementation of strategy X, are associated with favorabl~ outcomes. The original diagram may now be revised somewhat:

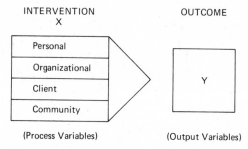

Specific process variables in carrying out a guideline might fall within social-psychological dimensions as follows:

Personal: interpersonal skill of the practitioner in convincing his agency superior to authorize him to institute an innovation; the kind of energy commitment he has in terms of this practice task; his sense of satisfaction with his job; or technical knowledge of the tasks involved in the intervention.

Organizational: the degree to which the board has a positive or negative posture toward change; the degree to which this task is consistent with the practitioner's general assignment in the organization; agency resources available to support new undertakings.

Client: the degree of general support for the practitioner by the clients; the extent to which clients have a negative or positive attitude toward the agency, based on their past experience with it; the degree to which the client group is homogeneous and mutually supportive in its point of view.

Community: the extent of community participation in the agency; homogeneity-heterogeneity of the community viewpoint; community interest in this particular program.

This suggests a wide range of contingency factors in typical practice situations that may be assumed to be salient in affecting intervention outcomes. Thus, R&D research tends to have the characteristic of extensiveness.

One may assume (in keeping with Rosenberg) that there are also certain antecedent variables that may affect outcome. These antecedent variables are predisposing contextual factors. Such factors may independently affect outcome, be inert, or interact with process variables in affecting, or being associated with, a particular outcome. For example, working with board members rather than peer agency staff (process variable) may more likely be associated with favorable outcomes if carried through by more experienced rather than younger practitioneers (antecedent variable).

Antecedent variables may be conceptualized in terms of the same four social-psychological factors (clusters of variables) involved in the process variables: (1) personal, (2) organizational, (3) client, and (4) community. Antecedent variables indicate the initial context or base from which the intervenor starts. This context might include the sex or age of the practitioner, his attitude toward clients or the intervention, whether his organization is centralized or decentralized, or the racial composition of the community in which the action takes place. These sectors may be measured through a battery of "baseline" instruments.

The earlier diagram may now be amplified:

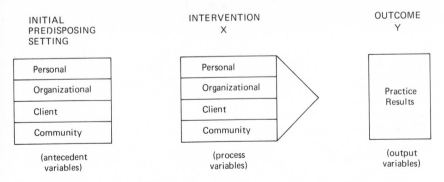

INITIAL PREDISPOSING SETTING	INTERVENTION X	OUTCOME Y
Personal	Personal	
Organizational	Organizational	Practice Results
Client	Client	
Community	Community	
(antecedent variables)	(process variables)	(output variables)

The social-psychological factors in both antecedent and process variable sets may have effects either on an independent bivariate basis or a more complex, interrelated basis.

This presentation underlines the earlier discussion in Chapter 3 regarding the need for complex, multivariate data processing methods in R&D undertakings.

Pilot work allows the testing of a development plan and its various facets at an early stage. In part it asks the question whether X can be brought into being, and, if it can, whether indeed Y is attained with sufficient frequency and adequacy as a consequence. It asks also by what means the necessary condition can be materialized and measured. The inherent complexity of a typical R&D project obviously calls for a careful initial pilot exploration.

OVERVIEW OF PILOT ELEMENTS

Pilot work marks the commencement of the development phase, and is the chief instrumentality for testing the feasibility and perfecting the methods of development. To recapitulate and crystallize what is involved, the overall objectives of development include the following:

1. Examining *if* an application concept/principle devised during conversion and design will work in action. Can it be brought into operational being under real world user conditions?

2. Determining *how* it works in action, that is, what it takes in human and material terms to operationalize the principle under such conditions. This involves specifying the detailed procedures of implementation.

3. Evaluating whether it works in action *effectively* and *efficiently*. Can it attain the objectives for which it is intended with a reasonable degree of success and reliability, and at an acceptable cost?

4. Devising means by which the specifications of operationalization can be captured and packaged in a form which permits easy *communication* and *replication*. In industrial terms this may mean mass production, in the human service fields it means widespread practice adoption.

Pilot work has the function of indicating in a small-scale exploration whether these objectives are likely to be achieved in a main field test. In this sense it serves to confirm or veto a large-scale implementation of the project. It also provides the tools and procedures through which the large-scale undertakings can take place.

In industrial product development, the burden of pilot work is mitigated to some degree through the use of simulations, particularly computer simulations. Through the use of Failure Mode and Effect Analysis, non-design qualifications (trouble spots) in ongoing and/or interactive stages and processes can be identified and therefore anticipated in real world settings. This permits the development of preparedness strategies and alternatives before working models are devised. Because of the complexity of human behavior and imprecision of measurement tools, this type of procedure in the study of group and organizational processes is generally not practical. Heavy reliance must be placed on the pilot study itself.

The pilot study should ideally provide an opportunity to examine beforehand on a small-scale basis every aspect of what will be undertaken in the full-scale development field test. In general this will cover a range of considerations such as the following:

The general plan or design of the field test

Administrative responsibilities, arrangements, lines of authority

Staff composition, functions, and size

Auxiliary staff needed

Staff supervision, training, support, relationships

Field settings

Field arrangements, expectations and limitations

Instruments for measuring process, outcomes, antecedent variables, participant characteristics, social structural variables, etc.

Sampling requirements and methods

Data analysis procedures

Data processing methods and costs

Materials handling

Space requirements

Finances, including salaries, equipment, operating expenses

Timing and duration of development

Communications

Relationships to the funding or sponsoring body

Procedural difficulties and design flaws

Others might be added to this list, but these should suffice to indicate the scope of technical, human and organizational concerns that typically must be encompassed. All of these cannot be addressed here but several of special interest will be selected for attention.

Fairweather (1967) has perhaps carried the notion of development as far as anyone currently working in the social sciences. He terms his approach "Experimental Social Innovation," and he evolves his action design concepts not from previous research but from observation of natural behavior. Thus, his approach forgoes use of a retrieval and conversion methodology as described here. Rather he constructs an innovative program or technique from an examination of the problem situation itself. Once an innovation or intervention has been formulated for dealing with the problem it is implemented in a manner having many similarities to a development undertaking. Some aspects of Fairweather's perspective as related to development are as follows:

Definition–defining a relevant social problem

Innovation–creating solutions to problems

Context–implanting innovative programs in natural social settings

Responsibility–assuming responsibility for what happens to participants, users, clients

Evaluation–carrying out innovative programs for a sufficient time to allow outcome and process evaluations to be made

Cross-disciplinary–using a cross-disciplinary approach consonant with the dimensions of the social problem under consideration. (Fairweather, pp. 20, 60)

From time to time we will refer back to Fairweather's observations as they are consistent in many respects with our own concepts of and experiences in social R&D.

STRUCTURING THE FIELD TEST

One of the first steps in any field test, assuming its purpose is clearly defined, is to obtain the necessary organizational arrangements and administrative commitments to proceed. These involve arrangements within one's own organization (whether this be a university, federal agency, or consulting firm) and user contexts (whether these be social agencies, mental hospitals, detention homes, etc.). Fairweather lists the following as essential ingredients of a start-up situation:

an adequate budget

appropriate personnel

work space

computer time

contacts with the user system

In part the pilot test will demonstrate what the ultimate dimensions of each of these factors must be for successful development.

The composition of the core headquarters staff is a key consideration to be dealt with in this phase. One aspect is the size of the key management and leadership group, the other is its composition. It seems necessary to incorporate three competencies in this core group, which perhaps can best be described in terms of three roles: a project director (analogous to a project manager in industrial R&D) who assumes overall direction of the undertaking and attempts to integrate the scientific and application elements; a director of field operations (analogous to a production manager in R&D) who is ultimately familiar with the practical aspects of the application problem and user settings; and a director of research operations who combines evaluation and operations research skills. The pilot phase should reveal how these three basic functions—overall integration and direction, practice knowledge and perspectives, research knowledge and perspectives

—can best be blended at the top level in the context of the development task.

The selection of specific, appropriate user settings is a critical aspect of the pilot phase. Appropriateness implies that these settings should be similar to settings in which the ultimate program or technique to be developed will be employed. A formal representative sample may not be required, but "typicality" should be sought. A specimen of each of the ultimate types of settings of concern should be brought into the pilot stage if at all possible. Settings may be outside the R&D organization (as for example in a university sponsored program) or part of the same organization (as with an R&D unit which is part of a national organization having local service branches). It is also possible for the R&D program to set up its own implementation outlets for experimental purposes.

Agreements and understandings need to be developed concerning the conditions of the relationship with application field settings. What kinds of programs can be carried out in the settings and with what limitations? What kind of data can be gathered, by whom? What time period is established for implementation? Who bears the costs of various components of the undertaking? In most human service settings the question of confidentiality will arise as an early issue to be grappled with. Locked files, use of code names or numbers for clients, and scrupulous discretion by research staff are some conditions which may allay the fears of professional practitioners in this area. Unless the genuine concern of these professionals over confidentiality is acknowledged and acted upon, this can be a continuing hindrance to project implementation. The pilot stage should allow for appropriate measure of confidentiality to be worked through in the particular application setting.

Because pilot work implies a close and intensive examination of the issues and problems involved in development, it seems appropriate to select settings that are close to the core headquarters staff. This permits the core staff to be intimately involved in the implementation/operationalization process and in the related aspects to measurement and evaluation. In addition to proximity, a small to moderate number of sites or implementations are conducive to this type of close examination of the pilot situation. On balance, intensity rather than scope or representativeness is an essential feature of piloting (Jahoda, Deutsch and Cook, 1955).

STAFFING AND SOCIAL ENGINEERING FUNCTIONS

Field staff or practitioner staff who operationalize research derived application concepts that are still in abstract or theoretical form are analogous to development engineers who perform a similar function in the physical sciences. There is difficulty in recruiting these personnel because the social sciences and social professions do not train such specialists in knowledge linkage and transfer as do the engineering schools. In the absence of such prepared cadres, pilot work requires procedures to select and train personnel in the execution of such functions.

A useful perspective for viewing engineering roles in the social fields is provided by Mackie and Christensen (1967). Their observations are based on a study geared to improving training programs in the Navy. They did this by describing "the processes involved in translating the results of psychological laboratory research into forms that would be meaningful and useful in operational settings." The authors begin by defining the task and indicating the need for appropriate professional roles:

There presently is no methodology for translating between the laboratory and real world contexts because of the inadequate development of common task taxonomy and consequent limited understanding of the process variables involved. To the extent that more translatable research is performed, there will be an increasing need for a corps of professionals who may be described as learning engineers. (pp. 7–8, 10)

They go on to quote Petrullo's observations regarding obstacles to the development of such roles:

There are very good reasons for not wanting to put some theories into immediate practice. Fear that they may not work is not a good reason, since the scientific method itself is based upon hypothesis testing. A good reason, however, is the knowledge that, before any theory can be applied, it must be operationalized; it must be subjected to a number of tests under experimental and real-life conditions. It must be taken out to the "proving grounds"; it must be restructured; the conditions under which it will work must be discovered; exact measurements and predictions must be made and validated; etc.
The technical reasons for the lag in application of theoretical results in the social sciences can thus be found in the lack of social engineers and technicians to develop operational concepts; in the non-existence of human proving grounds where the experiments can be conducted on such problems as leadership; and in the lack of methodology as to procedures to be followed in translating research findings. (p. 23)

Two main characteristics, and a third supplementary one, appear to be necessary for people with high potential for social engineering work. The first is ability to think in theoretical and abstract terms. Good preparation in the behavioral or social sciences is a basic route to such capability. A second characteristic is familiarity and competency in the area of professional practice involved in the action implementation. Appropriate professional practice training and/or experience is a requisite for this capability. The skill level, however, must be unusually high because of the uncharted and complex nature of this type of application task. Success or failure of the application concept must hinge on its intrinsic character rather than on inept or inappropriate implementation.

It is important that the field staff be intimately familiar with problems and processes in the real world of practice because only those acquainted with the problems of the application context can deal fluidly and well with the complexities of conversion. This contention is given strong support by Mackie and Christensen (1967):

Formulation of possible applications of research findings requires extensive knowledge of the operational problems in the field in which application is to be attempted . . . The learning engineer will require specialized knowledge of the subject matter, or operational tasks, in the field where application is to be attempted. Without such knowledge, he will not be able to identify the operational counterparts of laboratory variables nor understand the nature of the stimuli operating in the real-world situation [emphasis in the original.] (pp. 10, 106)

Roberts (1964), writing from a more established industrial R&D vantage point expresses the same idea:

The engineer, whose job is much more complex than that of a production worker, becomes more proficient when he knows the company procedures and policies; has learned the important formal and informal communication channels; has determined where he can obtain assistance in solving critical problems; is familiar with the technical aspects of the company's products; and has learned the technical errors which were made previously so that he can avoid the same pitfalls. (p. 134)

Familiarity with the application setting in itself is not sufficient for engineering functions, however. As we have said, a high level of practical and intellectual competence regarding these settings is necessary for the performance of creative, inventive conversion tasks in those settings. Mackie and Christensen state:

The tasks of relating theoretical, laboratory, and real-world variables, assessing the meaning of research findings and innovating applications, make it essential that the qualifications and training of these engineers be of a very high calibre. (p. 10)

Also, Roberts observes:

The most critical productive project resource (in R&D) is engineering manpower. (p. 129)

A third criterion for social engineering functions is the ability to observe accurately and record exactly and faithfully. Too often people in the human service fields become caught up in the flow of events and find it difficult to draw back for a time in order to record the details of the processes in which they are engaged. Activists, change agents and service providers find their orientation to people and to change is so strong that recording and reporting is an intrusion on these more salient, and appealing activities. For the social engineering functionary, however, this capability is vital. An engineer in industry who is not able to observe and keep accurate records of mechanical or other natural processes is useless, as is a social engineer in the human services who is similarly handicapped.

Three basic qualifications of social engineers, therefore, are the following:

1. *Conceptual thinking capability*—familiarity and facility with regard to theoretical writings
2. *Practice competency*—familiarity with and skill in dealing with application situations
3. *Dependability-reliability*—in reporting and task completion

Both our own pilot experience and literature support these criteria for the selection of field staff. These appear to be among the critical attributes of social engineering functions.

It's a transition leading into the next subject, i.e., training.

A daylong orientation meeting served to establish the role of the Field Operations Director as the "trainer" and to give the field staff a general introduction to the purpose and methods of the Project. Formal lines of authority and communication were established. The first phase of the Project was detailed and related to the Project as a whole. They were given a clear sense of the way research derived from literature had been translated into a form that could be "tried out" by practitioners in the field. All of these things combined to provide them with identification with the Project, an awareness of development objectives, and a sense of the partnership aspect of the work in which they shared.

In addition to acquainting them with pay arrangements, meeting schedules, expectations for written work, and communications arrangements, they were also introduced to a set of application concepts or "action guidelines." They received a simple description of the action concept in rather abstract form of each guideline and a general verbal illustration of how that guideline might be related to practice. For example, a typical action concept (or guideline) read:

Practitioners who wish to change an organization's goals may approach this by altering the structure of influence within the organization through increasing the power of those groups within the organization holding goals compatible with their own.

No other guidance regarding the application concept was provided. Each field staff member was expected to take steps to operationalize this guideline in the context of his or her specific agency situation. The operational nature of the engineering function is demonstrated in this illustration. The initial reaction of practitioners or potential users to the plausibility of such a design concept may provide early confirmation or doubt concerning its workability in the field.

Individual follow-up meetings were held by the Field Operations Director with each of the practitioners in the period immediately following the initial staff session. Also he visited each individual agency in which pilot work was taking place.

The basic pattern of ongoing training of practitioners involved two components: regular staff seminars (every two weeks at first, then monthly); and consultative meetings between the Field Operations Director and each practitioner. (These were held uniformly on a weekly basis initially and later on a variable basis.)

A series of General Staff Seminars were held in which there were two major task objectives. First, to help the practitioners to do a more effective job in using the guidelines (operationalization). And second, to help them to describe better what happened in the process of using the guidelines (recording and reporting).

These meetings or General Staff Seminars are of importance in several ways in controlling the developmental processes of a pilot study. Through them, communication between the staff practitioner and core research staff takes place in matters of mutual concern. They serve as an ongoing source of motivation and reinforcement for the practitioners. They are a mechanism by which to modify procedures or shift direction. They are forums in which general complaints can be raised and dealt with. They served as a vehicle for training, enlightenment, and improved task performance. This concerted interpersonal interaction seems necessary and valuable during early piloting and development work.

The pilot phase also revealed the necessity of a procedure to define or operationalize the various "elements" of an application concept. This approach of using the basic elements of the concept is helpful in determining whether it indeed has been operationalized, i.e., in order for the intervention X to be brought into being, each of the elements has to be specifically operationalized.

As an example, the previously stated guideline may be underlined as follows to indicate all key elements:

Practitioners who wish to *change an organization's goals* may approach this by *altering the structure of influence within the organization* through *increasing the power of groups within the organization holding goals compatible with their own.*

In order for a guideline to be considered satisfactorily operationalized, the staff practitioner has to indicate: first, a practice objective that involved changing an organization's goals; second, the structure of influence within the organization, along with how it would be altered; and third, the method of increasing the power of compatible groups. The pilot stage is invaluable in uncovering unanticipated operational and procedural problems such as failure to sufficiently break down the various parts of a design concept.

Another staffing problem that pilot work affords an opportunity to work through is the relationship of practitioners and administrators to research people. This may be described as research politics or, "rocking the administrative boat." Searching for a more effective or efficient way to do things often represents a threat to those who have carved out more or less secure niches in organizational settings. Observation and evaluation by researchers can pose a threat to operational people, a threat to which they may respond with emotions that lie anywhere along a continuum from grudging acceptance through hostile indifference to undisguised efforts at sabotage. The experience of Hiltz (1974) provides insight into the frustrations that can accrue to the conscientious researcher encountering this problem. In her situation the practitioners developed what she terms a "strategy of non-cooperation," characterized by the following (all too familiar) set of tactics:

1. Attack the validity of the proposed research. However, steadfastly refuse to offer any constructive suggestions.
2. Claim ethical considerations that make the research impossible.
3. Attack the researcher's credentials, ability, personal characteristics, or anything else that might stop the research.
4. Having lost the battle over whether there is to be any evaluative research, limit access of the researcher to the staff and data. (Assume the evaluator is the enemy and let the staff know this.) If the delays and frustrations are great enough, maybe the evaluator will give up. (p. 219)

This may seem like an extreme example; it is not. Those who choose to embark on social R&D applications must be fully prepared to meet resistance and hostility, sometimes in the extreme. Furthermore, the problem is not unique to the human services but exists wherever there is a team which ranges along a continuum with researchers at one end and appliers at the other.

A major function of a pilot study is to identify those circumstances where such problems might generally arise in a main field test and to develop in advance effective strategies for dealing with them. Some approaches to mitigating this problem may include the following:

shared decision making

full interpretation by researchers of purposes and methods

developing a team spirit

feedback of data during the process of development work
involvement of practitioners in interpretation of data
involvement of practitioners in instrument design
participation by practitioners in planning and conduct of training sessions
close contact by researchers with the application situation
use of personnel with joint research-practice backgrounds

Others may be added. Some of these may be useful and appropriate in one development project and not in another. Experimentation with various approaches in the pilot phase should indicate optimal arrangements for later work.

The nature of this relationship touches also on the nature of supervision, control and encouragement needed to guide "social engineers" through the implementation/operationalization process. Should monitoring be tight or flexible, should remuneration be based on "piece work" or a general task assignment, should modes of influence involve external expectations or internalized norms, should rewards be primarily monetary or should they include professional and personal satisfaction? Probably some balance needs to be struck that may be unique for each development venture, and which a careful pilot study can indicate. Aspects of monitoring and supervision will be discussed further in the next chapter.

INSTRUMENTATION AND DATA TREATMENT

One of the major tasks of the pilot phase is the production of instruments of various kinds necessary to implement development. Instruments will be discussed more fully in the next chapter, thus only a few remarks will be made here in relation to how this subject is implicated in pilot work. Two different types of variables must ordinarily be measured in development: process variables, and outcome variables.

Process variables pertain to the recording of how a guideline is operationalized. This may include the number of times a client is seen, the type of incentives given to encourage participation, the intensity of effort required by the practitioner in a given initiative, the form of communication used in implementing an action principle, the type of interaction that takes place between individuals or groups involved in the intervention, and so on.

Outcome variables pertain to evaluation of the results of implementing the intervention. What might be said to be the consequences of this type of intervention? Was it successful? To what degree?

Both process recording and outcome evaluating instruments may be of many types: obtrusive or unobtrusive, highly structured or open-ended, self-reporting or observational. Fairweather (1967) suggests the following types of scales for social innovation projects: behavior ratings, essay and open-ended questions, attitude and expectancy scales, economic records, administrative records, research journals. Instruments may also need to be developed on such variables as baselines, characteristics of practitioners, clients, agencies, etc.

The pilot phase allows for testing the general approach most suited to the task at hand, the types of specific items that most effectively yield information, timing in data collection, who should gather the information and under what circumstances. In working with practitioners in the field, data collection must blend to some degree with the tasks of practice, and must not intrude upon the practice so as to distort or hinder it. Synchronizing data collection and intervention requirements may require considerable trial before the right balance is achieved. In our own work, for example, we commenced the pilot stage with requiring field staff to fill out a weekly log form detailing a range of variables related to implementation. Through the pilot stage we learned that this amount of recording imposed what practitioners perceived to be a heavy burden of recording on them. In experimenting with a bi-weekly recording arrangement we found that practitioners could tolerate this more easily, and there was little or no loss of information on the flow of interventive process. The modification also eased the data processing load at project headquarters. A function of the pilot stage is to indicate the amount and level of detail needed to study the operationalization process. These procedures were usefully carried forward into the main field test.

Because of the great number of variables ordinarily involved in social R&D, data processing and data handling comprise complex technical and administrative problems. It is useful to have both research and operations staffs involved in assessing these procedures, as they involve both facets of the endeavor. During pilot work data should be reviewed in terms of such factors as:

Relevance—is the answer responsive? Does it have a direct relationship to project objectives? Does it "make sense?"

Completeness-specificity—is there enough ("full") information in sufficient detail?

Clarity—can the response be understood? Is it intelligible and comprehensible?

Processability—is the response in a form that it can be aggregated, coded, and analyzed appropriately? Can it be treated within customary research procedures?

Such a review can lead to elimination of defects that might be damaging in the main field test.

Several other uses of pilot work can be illustrated through the CIP experience. At an early seminar, a pattern of feedback reporting to the practitioners on the status of data gathering and the analysis of baseline factors was introduced. This was carried throughout the pilot study and proved to be a useful mechanism for sharing findings and maintaining practitioner interest. Helmstadter (1970) points out that open communication and common goals with frequent feedback and reports on progress are important to maintaining morale and motivation in research-related tasks.

Much later in the pilot year we realized that the simultaneous execution of several guidelines by a practitioner, though interesting for its practice potential, also made it extremely difficult from a monitoring standpoint to partial out the effects of each guideline on the desired outcome. We decided that from that point onward, practitioners would be required to implement guidelines separately and serially.

The extent of pilot work in a given project depends in part on the state of the art in the field. When instruments, procedures, and conventions are well established, less is required of a pilot venture. Gibson (1964) observes in discussing methodological problems:

An important factor in determining the reduction to public practice of new knowledge or developments is the "technological environment" prevailing at the time . . . This comprises the sum total of all the know-how, skills, techniques, tools, materials, and appurtenances that are items of commerce, readily available for producing a new device or perfecting a service, so that it can be presented to the using public in simple, reliable, and economical form. For example, if we wish to make a modern loudspeaker cabinet, the technological environment that affects us is the kind of wood we have available, the hand or power tools we have, the screws, the glue, the paint that we can obtain. (p. 43)

Gibson also offers the following with respect to technical aspects of field testing:

It was many years after Newcomen first demonstrated the feasibility of a steam engine that artisans were able to bore a cylinder more than eight inches in diameter, round enough to accommodate a tight-fitting piston. The introduction of the steam engine into public practice was delayed for a long time. Indeed, one can say without exaggeration that the interactions with the technological environment have played a dominant role in determining the direction of technological progress. (p. 44)

The rather underdeveloped technological environment in which social R&D must take place should predispose those who would utilize social R&D toward a lengthy and intensive period of pilot work in most instances. To ignore or play down the pilot effort is to jeopardize the basic development endeavor. Pilot work should pave the way to a productive and efficient main field testing development phase, the character of which we shall now examine.

BIBLIOGRAPHY

CAMPBELL, DONALD T., and JULIAN C. STANLEY, *Experimental and Quasi-Experimental Design for Research.* Chicago: Rand McNally, 1966.

FAIRWEATHER, GEORGE W., *Methods for Experimental Social Innovation.* New York: John Wiley & Sons, 1967.

GIBSON, R. E., "A Systems Approach to Research Management," *Research, Development, and Technological Innovation: An Introduction,* ed. James R. Bright, pp. 34–57. Homewood, Ill.: Richard D. Irwin, Inc., 1964.

HELMSTADTER, G. C., *Research Concepts in Human Behavior.* New York: Appleton-Century-Crofts, 1970.

HERSEN, M., and D. BARLOW, *Single-Case Experimental Designs: Strategies for Studying Behavior.* New York: Pergamon, 1976.

HILTZ, S. ROXANNE, "Evaluating a Pilot Social Service Project for Widows: A Chronicle of Research Problems," *Journal of Sociology and Social Welfare,* 1, no. 4 (Summer 1974), 217–224.

HOWE, MICHAEL W., "Casework Self-Evaluation: A Single Subject Approach," *Social Service Review,* 48 (March 1974), 1–23.

JAHODA, MARIE, MORTON DEUTSCH, and STUART W. COOK, *Research Methods in Social Relations, Part One: Basic Processes.* New York: The Dryden Press, 1955.

MACKIE, ROBERT R., and PAUL R. CHRISTENSEN, *Translation and Application of Psychological Research,* Human Factors Research, Inc., Santa Barbara Research Park, Goleta, California, January 1967. Technical Report 716–1.

MCCRORY, R. J., "The Design Method—A Scientific Approach to Valid Design," *Technological Planning at the Corporate Level,* Proceedings of a conference sponsored by the Associates of the Harvard Business School, September 8–9, 1961, ed. James R. Bright. Cambridge, Mass.: 1961, pp. 59–67.

MOSER, C. A., and G. KALTON, *Survey Methods in Social Investigation,* pp. 47–51, 93, 264, 310, 319, 348, 375. London: Heinemann Education Books, Ltd., 1971.

ROBERTS, EDWARD B., *The Dynamics of Research and Development.* New York: Harper and Row, 1964.

ROSENBERG, MORRIS, *The Logic of Survey Analysis.* New York: Basic Books, 1968.

SCHUTZ, RICHARD E., "The Nature of Educational Development," *Journal of Research and Development in Education,* University of Georgia (Winter 1970), 39–64.

STEELE, SARA M., *Contemporary Approaches to Program Evaluation and Their Implications.* Washington, D.C.: Capitol Publishers, Inc., 1977.

Main Field Testing I
Purpose and
Functions

All Laboratory products undergo a rigorous research and development cycle prior to release for reproduction and distribution by other agencies. At least three phases of field testing—work with a prototype, a supervised performance field test, and an operational test under normal conditions without Laboratory participation—precede formal external review and an official decision on acceptability. In view of this thorough evaluation, those who adopt Laboratory products and processes can know with certainty the kind of outcomes they can anticipate in their own educational setting.

> John K. Hemphill, Laboratory Director
> The Far West Laboratory for Educational
> Research and Development

THE NATURE OF MAIN FIELD TESTING IN DEVELOPMENT[1]

Development is at the heart of R&D, and main field testing is the essence of development. Novick (1961), head of cost analysis for the Rand Corporation, estimates that "improved application," or development, amounts to approximately two and a half times the costs of all other aspects of R&D.

[1]Portions of this chapter appear in the CIP technical report, Jack Rothman, Joseph G. Teresa and John L. Erlich, *Developing Effective Strategies for Social Intervention: A Research and Development Methodology* PB-272/454 TR-1-RD, National Technical Information Service, Springfield, Virginia, 1977, with special reference to chapters 2 and 3; and in Jack Rothman, "Harnessing Research to Serve Practice," Paper presented at the National Conference on the Future of Social Work Research, sponsored by The National Association of Social Workers, San Antonio, Texas, October 15–18, 1978.

127

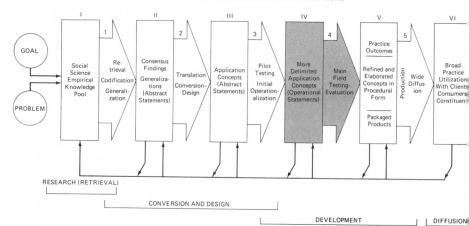

According to McCrory (1961), "development tasks are extremely demanding in terms of engineering skills and usually involve the major expenditure of funds and time" (p. 44).

Development requires the full working through, evaluation, and detailing of an application concept so that it can be used in developed form with ease and dependability. This is what makes it so difficult and demanding. Radnor et al. (1976), of the Center for the Interdisciplinary Study of Science and Technology, point out that readiness for use is *the* distinguishing characteristic of development:

Development involves a process of converting knowledge into *User-ready* products. The emphasis or focus of development is on the User. The end-product must be something the User can use (with at most some minimal fitting or tailoring). [emphasis in the original] (p. 72)

Thus, while "testing" distinguishes pilot work, "perfecting" characterizes main development work.

The concept of "user-ready" materials, techniques, and programs is elementary and important, yet we find it virtually absent in the social sciences and in the human services. Typically, a new policy or program is conceived and promulgated by a policy group or administrative staff. In the usual practice, it is widely diffused without formal evaluation regarding performance criteria or effectiveness. Occasionally, some preliminary pilot or "demonstration" is conducted; but, ordinarily, this is at a level involving only the notion of feasibility. Hundreds of programs sponsored by HUD, the Labor Department, and HEW in such areas as housing, job placement, or rehabilitation are carried out in this way. Occasionally, evaluation is encouraged or mandated, as with O.E.O. Community Action Programs, or, more recently, in Community Mental Health. Evaluation typically occurs *after* the programs have been described and are in widespread—often national—operation. Often these are programs involving millions of clients but with no clear-cut, systematic procedures for feedback of evaluation findings to redirect program design. Compared to industrial R&D, these procedures are primitive, inept, and wasteful.

Why development has been overlooked in the social field is an enigma. There has been some codification of research and shaping of application concepts into propositional inventories at the retrieval end of R&D. There has also been a considerable amount of research and theory building on the diffusion end. Program evaluation has also been receiving increasing attention. But the bringing to bear of these techniques and insights in a coherent development program has been extremely rare and scattered. It remains a huge intellectual and technical void in the social sciences and allied professions.

A sad, but unfortunately typical, example of what occurs when development is neglected is reported by Gross et al. (1971) in attempting to implement a new instructional approach (called the "catalytic role model") in a public school system. The innovation is described as follows:

This role is to maximize the potential talents and interests of each child, to help children to develop their interests and capacities, to help them learn how to learn, and not to teach them a set of standard concepts or facts. Children are seen as different types of candles to be lit; the task of the teacher is to light each candle ... The teacher's task is to create the type of classroom atmosphere in which children feel free to pursue their own interests, to learn what they, not the teacher, view as important. To do this, the teacher is expected to flood the classroom with a variety of educational materials, primarily self-instructional, that are based on "pedagogically sound" ideas so that whatever materials a child decides to work with will make a contribution to his education ... The teacher is expected to facilitate contact between children and the self-instructional materials; she is also expected to encourage children to teach each other. (pp. 12–13)

After eight months the attempted innovation ended in failure, leaving the staff disillusioned and cynical:

Our findings showed that the failure to implement the innovation was attributable essentially to a number of obstacles that the teachers encountered when they attempted to carry it out [including] ... lack of clarity about the new role model ... lack of the skills and knowledge required to carry it out ... unavailability of required materials and equipment ... a set of organizational arrangements that were incompatible with the innovation. (pp. 196–98)

Here is a case of a design concept being imprecisely drawn. Kinds of role performance were only generally stated, expected outcomes of innovation implementation were not clear, and there was no basis for providing the new skills and resources that would be needed for teachers for the implementation. All of these things would be immediately discernible with an R&D approach. The innovation would have been initially stated in prescriptive form, and the procedures and circumstances for successful implementation would have been established first through a pilot test, then through a full field test of the innovation. When development was complete, the innovation would have been user-ready in its detailed prescription; and there would have been a greater likelihood of a positive outcome. Cost, energy, and thought requirements would have been higher, no doubt, but so, too, would have been the probability of success.

Main field testing in development involves a number of interrelated purposes and methods. A larger number of users and user settings, for example, are usually required for the main field test than were employed in the pilot study. Quite obviously, it is necessary to determine whether the applications will work fairly broadly and under less purely experimental circumstances than are found in the pilot situation. It involves, too, more refined and sustained attention to the component items in the framework of development that were discussed in the previous chapter.

In our own work we used a limited number of field staff during our pilot phase. These worked only with the general statement of the application concept. There was no manual or handbook available to them, and they used open-ended log recording forms to report their experiences. We may speak of these participating practitioners as "front end" social engineers, or development engineers, because it was necessary for them to work closely at the edge of theory. Their tasks consisted of converting aspects of theory into real world processes.

The core development work was done during the main field study with an expanded field staff. This group had not only the application concept to work with, but also a preliminary version of the handbook that had been composed from the experience of the pilot year. This group employed more structured, check-list type recording instruments with categories from pilot study log data. This group also had a well-defined methodological procedure to guide their efforts.

While still performing social engineering functions through converting and operationalizing theoretical formulations, the main field study participants had materials to work with that had already begun to take formative, operational shape. Thus, they needed somewhat less theoretical competency and required a lesser degree of project supervisory support than did the pilot group. In addition, during this stage more rigorous evaluation procedures were employed to determine the extent to which practitioners attained their intended goals in implementing guidelines. In this way it was possible to relate particular types of implemental activities to goal attainment. It was also possible to structure information in the final handbook in terms of practices that had demonstrably achieved favorable outcomes.

Through the process of performance testing in the field, one attempts to specify the conditions that will predict the greatest likelihood of favorable outcomes in carrying out a particular application concept. The precision and repetitiveness of predicted outcomes prevailing in the physical sciences is missing (some may add, thankfully, for the flexibility and autonomy of human behavior is not a matter to be depreciated). Nevertheless, some approximation of the careful and systematic procedures of the physical sciences is both possible and beneficial. There has been experience with performance testing in educational R&D (Sanders and Sachse, 1977). It usually signifies measuring student capabilities in a real or authentic test situation, rather than the rigorous performance standards suggested here.

The result of such performance testing is the determination of the specifications—parameters and central tendencies—of applications: patterns of implementation, numbers and types of individuals and groups to be involved, etc. When "captured" by reliable recording procedures, such specifications can be set down in an appropriate medium of communication—manual, guidebook, chart, film, etc.—that enables a new user to replicate the implemental activities in such a way as to obtain a similar outcome. Furthermore, the new user should obtain these outcomes with greater ease, less need for trial and error, and a higher success rate than if development work, and its systematic encapsulation had not occurred.

The product of CIP's efforts, a practitioners' handbook, projected us into the next operational step of the R&D process. Here this handbook was given a terminal field test in a more informal way. Potential users—practitioners, students in graduate training, faculty—were asked to review or to use the handbook as a planning and/or training instrument. The field sample in this instance was not made up of social engineers, but approximated the intended ultimate target population of users. At this step one can discern user reactions, bugs, and potential improvements, so that corrections and modifications can be made in the final version. The basic cyclical character of development is revealed in such a pattern.

PERFORMANCE TESTING
AND THE DEVELOPMENT OF SPECIFICATIONS

Few men of letters enjoyed Oscar Wilde's reputation for mastery of the spontaneous epigram and witty, insightful aphorism. Few men worked harder at being "spontaneous." He contrived his ideas, wrote them out carefully, committed them to memory, tried them out on a few close and trusted friends, assessed their impact, made any necessary adjustments to improve their effect. He would then spring them nonchalantly and "spontaneously" on lecture audiences or large social gatherings. Oscar Wilde, without realizing it, was practicing performance testing in wit engineering.

The effectiveness of the personal measurement and evaluation techniques used by Wilde can be seen in the effectiveness of his performances. All field testing requires procedures for measurement and evaluation. In R&D this is usually referred to as "performance testing." In the social sciences the closest analogy is program evaluation.

The need for a measurement of goal attainment ought to be self-evident when viewed in the light of R&D objectives. R&D seeks to associate certain variables involved in the *process* of implementation of a guideline (X) with the relative success in the achievement of the intended objectives (Y). In any situation where the assessment of outcome as a function of process is important, dependable outcome measures are indispensable. It is essential to find out if the solution works.

Those in more conventional industrial R&D carry this analysis a step further. They hold that evaluation not only indicates whether the solution works, but also its reliability and the conditions under which it works. This has given rise to the field of reliability engineering which tries to establish methods and test procedures for measuring and assessing reliability parameters. When viewed as simply the capability of a specified performance within a given set of operating conditions and environments, reliability proves to be as useful a notion in social R&D as it is in industrial R&D.

Gibson (1964), in discussing product development, appears to be making a similar point:

Its promised performance must be realized with safety, reliability and ease of operation when it is placed in the hands of the using public . . . All these attributes must be engineered into the commodity before it can be said to be *reduced to public practice.* [emphasis in the original] (p. 43)

Five important factors need to be examined in connection with performance testing. These are: outcome evaluation, process evaluation, instrumentation, quantitative analysis, and specification formulation. An examination of each of these factors points up the extent of the parallelism of the pilot and main field test steps, a relationship that is one of similarity and not of congruency.

Outcome Evaluation

Program evaluation theory is the main body of literature available for guiding outcome assessment methods in the social field. There has been an outpouring of theory and method literature about evaluation in the last decade or so by such scholars as Caro (1977), Guttentag and Struening (1975), Weiss (1975), Rossi and Williams (1972), Suchman (1967), Isaac and Michael (1971), Epstein and Tripodi (1977), Tripodi, Fellin, and Epstein (1971), and Steele (1977). Among these authors there does not seem to be much disagreement on the definition and purpose of evaluation research, only slight differences in emphasis. Weiss (1972), for example, sees the purpose of such research as a way of measuring the effects of a program against the goals it set out to accomplish. This provides useful input for decision making about the program and for improving future programming. Caro (1977) agrees, stating, "[evaluation research] attempts to provide a program administrator with correct information in the consequences of his actions" (p. 88). Tripodi, Fellin, and Epstein (1971) define evaluation as a management technique for the sytematic feedback of information to be used to improve social programs.

Others emphasize the scientific function of allowing inferences to be made about effects of given inventions. Suchman (1967) statess the evaluation hypothesis as "activities A, B, C will influence the process producing X, Y, Z" (p. 38).

A useful general orientation is provided by Weiss' (1972) delineation of basic components of evaluation research:

1. the use of a *systematic methodology,*
2. the *assessment of the outcomes,*
3. the establishment of *specific criteria* upon which to base objective outcome assessments, and
4. the contribution of this information to *social purposes* (as an aid to decision making regarding the efficiency of different interventions in bringing about different social ends). (p. 4)

These notions highlight a particular feature of evaluation research: the use and adaptation of scientific methods to further practical social goals. This is the same blend we have described as a characteristic of R&D. At the development stage working and workable forms of evaluation should have evolved from the pilot phase.

Ample technical information is available about evaluation methods and will not be repeated here. For our purposes we wish primarily to locate evaluation as a function within the R&D model.

Process Evaluation

While outcome evaluation concerns itself with the results of an intervention effort, process evaluation concerns itself with the means. Outcome evaluation asks the question: to what degree are application concepts successful when applied in the field? Process evaluation asks: can you assure that the application concepts are implemented in such a way as actually to bring into being the inherent strategy or initiative embedded in the concept? This examines whether the concept materializes (i.e., that X is actualized). The concreteness and coherence of "means" are less tangible in the social field than in the physical. It is often more difficult to be clear about the operational reality of a social program than of a machine.

Process evaluation has not received the same degree of attention in the literature that has been lavished on outcome evaluation, but this has been on the upswing. The literature deals with the nature of the means (treatment, program, intervention) used to bring about a given outcome. As Chommie and Hudson (1974) state:

An alternative and complementary strategy of evaluation aims to conduct research that facilitates program changes and enhances understanding of it. This strategy looks at program processes to explain outcomes and in general to learn more about intervention. (p. 682)

Hesseling (1964) sees process evaluation as taking place during the progress of a program. In his view it involves a "systematic observation and recording of the activities of a program" (p. 19). The following kinds of activities are related to process evaluation:

1. identifying and monitoring potential sources of failure;
2. delineating project staff pre-program decisions and their logistical requirements;
3. describing what actually takes place;
4. determining the congruence between what is intended and what is actually observed;
5. determining the logical consistency between a program's objectives and its planned activities.

Specific methodological details can be found in the evaluation literature and in the CIP technical report.

Instrumentation for Recording the Process of Implementation

One does not approach social science research in any form without realizing that he is dealing with intricate and complex phenomena made up of multi-layered, often convoluted, rational and irrational human interactions. The social process not infrequently appears on its surface to be some sort of intermingling of the intelligible and the unfathomable. Yet, out of the apparent chaos, careful observation often reveals a modicum of predictable consistency to social process. It is this fact that encourages the social scientist that useful, interesting data may be derived from controlled examination of social phenomena. In the pilot phase instruments for such examination are *experimented* with; in the development stage they are *employed* in operational form.

There are three important ways of gathering the useful and interesting data the social scientist seeks: direct observation, interviewing (directly or through questionnaires) those participating in the experience, and self-reporting by those participating in the experience. Straight observation requires the observer to be on hand in the immediate environment. It runs the risk of distorting the social process, for the observer may be an intrusive, causative element in the experience being reported. Interviewing lessens this risk, for the interviewer intrudes only periodically and this can be done outside of the actual interventive situation. Interviews, however, are less able to capture subtle changes in direction, thought, or process that are readily apparent in ongoing observation. Self-reporting offers a natural way of gathering data on complex, internal thought processes. Yet, self-reporting also offers opportunity for distortion. The participant may not perform his reporting tasks with the expected diligence, he may view his experience with various distortions of ego and/or stress, or he may even report what he believes the experimenter wants to hear without regard to the true facts of the situation. In any case, as Trow (1957) observes:

Different kinds of information about man and society are gathered most fully and economically in different ways, and . . . the problem under investigation properly dictates the methods of investigation . . . The inferences we make from data, and the theory from which they derive and to which they contribute, may, indeed, be nothing more than "educated guesses"—but that is the nature of scientific theory. Our aim is to make them increasingly highly educated guesses. (pp. 33–35)

The full range of measuring instruments available to the social sciences for knowledge-building purposes can be drawn upon to serve R&D purposes. An indication of some of them was given in the previous chapter. A period of careful experimentation and creative guesswork lies ahead in matching up such instruments to the peculiar requirements of social R&D.

Analysis Requisites for Development

The objective of developmental work is to observe intervention behavior in its natural setting in order to facilitate successful future intervention by others in those same types of settings. The rationale for this is provided in part by Mackie and Christensen (1967):

To the extent that stimulus conditions differ in research and real life contexts, the need for translation and confirmatory research increases. When stimulus conditions are highly abstract, or nonsensical, the findings of a study can do little more than generate hypotheses for validation studies; i.e., translation is not possible.

In general, studies will be more translatable and have a higher likelihood of application if the investigator employs "natural" stimuli (stimuli as they exist in some operational environment). The use of "natural" stimuli, or carefully constructed facsimiles, should be encouraged: the temptation to invent stimulus (task) conditions to suit one's convenience, experimental apparatus, or theoretical viewpoint should be resisted. (pp. 39–40)

The consequence of studying natural phenomena is the production of multivariable research situations. This circumstance (and its particular virtues) is analyzed by Stagner (1966) with regard to using learning research to improve classroom teaching:

The research strategy of the "pure" experimentalist is typically designed around the single criterion; and, indeed, if the environment so constrains the organism that only one dimension of behavior variability is permitted (e.g., speed of running down an alley), not much more can be gotten. But anyone who has done learning research knows that different criteria of learning often give different outcomes. The experimenter cuts this Gordian knot by arbitrarily choosing one and discarding data relevant to the others. But he, too, might achieve more penetrating insights into the consequences of his independent variables if he adopted a multiple-criterion approach to his dependent measures. (p. 2)

Data analysis in these circumstances is complex and sometimes perplexing. Some difficulties and requisites of this approach are spelled out by Guetzkow (1959):

Many social situations have large numbers of highly interrelated variables with feedbacks. Instead of being able to work with quasi-isolated miniature models—as the natural scientist does—the user of social science must immediately work with an interrelated system. Even though scientist and applier try to simplify, both are forced to reckon with the interplay among their variables, because variables often cannot be held constant without disrupting the social process itself. (p. 70)

Tukey (1962), an expert in multivariate analysis, has suggested that analysis techniques should "seek for scope and usefulness" rather than the security of established and neat procedures. He speaks of multivariate heuristics involving a kind of venturesome detective work. Such analysis is concerned with the dynamic relatedness or jointness of measures of given subjects or phenomena. Another specialist, Kendall (1957), defines the technical analysis task in this way: "The variates are dependent among themselves so we cannot split one or more off from the others and consider it by itself. The variates must be considered together. Procedures for combining the variables in an optimal way need to be formulated" (p. 5). There is no question but that this places a strain on statistical technology.

Multivariate analysis involves such complex and interrelated procedures as factor analysis; canonical, multiple and partial correlation; multivariate analysis of variance; and discriminant and classification functions. Matrix algebra is an indispensable tool for carrying out these analysis procedures, as is the use of appropriate computer programs. Fortunately, methodological advances have provided assistance, as can be seen in works by such authors as Tukey (1977), Horst (1965), DuBois (1957), Fienberg (1977), Bock (1966), Rulon, Tiedman, Langmuir, and Tatsuoka (1967), and Harris (1975). Some of these are specialized (Horst in factor analysis, DuBois in correlational analysis, Rulon in discriminant analysis). Others, Harris for example, treat the subject generally.

It is evident that R&D programs need to contain within their staff complements not only able program evaluation specialists, but also research analysts with specialized competency in multivariate techniques. Alternatively, the R&D program must make provision for ample consultation by such experts. Doubtless, the expansion of social R&D will be a stimulus to improved multivariate statistical techniques. At the same time, social R&D will be dependent upon such advances for its own development.

Formulation of Specifications

Specification of performance levels is a standard step in the development of a new automobile, for example, or a new solar powered electrical generator. This standard is virtually absent in the development of new social programs or practice techniques. Because of this lack, it is difficult to communicate the concept of specifications in social intervention. It may be useful, therefore, to illustrate the notion through the CIP experience. This material follows closely the Project technical report (Rothman, Teresa and Erlich, 1977, pp. 6:12 through 6:22). We will refrain from full methodological explication, as this is accessible in the technical report.

Lest one become confused or sidetracked by what is to follow, let it be clear that the purpose of the analysis in R&D is not to arrive at broad scientific generalizations. Rather, the aim in our situation was to develop specifications for guideline implementation (parameters and central tendencies of successful implementation) so these might be included in a handbook to assist other practitioners in guideline implementation.

With this caveat in mind, we will now proceed with a two-fold presentation of our data analysis. (Qualitative analysis is equally important and will be discussed in chapter nine.) The first aspect will be what we have called a "profile of successful practice." This profile will be a descriptive analysis of 15 of 21 practitioners who were rated as achieving a high level of success in implementing the innovation guideline. The second aspect will be a discussion of the multivariate discriminant analysis between more successful and less successful practitioners. We will then present an action profile of specifications for implementation. The innovation guideline uses the application concept of "partialization" in establishing a new service program (see p. 174–76).

Our data were derived from a self-reporting final summary log that was filled out by the field staff upon full completion of implementation.

DESCRIPTIVE ANALYSIS:
A "PROFILE OF SUCCESSFUL PRACTICE"

We began with a panel of expert judges assessing the degree of goal attainment in implementing the guideline on a 1 to 5 scale for each of the practitioners who completed implementation. A rating of 5 meant the field staff member had achieved complete success in implementation; i.e., the goals the member had established had all been met. Lower ratings indicated less success. We defined what we shall refer to as the "success profile" group, consisting of those fifteen practitioners receiving either a 4 or 5 rating—"complete" or "almost complete" success. There were eleven field staff members who received a rating of 5, and these we shall refer to as the "more successful" group. Ratings of 4 down to 1 indicated decreasing levels of success in implementation. Nine practitioners fell within this range, and we shall refer to them as the less successful group.

In constructing our profile of successful practice, we were particularly concerned with three areas: which and how many key community groups did the field staff member contact in the process of implementation, which and how many key individuals were contacted during the implementation, and what factors either facilitated (enhanced) or limited (inhibited) implementation. While the first two of these could be ascertained objectively (recording actual numbers), the facilitating and limiting factors were particularly a matter of subjective judgment on the part of the field staff. To ascertain the degree of facilitation or limitation, each field staff member rated the variables in each sector (personal, agency, community, clientele) on a "none" to "high" (0 to 4) intensity scale. A tendency was noted when an intensity of 3.0 or more was found for facilitating factors and when an intensity rating of 2.5 or higher appeared for limiting factors. This was an arbitrary decision on our part and was based on the way in which the intensity scores tended to cluster for facilitating and limiting factors.

KEY COMMUNITY GROUPS CONTACTED The descriptive analysis indicated that the profile of success group (those fifteen of twenty-one implementers who achieved "complete" or "almost complete" success) contacted from zero to twenty community groups (parameter). Approximately 47% considered one to five groups (central tendency) to be important to the implementation.

Public agencies were considered most important by the largest percentage (53%) of successful practitioners. Contact with such organizations was made primarily for reasons of immediate participation (13%), legitimation (13%), or future participation (10%). The data indicate that voluntary associations were considered important for reasons of information and guidance (13%) and public relations (10%), and that immediate participation (10%) was sought from these agencies.

We should point out that a tendency was noted whenever percentages of 10% or greater appeared. A very large number of cells were involved in the analysis and 10% was more than expected on a probability basis in any given cell. Thus, when encountering percentages of this magnitude, they were regarded as indicating a tendency to be recognized.

KEY INDIVIDUALS CONTACTED The data indicate that this sample of practitioners used more individuals than groups in carrying out the guideline. The mode (33%) was eleven to fifteen (central tendency) with a range (parameter) of from one to thirty contacts. It is interesting to note that the more successful practitioners considered a fewer number of individuals important, apparently focusing their efforts on selected, influential actors.

Successful practitioners most frequently considered the agency executives (67%) to be important. Agency executives were most frequently contacted primarily for reasons of legitimation (17%), immediate participation (17%), and future participation (10%). Other trends included the contacting of relatively larger numbers of board members for reasons of legitimation (17%) and community people for immediate participation (10%). Board committee members, agency peers, and community leaders were also contacted in relatively larger numbers.

FACILITATING AND LIMITING CONDITIONS Successful practitioners gave a mean score rating to facilitating factors of 2.9 and to limiting factors of 1.4 in influencing outcome of implementation (on the 0 to 4 intensity scale). For each of the social psychological spheres (Personal, Agency, Community, Client), limitation was rated lower than facilitation as a consideration in implementation.

MULTIVARIATE DISCRIMINANT ANALYSIS

In this analysis we compare those field staff members who were "more successful" in implementing the guideline (i.e., our panel of judges rated their implementation experience 5, complete goal attainment, on our outcome scale) with those who were "less successful" (i.e., who received a 1 to 4 success rating). In this comparison the facilitating and limiting factors take on a special dimension of importance.

FACILITATING FACTORS   The discriminant data analysis indicated that a mode of significant differences existed between the "more successful" and the "less successful" practitioners on the Personal factor (p = .007). This suggests a particularly important function for Personal facilitating factors.

When "more successful" and "less successful" practitioners are compared, it is seen that the "more successful" gave higher ratings to the following factors: *good reputation, self-confidence, knowledge of clients,* and *good relationships with agency staff and administrators. Position or role* in the agency also proved to be an important factor. *Commitment to the program, knowledge of community,* and *enjoyment of job* did not contribute to the discriminant function. This was true, however, because these factors were all rated high in intensity by both the "more successful" and the "less successful" groups.

The mean score intensity level of the Personal facilitating sector variable was $\overline{3.6}$. Those of the other sector variables were lower and clustered at a similar level of intensity: Agency = $\overline{2.7}$, Client = $\overline{2.5}$, and Community = $\overline{2.7}$. Significant differences (p. = .03) were found between the "more successful" and "less successful" groups on the Community variable. In particular, the "more successful" practitioners rated voluntary participation high.

While the Agency did not rate high in facilitation for the descriptive analysis, certain organizational factors merit note. *Support by the administrative hierarchy* (supervisor, administrators, board) was singled out as an important consideration. In addition, *practitioner assignments being consistent with the effort* was rated high in intensity by both "more" and "less successful" practitioners.

LIMITING FACTORS   Agency rated highest in limitation. Furthermore, significant differences (p = .01) were found between the "more successful" and the "less successful" groups. Three factors were mentioned by a higher percentage of successful practitioners. These also discriminated between the "more" and "less successful." "More successful practitioners generally gave higher intensity ratings to: *lack of power or authority of their organization, unclear or shifting goals, programs and assignments within the organization,* and *lack of support of affiliated organizations.* The first two factors were also mentioned by a higher percentage of successful practitioners in the success profile (that group of fifteen who rated 4 or 5 on implementation success). Systematic limitation in the mandate or structure of their sponsoring organization, rather than overt hostility or resistance within it, seemed to be the constraining elements. Consistent with this tendency, the cross section of successful practitioners in somewhat higher percentages mentioned the following additional limitations: *a hindering agency structure* and *lack of resources and of staff.* It is interesting to observe that the "less successful" field staff members differed from the "more successful" in being limited not by these general systematic constraints, but by lack of support from their supervisors and from lack of knowledge by the agency of clients and/or community. These latter appear to be more accessible and manipulable variables—variables the "more successful" practitioners may be able to manage and the "less successful" unable to deal with well.

Personal factors were rated relatively high among limiting variables and were significantly different (p = .03) between the two success level groups. "More successful" practitioners gave a higher intensity rating to *fatigue* than did "less successful" ones. One inference might be that successful practitioners felt incapacitated by limitations in their energy level rather than by inadequacies in personal capacities. "Less successful" practitioners included *poor relationships with the agency board* and *lack of knowledge of the community* as sources of limitation, factors that partially relate more to personal deficiencies. At the same time, these practitioners also include general restrictions such as *personal loss, lack of time,* and *over-involvement*— some of which were also mentioned by a relatively high percentage of the success profile group.

A considerable number of Personal factors from the success profile were not limiting at all. Among these were *poor relationships with various groups, lack of knowledge of the community or programs, not enjoying the job, professional disinterest,* and *personal loss.* The emphasis in personal limitation as expressed by the field staff appears to be on the pressures and demands in the work environment of human relations agencies, including fatigue, over-involvement, insufficient time, etc.

AN ACTION PROFILE OF IMPLEMENTATION SPECIFICATIONS

By carefully considering the implications of the information our examination of the data has provided us, it now becomes possible to construct an action profile for optimizing successful implementation of the innovation guideline. The action profile specifying intervention behaviors represents, in effect, a prescription for successful action, derived from demonstrated, real world success of others in similar situations who were implementing a strategy derived in the first instance from existing research. Development permits us to mold that strategy into its most effective, user-ready form.

In implementing the partialization strategy of the innovation guideline, the change agent may anticipate contact with a moderate number of key community groups, typically in the one to five range. Public agencies might be given attention, especially to obtain their participation or to gain their legitimation for programs and activities. Voluntary associations may also be important, especially for assistance in information and guidance or for public relations purposes. Immediate participation may be sought from private agencies.

A larger number of key individuals will likely be contacted, ranging in number from one to thirty. Care should be taken to limit such contacts to the number required, lest unnecessary energy be expended. The agency executive is an especially important contact to consider, particularly to gain his participation in, or legitimation for, the innovation program being planned. Board members may also be anticipated as sources of legitimation and community people as potential participants in the program.

The user would do well to place emphasis on the positive, facilitative factors in the situation, rather than to dwell on limitations and resistances. These latter should not be completely ignored, however.

With regard to facilitation, it is important to take stock of one's personal capacities and resources. One's attitude toward the program being promoted is important to consider. The practitioner should attempt to select a program for which he has a personal commitment or one for which he can develop such a commitment. One's position or role in the agency is of importance. Hence, a program should be selected that is compatible with his place in the agency. These considerations have to relate, of course, to client and community needs. He should also take care to acquire sufficient personal knowledge of the community in which the innovation is to take place.

A good reputation and self-confidence will help. Good working relationships with colleagues and administrators will also be of assistance. Knowledge of the client group for which the innovative program is intended is another key consideration.

Attention should be directed at gaining administrative support within the agency and voluntary participation in the outside community. Internal support may be engendered if the program selected is consistent with the practitioner's already-existing assignments. In this way the innovative program and normal work responsibilities may reinforce one another.

Aspects of the agency structure may stand in the way of success; for example, lack of power or authority of the agency. A cautious, but possibly effective, tactic may be to select a program that falls naturally within the existing mandate of the agency—at least, perhaps, as a first attempt in using this guideline. One should be alert to possible shifts in agency goals and arrangements, perhaps planning contingency approaches for various possible changes that may be projected. Lack of resources and of staff can be incapacitating; hence, one should plan a program that lies within existing agency capacities or one for which specific available resources exist in the community. Alternatively, some considerable time and energy should be pre-allocated to the accumulation of necessary resources and personnel.

Since fatigue, over-involvement, and lack of time may inhibit progress, careful, focused planning of time and energy is critical. Some of the previous suggestions may assist in this—choosing a program for which there are existing resources, one which is consistent with current job assignments, and which supplements or reinforces one's basic role and position in the agency as perceived by superordinates. Making sure to cultivate suitable relationships with board members and acquiring adequate knowledge of the community (already mentioned) will preclude stumbling over obstacles commonly encountered by others.

Because of limitations of social R&D at this point in time and of our own particular endeavor, the user of the handbook was warned to be cautious in carrying out these practice directives. He was also cautioned to test them carefully against the practice situation and his own experience and professional judgement.

Perfecting the formulation of specifications in social R&D is an uncompleted task; indeed, it is one that has barely started. What was given here is meant to suggest potentialities and directions for further development.

SOME FIELD PROBLEMS IN DEVELOPMENT

The key to effective operationalization of application concepts, or action guidelines, lies in proper conceptualization. This demands clear goal specifications and a clear understanding of the guideline elements. It is a disciplining process, intellectually, requiring a level of planning and organization brought to the work experience of the practitioner that may not have previously existed. The possibilities for increasing practice effectiveness through participation in development field testing are intriguing.

While the use of field staff who are functioning in their natural settings for R&D purposes holds potential for yielding data of immense value, the very dynamics of that setting may interfere with the goals of an R&D project. When job requirements conflict with development requirements, it is the latter that may suffer. If a new program is starting up within the agency, or a critical incident occurs in the community that affects the agency, or a particular problem arises concerning a particular client and demands special attention, or special preparation is needed for an important board meeting of the agency: these are only a few of the circumstances that can place the field staff member in a project-job conflict. Under such circumstances it may well be difficult keeping the field staff going. This can be an oppressive problem to solve. Financial remuneration does not appear to be a sufficient motivator in working with professionals. Some strategy for the internalization of the goals of the project seems clearly indicated.

Goal Specificity

Another major concern has to do with goal specificity. It is obvious that a clear indication from practitioners of their intended goals in using guidelines is needed if one is to assess with any accuracy whether the *results* of intervention were in the same "ball park" with the *intention* of intervention. The *need* to define goals clearly is a theme that pervades the evaluation literature. Kiresuk and Sherman (1968) and MacMahon, Pugh, and Hutchinson (1969), for example, make it clear that generalized goal statements when one is concerned with assessing outcomes are simply inappropriate. As the latter group of authors puts it:

Programs having as their objective a higher level of "positive mental health," for example, stand no more chance of being successfully evaluated than would a program of venereal disease control that is based on the objective of fostering positive genital health, however admirable such an objective may seem. (p. 56)

Rossi (1971) goes even further:

A social welfare program (or for that matter any program) which does not have clearly specified goals cannot be evaluated. (p. 18)

Yet, as with so much in the social services, some perverse pixie seems to keep whispering in our ear, threatening us with internal discomfort if we should dare to speak in anything other than generalities. The result, as we discovered in our pilot work and throughout the main field test, was that our field staff found it quite difficult to indicate a clear, definite, uncontaminated goal in employing a guideline that could be cleanly evaluated. This shouldn't have surprised us for Riecken (1972) rates the operational statement of objectives as the most difficult task in conducting evaluation studies. Furthermore, in the human services, we have a long and noble tradition of fuzzy goal statement construction. As Weiss (1972) points out:

Program goals are often hazy, ambiguous, hard to pin down. Occasionally, the official goals are merely a long list of pious and partly incompatible platitudes. (p. 25)

Aronson and Sherwood (1967) support this belief by offering a vivid depiction of the problem in a specific program evaluation project.

In the CIP we became aware of the problem during the pilot test and remained sensitive to it throughout the main field test. To counter it, our field staff were given very strong direction, training, and supervisory support to enable them to indicate a specific, focused, clear, short-range goal. The initial log was the main vehicle through which this was accomplished.

144

No initial log was approved until the staff review panel agreed that the goal was properly stated for evaluation purposes. In addition, the preliminary handbook was used to reinforce this objective recurrently with instructions, examples, etc. The second item in the initial log for the innovation guideline, for example, specifically asked: "What is your goal (i.e., the innovation) in using the guideline? Be as specific as possible. Keep a short-term time perspective." Furthermore, in the handbook there appeared a specific section headed "Getting Started" in which the field staff member was carefully guided through a series of goal setting steps geared toward establishing goals of considerable specificity.

Three factors appeared to contribute to this proclivity for goal obfuscation. First, because of the uncertainty and unpredictability of the practice environment, together with the underdeveloped state of social science and practice knowledge, there is merit in maintaining an open and flexible set with respect to goals. In this way the practitioner can shift as information becomes available or as developments evolve or crystallize. Open-ended goals may be viewed as functional and desirable in such practice settings. We might call this the factor of *adaptability*.

Second, because the practice environment is often volatile and unpredictable, vague, broad, and multiple goals provide a shield for the practitioner. Since he cannot guarantee the outcome of his efforts, amorphous goal definitions allow for claims of success that cannot be easily refuted. This provides both a defense against detractors and a basis for self-assurance and self-confirmation. We might call this the factor of *self-protection*.

Third, many practitioners do not treat their practice situation with a high degree of conceptual rigor. Such demands are not commonly placed on them in human service practice situations (although the "accountability" trend may counteract this), and training in many human service professions does not socialize professionals to thinking along these lines in the same way as does, say, training in law or engineering. Further, the pressures, confusions, and uncertainties of practice environments invoke hasty, multiple responses not conducive to deep, unhurried, deliberation. Indeed, this may be functional and necessary for success. Call this the factor of *conceptual looseness*.

Weiss (1972) suggests a fourth, "political" explanation as well:

Support from many quarters is required to get a program off the ground, and the glittering generalities that pass for goal statements are meant to satisfy a variety of interests and perspectives. (p. 27)

The needs of the practitioner for flexibility and a shield appear to clash with the researcher's need for consistency and task rationality. Intellectual style regarding rigor and explicitness may also result in differential functioning in common tasks. Further, the nature of the relationship between the researcher and the practitioner may create problems, particularly if outside the research context that relationship is one of peers and/or friends. Not only is an element of dominance and control brought into that relationship where it may not have existed in the past, but the practitioner may find himself faced with conflicting directions: those normally coming from his agency and those now coming from the researcher.

There are several ways to counter this tendency toward generalized goal specification. Keep the time perspective short, for example, and demand short-range goals. Such short-range goals help practitioners to focus more clearly on their goal statements. During the main field test, our field staff were specifically instructed to gear intervention goals to an approximately six-week time frame (roughly a four- to eight-week period). In addition to assisting with timely execution of guidelines, this common standard makes for relative uniformity in the scope of goals pursued, thus aiding analytic comparability among different interventions. This use of short range goals finds support from such evaluation research specialists as Daniels (1965):

Only by such statements is it possible to establish intermediate steps and assess progress toward ultimate goals or to evaluate alternative paths. (p. 225)

A second effort at combating this tendency toward generalized goal statements lies in restricting the goal statement to a single, focal goal. We adopted this policy when our pilot experience demonstrated to us that permitting a hierarchy of goals (an overall goal with one or more sub-goals) or permitting multiple goal statements made it extremely difficult to identify the relative importance and interrelationships among goals. Such multiple goal seeking is common in practice, but it is a disaster for R&D.

BIBLIOGRAPHY

ARONSON, SIDNEY H., and CLARENCE C. SHERWOOD, "Researcher Versus Practitioner: Problems in Social Action Research," *Social Work*, October 1967, pp. 89–96.

BOCK, R. D., "Contributions of Multivariate Statistical Methods to Educational Research," in *Handbook of Multivariate Experimental Psychology*, ed. R. B. Cattell. Chicago: Rand McNally, 1966.

CARO, FRANCIS G., *Readings in Evaluation Research*, 2nd ed., New York: Russell Sage Foundation, 1977.

CHOMMIE, P. W., and J. HUDSON, "Evaluation of Outcome and Process," *Social Work*, vol. 19, 1974.

DANIELS, R. S., "Guidelines for Community Mental Health Plans and Programs," *Community Mental Health Journal,* vol. 5, no. 3, 1965.

DuBOIS, P. H., *Multivariate Correlational Analysis.* New York: Harper & Row, 1957.

EPSTEIN, IRWIN, and TONY TRIPODI, *Research Techniques for Program Planning, Monitoring and Evaluation.* New York: Columbia University Press, 1977.

FIENBERG, STEPHEN E., *The Analysis of Cross-Classified Categorical Analysis,* Cambridge, Mass.: MIT Press, 1977.

GIBSON, R., "A System Approach to Research Management," *Research, Development, and Technological Innovation: An Introduction,* ed. James R. Bright, Homewood, Ill.: Richard D. Irwin, Inc., 1964.

GROSS, NEAL, JOSEPH B. GIACQUINTA, and MARILYN BERNSTEIN, *Implementing Organizational Innovations: A Sociological Analysis of Planned Educational Change.* New York: Basic Books, 1971.

GUETZKOW, HAROLD, "Conversion Barriers in Using the Social Sciences," *Administrative Science Quarterly,* vol. 4, 1959.

GUTTENTAG, MARCIA, and ELMER L. STRUENING, eds., *Handbook of Evaluation Research,* vols. 1 and 2. Beverly Hills, Calif.: Sage Publications, 1975.

HARRIS, RICHARD J., *A Primer of Multivariate Statistics.* New York: Academic Press, 1975.

HESSELING, P., "Principles of Evaluation," *Social Compass,* vol. 11, 1964.

HORST, P., *Factor Analysis of Data Matrices.* New York: Holt, Rinehart and Winston, 1965.

ISAAC, STEPHEN, and WILLIAM B. MICHAEL, *Handbook in Research and Evaluation.* San Diego: Robert R. Knapp, Publishers, 1971.

KENDALL, M. G., *A Course in Multivariate Analysis.* London: Charles Griffin and Company, 1957.

KIRESUK, T. J., and R. E. SHERMAN, "Goal Attainment Scaling: A General Method for Evaluating Comprehensive Community Mental Health Programs," *Community Mental Health Journal,* vol. 4, no. 6, 1968.

MACKIE, ROBERT R. and PAUL R. CHRISTENSEN, *Translation and Application of Psychological Research.* Goleta, California: Human Factors Research, Inc., January 1967. Technical Report 716-1.

MACMAHON, B., T. F. PUGH, and G. P. HUTCHINSON, "Principles in the Evaluation of Community Mental Health Programs," *Program Evaluation in the Health Fields,* H. C. Schulberg, A. Sheldon and F. Parker, eds. New York: Behavioral Publications, Inc., 1969.

McCRORY, R. J., "The Design Method—A Scientific Approach to Valid Design," *Technologial Planning at the Corporate Level,* Proceedings of a conference sponsored by the Associates of the Harvard Business

School, September 8–9, 1961, ed. James R. Bright. Cambridge, Mass.: 1961.

NOVICK, DAVID, "What Do We Mean by 'Research and Development'?" *Technological Planning on the Corporate Level,* Proceedings of a conference sponsored by the Associates of the Harvard Business School, September 8–9, 1961, ed. James R. Bright. Cambridge, Mass.: 1961.

RADNOR, MICHAEL, et al., "Agency/Field Relationships in the Educational R/D & I System: A Policy Analysis for the National Institute of Education," *A Policy Analysis for the National Institute of Education,* Evanston, Ill.: Center for the Interdisciplinary Study of Science and Technology, Northwestern University, October 1976.

RIECKEN, H. W., "Memorandum on Program Evaluation," *Evaluating Action Programs: Readings in Social Action and Education,* ed. C. H. Weiss. Boston: Allyn and Bacon, Inc., 1972.

ROSSI, P. H., "Evaluating Social Action Programs," *Readings in Evaluation Research,* ed. F. G. Caro. New York: Russell Sage Foundation, 1971.

ROSSI, P. H., and W. WILLIAMS, eds., *Evaluating Social Programs.* New York: Seminar Press, 1972.

RULON, P. G., D. V. TIEDMAN, C. R. LANGMUIR, and M. M. TATSUOKA, *Multivariate Statistics for Personnel Classification.* New York: John Wiley and Sons, 1967.

SANDERS, JAMES R., and THOMAS P. SACHSE, "Applied Performance Testing in the Classroom," *Journal of Research and Development in Education* 10:3, Spring 1977, pp. 92–103.

STAGNER, ROSS, "Presidential Address to Division 14 (Industrial Psychology) of the American Psychological Association," Newsletter of the Division of Industrial Psychology, vol. 3, no. 4, 1966.

STEELE, SARA M. *Contemporary Approaches to Program Evaluation and Their Implications.* Washington, D.C.: Capitol Publishers, Inc., 1977.

SUCHMAN, EDWARD, *Evaluative Research: Principles and Practice in Public Service and Social Action Programs.* New York: Russell Sage, 1967.

TRIPODI, TONY, PHILLIP FELLIN, and IRWIN EPSTEIN, *Social Program Evaluation: Guidelines for Health, Education and Welfare Administrators.* Itasca, Ill.: F. E. Peacock Publishers, Inc., 1971.

TROW, MARTIN, "Comment on Participant Observation and Interviewing: A Comparison," *Human Organization,* vol. 16, 1957.

TUKEY, J. W., "The Future of Data Analysis," *Annals of Mathematical Statistics,* vol. 23, 1962.

TUKEY, J. W., *Exploratory Data Analysis.* Reading, Mass.: Addison-Wesley Publishing Co., 1977.

WEISS, C. H., *Evaluation Research: Methods of Assessing Program Effectiveness,* Englewood Cliffs, N.J.: Prentice-Hall, Inc., 1972.

Main Field Testing II
Staffing and
Organization

The melding and interweaving of professionals and professional knowledge required by complex (R&D) endeavors challenges the manager to find ways of uprooting the professional yet allowing him to maintain his ties to his field of expertise. . . . [This role] is best described by the analogy of a metronome, a time keeping mechanism which is designed to keep a number of diverse elements responsive to a central "beat" or common rhythm.

Leonard R. Sayles and Margaret K. Chandler,
Managing Large Systems: Organizations for the Future

STAFFING AND CONCOMITANT ORGANIZATIONAL STRAINS

An R&D capability requires a staff group that is typically very diverse and fairly large. Diversity relates to the many different types of tasks involved in various aspects of the R&D process. People from a range of specializations with differing competencies are necessary, from those with the facility of working close to the margin of science to those with ease in communicating with and understanding the operational problems of people engaged in application tasks. In addition, a wide variety of supplementary technical and administrative staff play a role. Since the essential experience in staffing and structuring R&D effort has taken place in the

TABLE 8-1
PERSONNEL PARTICIPATING IN THE HOSPITAL-COMMUNITY STUDY
WITH THEIR PRIMARY INSTITUTIONAL AFFILIATION

hospital		university		nonprofit rehabilitation corporation
Service	Research	Consultants	Research	Service
One psychiatrist One social worker Two nurses Four nursing assistants	One chief social innovative experimenter (principal investigator) One experimental assistant	Legal Accounting Insurance Statistical Computer Medical Janitorial	One chief social innovative experimenter (principal investigator) Two social innovative experimenters Three experimental assistants	Board of Directors

physical sciences and in industry, we will draw heavily from those fields in this discussion.

In industry the types of specialized roles have been described as including design, drafting, model shop, technical testing, and so on. Accomplishment of task demands calls for staffs of considerable number. In his work Fairweather (1967) required a staff of twenty-three in service, research, and consultation functions. These were drawn from a hospital and a university, and included the involvement of the board of directors of a nonprofit rehabilitation corporation. The range of specializations is great, as Table 8–1 indicates. Managerial problems arise in blending these multiple actors within an organization of considerable scale and complexity.

Shepard (1963) discusses staff diversity in terms of "locals" and "cosmopolites," drawing on Merton's original terminology. The locals are company men concerned with the concrete value of activities for the firm for their advancement within it. Cosmopolites identify with a professional reference group and are concerned about contributions to knowledge and externally allocated prestige. R&D efforts require both the maintenance and creative orientations, however discordant, represented in these two types.

According to Villers (1974), specialization is a growing and inevitable trend in R&D:

The increase of specialization reduces more and more the area of activities of each specialist, but the rate of increase of technical progress extends more and more the depth of his accomplishments. (p. 6)

Schutz (undated) feels the specialized role is both necessary and desirable:

The conduct of development in education requires highly competent specialists, not prima donna generalists. Now, and likely forever, personnel qualified as journeymen contributors to development in education are likely to be trained and to identify themselves as discipline specialists rather than as "developers." (p. 37)

A sense of staff composition is conveyed in this report by Klausmeier (1968) of an educational R&D center:

Execution of the Center programs requires proper interdisciplinary staffing. The Center subscribes to the philosophy that the most productive research and the development of effective instructional systems will derive from teams composed primarily of behavioral scientists, subject-matter specialists, and experts in curriculum and other areas closely related to educational practice. The behavioral scientist contributes his research skills and knowledge of the subject field; the experts in curriculum and other fields contribute knowledge about methodology and other relevant instructional variables. (p. 153)

There have been two points of view expressed about project organization in response to the highly diverse environment of R&D. One is to move in the direction of decentralization and unit autonomy. In other words, in order to preserve and enhance the unique character of the various subgroupings involved in the total process, one might set them off and give them a somewhat insular and sheltered setting to work within. David B. Smith (1961), a vice-president of technical affairs for Philco, state this position as follows:

In my opinion, in a decentralized company the best way to obtain this [creative] environment is to have a central research laboratory, separate from the line divisions. . . . It must be protected from the distractions of current problems. Management must have patience and not expect immediate results. (p. 37)

Roberts (1964) decries this tendency in R&D on the basis that it not only interferes with the effective functioning of an R&D program, but it also clouds an understanding of the systemic nature of R&D. Overcompartmentalization takes place, he says, in three ways: The research laboratory and staff become isolated either organizationally or geographically; the research staff, itself, may be subdivided by discipline or by function (proposal preparation group, design group, advanced developers); the engineering staff may be segmented by specialization or product sub-system (combustors and control systems, for example). This "erects solid walls in the paths of managerial vision of the organization as a whole" (p. xvii). Roberts goes on to explicate the problem:

The multidepartment division of R&D creates the appearance of a multitude of "special problems." The personnel department sees the "special problems" of recruiting, training, evaluating, and retraining engineering and scientific manpower. The finance department has the "special problems" of government contracting, progress measurement, and project funds control. The manufacturing department concentrates on "special problems" of the many change orders that must accompany early production. The "special problems" that the marketing department treats relate to the few sources of contracts, the need for major technical-financial proposals, and the all too often boom or bust nature of market participation. All these "special problems" obscure from managers the integrated aspects of the research and development process. This compartmented organization structure has been one of the foremost restrictions on management's comprehension of research and development. (pp. xvi-xvii)

The cross pressures of requiring specialized capabilities and common endeavors are articulated by Schutz (undated) as follows:

A major paradox . . . is that effectiveness in development programs requires a high order of responsible autonomy and the opportunity to innovate and even to change plans. But large scale projects . . . also require unbelievably precise integration and coordination among the parts. . . . Thus, a wide array of intellectual and economic commitments must be simultaneously focused on a very explicit task without destroying the motivations that release energy and commitment. (p. 32)

This paradox must be met by a delicately balanced R&D organization.

CHARACTERISTICS OF R&D STRUCTURES

The paradox has been explored in a research study conducted by Lorsch and Lawrence (1965). They examined two plastics firms (Rhody and Crown) engaged in innovative product development, looking at structural features and sales resulting from new products. One of the companies, Rhody, operated *both* at a higher level of specialization and more effective coordination:

The effective coordinating unit and cross-functional coordinating committees allow members at Rhody to concentrate on their specialties and still achieve a unity of effort. Sales, research, and production specialists are each able to address their separate departmental tasks and work in a climate which is conducive to good performance. At the same time, the men in the coordinating department, who have a balanced orientation toward the concerns of the three departments of specialists, help the three units to achieve a unity of effort. The cross-functional committees also provide means by which the specialist groups and the coordinators can work through their differences and arrive at the best common approach. (pp. 120-121)

At Rhody, products developed in the most recent five year period accounted for 50% of sales. At Crown the figure was about one third of that.

The researchers infer two organizational ingredients of R&D success: first, specialists oriented to particular tasks working in an organizational structure conducive to specialized task performance; and second, effective means of coordination that allow persons with differing knowledge, attitudes, and skills to pool their efforts toward a shared objective. This arrangement, the authors point out, is not meant to eliminate conflict. Rather, it provides a means by which conflicts among different functionaries can be brought to the surface and resolved in an orderly way. Accordingly, energies can continue to be focused on innovative processes:

The challenge ... is to work at developing means of coordination which permit effective specialization *and* effective coordination. This is the combination that is necessary. ... (p. 122)

One might view the coordinating committee or unit as a reconciliating mechanism, the need for which Villers (1974) discusses:

It is now recognized that the effectiveness of R&D operations should be improved, especially by reconciling various points of view. Research scientists and engineers must know that they will receive the full recognition they deserve for their technical accomplishments and it will help them to be successful if their freedom of thinking is stimulated by giving them some opportunity to work on their own. The need for providing the conditions of operation wanted by the research scientist and engineers has to be reconciled with the need of the company for profit-making now and for meeting future competition. (p. xi)

Villers goes on to take a highly practical look at the issue suggesting that integration be accomplished by focusing on the central problem at hand:

Because of the growth of specialization, the scientists and other specialists find it more and more difficult to understand each other and to coordinate their activities at the right time and at the right cost. From a technical point of view, the engineers and scientists can successfully contribute to profit-making only if they can reconcile the need for technical success with the need to contribute effectively to the success of operations conducted by other specialists. For instance, research work must serve the needs of the salesman who has to satisfy the customer with regard to delivery time, price and quality of the product. (p. 17)

Villers further suggests that communication among the specialists can be improved through such efforts as holding meetings and organizing committees for the purposes of exchanging views and information.

Another way of addressing this issue has been suggested by Jack A. Morton, who has served as Bell Lab's head of components research and engineering. According to Morton (1969), the operations of an R&D system must be analyzed in terms of organizational *barriers* and *bonds*. He suggests that the R&D process be thought of as a machine for processing information, a machine made up of a well defined series of steps linked together in a precise order. Should any of these steps be missing, or fail to function properly, then the machine will fail to perform:

> When we think of our machine as a "people system" for processing information, we see that we can do things that will inhibit the flow of information and other things that will encourage it. Just as in an electronic circuit, you use insulators, conductors, semiconductors, to build barriers and bonds to the flow of electrical information.
>
> And sometimes you want to build both . . . For instance . . . if I allow the feedback loop from design or manufacture to basic research to get very strong, the feedback will stop the basic research. And it won't be long before I've lost my research and perhaps my research people. So we purposely put a barrier between manufacture and basic research—either a space barrier, an organizational barrier, maybe both. (p. 84)

The sort of "people system" Morton describes in the management of a research organization, then, must contain certain bonds to facilitate the flow of information and certain barriers to limit it.

SPECIFIC STRUCTURAL ARRANGEMENTS

There is some difference of view within the R&D field concerning what type of structural arrangement will generate the kind of creativity and productivity discussed above. Shepard (1963) indicates that there are two basic structural approaches: functional groups or project groups. Functional groups are organized around specialist criteria. Project groups are more ad hoc collectivities, comprised of diverse specialists working on a given developmental undertaking. Sayles and Chandler (1971) illustrate that what is advantageous for one form is generally disadvantageous for the other (p. 185):

PROJECT GROUPS	FUNCTIONAL (SPECIALIST) GROUPS
Advantages:	*Disadvantages:*
Full-time attention of personnel to the project	Part-time attention to any one project
Single focal point for sponsor and contractor for all project matters	No single focal point for a given multidiscipline job
Project visibility	Poor visibility of a given job

Cradle-to-grave responsibility for a given job	Diffused responsibility for a given job
Flexible level of reporting for project	Department reporting level relatively fixed
Tailor-made to fit the job	Must accommodate full range of interest for each specialist

Disadvantages:	*Advantages:*
Personnel experience limited to project experience	Reservoir of personnel skilled in a given functional area
Little interchange with similar functions outside the project; tendency to "reinvent the wheel"	Automatic interchange of ideas and solutions in a given functional area (prevents "reinventing the wheel")
Massive requirements for facilities for short periods	Amortizes large facilities over extended time
Fluctuating manpower levels and skills mix	Work base spread over many projects; therefore, relatively stable manpower level
Job performance very sensitive to organizational structures, skills, and ability of personnel	Overall performance relatively insensitive to structures—largely dependent on quality of personnel

According to Shepard (1963), neither of the two approaches has been found to be superior to the other:

In most laboratories, some *combination of functional organization and ad hoc team organization* is used. Each appears to have its advantages and disadvantages from the point of view of administration, productivity, creativity, and satisfaction in work. (p. 350)

We will project a model for a Human Services Lab (in Chapter 11) which attempts to incorporate a combined structure, using still another organizational form that has been identified by Sayles and Chandler, "structure based on work-flow stages" (i.e., the different phases of the R&D processes—retrieval, conversion-design, development, diffusion). While the process-based structure is not among the most common arrangement, it seems to offer advantages, particularly in a small-scale lab. Various "specializations" (such as information retrieval or media preparation) can exist as separate "departments." At the same time all of the specialists are related to one another in all projects through the project managers, who would hold a somewhat elevated position on the organizational chart. In a small lab the entire staff can meet together to discuss general progress and situations in specific projects. The manager might put together a particular configuration of staff for a given developmental project who would meet together regularly and intensively around this undertaking. At the same time staff might be working with others across specializations under another manager with regard to another project. A media person, for example, might be working on a handbook, a chart, and a form at the same time for different projects.

It would seem advisable for a team assigned to a given project, who represent skills across the entire R&D process spectrum, to meet together just after the project has cleared a screening committee. Thereafter, the assigned project manager might meet more intensely with the staff related to certain stages. For example, in the early period, much interaction would be necessary between the retrieval and field staff. Later, the intensity might shift to interaction between media and diffusion staff. But even here, the development people would need to be present to confer on whether the product is being presented in the proper written form or in an appropriate mode of training. The project manager thus plays a key role in linking, bonding, and coordinating. This role is analogous to the coordinating unit described by Lorsch and Lawrence (1965), but most of the actual integration comes through coordinating committees orchestrated by him.

R&D MANAGEMENT AND SUPERVISION

The critical role of the project manager has been portrayed in the foregoing. Two additional comments regarding this key actor merit comment here. One has to do with background qualifications; the other, with leadership style.

From our experience we conclude that the manager should be an individual with joint qualifications in a field of social science and in an applied practice field. His responsibilities range across the R&D spectrum, from involvement in retrieving and evaluating scientific literature, to involvement with applied people in operationalizing and assessing practice techniques. He should be able to speak the language and understand the problems of both an academic social scientist and the pragmatic human service professional (direct service worker, manager, planner, policy maker). Ideally, he should be trained in both an academic discipline and a professional service field, and, if possible, he should have experience in both areas. Typical combinations that come to mind are Ph.D./M.S.W., Ph.D./M.P.H., Ph.D./M.Ed., R.N./M.P.H., etc. If persons with formal training in two fields are not available, one might seek individuals with formal training in one of the areas and considerable interest, aptitude, and experience in the other. It may be possible to obtain as strong or stronger managers from the latter groupings. On strictly a probabilistic basis, however, the person with dual qualifications stands a better chance of bringing the necessary competencies to bear in R&D management. The analogy to industrial R&D is there. R&D managers often come with joint backgrounds in areas such as physics and engineering, engineering and business administration, etc.

The leadership style of the manager is as important as his background qualifications. The administrative task is complicated by the heterogeneous composition and cross-pressured climate of R&D. Some of the fundamental norms of those identified with social sciences and research are different from those who are identified with the service delivery professions. Shepard (1963) has analyzed the situation well. If we substitute human service bureaucracies for industry, the analogy will be useful:

Two organizational traditions, the professional and the [bureaucratic], meet in the laboratory . . . Certain conflicts between the two traditions can be pointed out here. [Bureaucracy] respects certain kinds of orderliness in productive organization, and takes them as evidence of efficiency. Thus centralizing services, controlling hours of work, budgeting time, controlling expenditures and decision making by graduated delegation of authority from top to bottom, and many other practices are regarded as elementary principles of good organization.

The scientific and professional organizational traditions are based on assumptions that are different from those of [bureaucracy] in some respects. In the first place, power is supposed to be exercised not from top to bottom, but sideways. Achievement is evaluated by "the weight of scientific opinion." Unless a colleague's competence or honesty becomes suspect, he is expected to make all decisions relating to his work for himself. The idea of a boss is anathema, as are the other external controls imposed by [bureaucratic] methods of organization—in fact, they are held to be inconsistent with the basic tenets of professionalism. (p. 348)

Individuals coming from such divergent backgrounds will expect different types of supervision from those above them in authority. In his studies of R&D supervisors, Pelz (1967) found that personnel performance was highest where the supervisor had a leadership style that gave neither complete autonomy nor excessive direction. Frequent interaction with staff and a participatory climate produced most effective work. Thus, both the extremes of laissez-faire and domination seem inappropriate. Dominating supervision brings forth apathy and resistance; laissez-faire leadership brings about dissatisfaction and low productivity. The preferred leadership may contain aspects of both "security" and "challenge," the climate Pelz found conducive to creativity. Pelz points out that it is the existence of *both* security and challenge at the same time, not a mid-point between them, that is effective. The challenge to R&D leadership is to find a way to keep a heterogeneous group of people fixed on a predetermined common goal, and at the same time to leave room for individual and group imagination and autonomy. Leadership must somehow blend freedom and flexibility with structure and bureaucratic expectation. These same requisites fall on the overall lab director.

SUPERVISION AND ALTERNATIVE DEVELOPMENT RATIONALES[1]

In the CIP experience we found that supervision was a critical but delicate problem. On the one hand, we had to insure that field staff were actually carrying out the application concept or strategy of the guideline. This required supervision that was both directive and firm. On the other hand, we sought the implementation of the guidelines in as naturalistic a fashion as possible. This meant the practitioner had to be free to function in a manner most consistent with his or her professional judgement and experience. This necessitated supervision that was supportive but essentially non-directive. This is not the paradox it may seem. The practitioners were recruited for, and agreed to operate within, a system whose boundaries were well defined. In a sense, we defined the game and established the rules: we specified in clear-cut, general terms the goals of the main field study; we imposed time constraints for the accomplishment of those goals; and we supplied the tools (action guidelines) for the accomplishment of those goals. Within these parameters, the practitioner was allowed considerable freedom for the creative development of strategies for playing the game. Each practitioner in our study was encouraged to engage in the process of guideline operationalization in a manner most appropriate to his or her particular situation. It was necessary for us to monitor them periodically, to make sure that they were not breaking the rules as we initially defined them; i.e., they were expected to stay within the confines of the application concept ("X") in implementation. When we discovered a broken or altered rule, it was necessary for us to institute corrective action, to guide the practitioner back to the specified route (or strategy) to goal achievement.

Unlike the situation in most social research undertakings, we were not interested in letting matters take their natural course in an "uncon-

---

[1]This portion of the chapter relies on the CIP technical report, Jack Rothman, Joseph G. Teresa and John L. Erlich, *Developing Effective Strategies for Social Intervention: A Research and Development Methodology* PB-272 454 TR-1-RD, National Technical Information Service, Springfield, Virginia, 1977.

taminated" way and then observing what occurred. The objective of development is to bring about desired outcomes and products and to study closely variables associated with creating such ends. R&D effort is not concerned, for example, with comparing the characteristics of staff practitioners who are or are not able to bring about successful outcomes, or factors that inhibit successful social intervention. As fascinating as such topics may be for disinterested social scientists, they are not the stuff of development work.

Urban (1976) has undertaken R&D activities in the psychological area. His understanding of what is involved is useful. This work, he states:

> ... does not start out with the question of whether or not one can achieve desirable client effects; it is directed toward maximizing the probability that one will do so. As such it eschews an experimental or quasi-experimental design framework, and the inferential statistics associated with it. It is a design effort oriented toward the development of that configuration of elements which has the highest probability of generating effects which people desire. (p. 8)

This flexible, goal-directed approach to supervision may be linked back to certain existing practices in R&D work. There are two different postures regarding the nature of the development process. One has a strongly predetermined cast, and assumes that one or more optimal solutions are conceived in the conversion and design phase. This perspective, influenced by the systems engineering school of thought, sees development as achieving effective operationalization of a previous calculated means of goal achievement. The use of computer modeling technology assists this approach. The other posture encourages the development engineering staff to fabricate some range of alternative means for going the course while manipulating the basic materials; at a later point, there is an evaluation of the relative merits of these alternative operationalized solutions.

These approaches can best be described by R&D specialists. Low (1961), a member of the Advanced Planning Staff at the MITRE Corporation, outlines the predetermined approach:

> First, specify as clearly as possible the basic ... objectives ... examine the goals ... seriously and imaginatively survey in the above contexts all possible interesting results which might be achieved if various specific engineering problems were solved ... rank the hypothetical capabilities (as studied in the third step above) in order by value, in terms of their potential contribution to achievement of the specified goals ... outline the principal technological steps which would be required in order to reach these capabilities which would have been rated as having high value ... select a small number of high value capabilities which have "reasonably" well specified steps for further examination and possible recommendation for full scale study and research and development. (pp. 110–112)

Kline and Meckling (1958), also speaking from an industrial, physical science standpoint, present a contrasting perspective and way of work:

[The Manager's] strategy reflects a deliberate effort to keep his program flexible in the early stages of development so that he can take advantage of what he has learned. He undertakes the development of a menu of sub-systems and components, but does not undertake these as hardware construction in the final form. . . . Thus, as development proceeds, he progressively narrows the range of alternatives on the basis of information acquired and eventually arrives at the construction of a specific system. (p. 357)

While the above pertains to production of fighter bombers, this aspect of the R&D process has relevance to social R&D as well. In one formulation, the preferred operationalization of an applied principle takes place on the drawing board through a cognitive process, perhaps aided by computer modeling. In the other, it evolves through direct engineering staff experience with basic materials and problems.

The state of knowledge in the social sciences and in the human services is such as to preclude, in many circumstances, firm *a priori* predictions concerning the effects of a particular means of intervention. For this reason, our own choice was to allow practitioners flexibility in determining their own forms of operationalization of the action principle (while constrained to work within the logic of the principle). Through use of systematic evaluation, we would then be in a position to assess *a posteriori* which of several operationalizations or solutions were effective in bringing about the intended outcomes. Schutz (1970), discussing R&D in the field of education, also supports the more flexible, evolving procedure. This suggests that for the social fields, this may be the preferred approach, a reflection of both their level of scientific development and the fluidity and complexity of human behavior. However, some simpler human service tasks, involving fewer variables, and more stable, predictable relationships might be preprogrammed; for example, helping welfare families keep tighter controls on their budgets or aiding young people in preparing for their first employment interview. The question is one that requires further clarification through experience and empirical investigation.

AUXILIARY STAFF SUPPORT

Backup organizational support is necessary to facilitate the work of core R&D personnel. Villers (1974) enumerates the main services and specialized functions that need to be built into an R&D program. These include the following:

Administrative assistance—A variety of administrative services can be helpful—preparing schedules, arranging for equipment and rooms, ordering and distributing supplies, setting up field visits, preparing budget statements, preparing or processing reports, etc. All these activities, if not accounted for, impose on the available professional and technical time of R&D staff. In the model structure (in Chapter 11) a top administrative manager and assistants for each program area are placed in the organizational chart to serve these ends. Clerical and secretarial assistance is also implied.

Technical assistance (and adequate facilities)—Technical assistance in the physical field can include such things as drafting, helping with the building of models, routine testing, etc. In human services R&D such assistants might assist in data processing, interviewing, or conducting group-testing sessions, checking and coding questionnaires and other data gathering instruments, routine charting of progress on tasks, etc. Certain clerical, research assistants, and aides at each program level serve these purposes in the model structure.

Reliability, value analysis, standardization—Here Villers is referring to activities that deal with the effectiveness of research activities. He is concerned largely with services that facilitate performance testing and efficiency of operating from a benefit-cost standpoint. In the model organizational chart a specialist in evaluative research and another in operations research are included to fulfill these functions. The latter will receive further discussion in the next section.

Some other unique auxiliary roles in industry are also indicated by Villers; e.g., legal assistance for patent protection. Human services R&D might entail copyright issues and possibly a range of other problems needing special aid. A clear picture of such roles awaits further experience in various sub-fields of human service work.

OPERATIONS RESEARCH AND MANAGERIAL CONTROL

The kind of resources that are necessary for the R&D effort is only one aspect of the entire R&D process. Another is the allocation and planning of those resources to achieve both efficiency and impact.

We contend that a stable organizational resource base is necessary to counteract the inherently volatile character of R&D. Careful process planning and managerial control is another important ingredient in this connection. This element of rigorous precision in sequencing and timing of activities may be viewed not as in contradiction to the fluid and emergent nature of R&D, but rather as a countervailing force that contributes to the creative tension of the situation.

As we pointed out in Chapter 3, the dynamic character of R&D contributes to an environment that can best be described by the one word: *turbulent.* As Schutz (undated) notes:

Modern development programs have life histories filled with unanticipated crises, unpredicted barriers, and impediments. (p. 31)

While nerves of steel, the patience of Job, and a heart that does not quail over complete reversals of federal program priorities are not absolute essentials for one who would engage in social R&D work, one is at a distinct advantage if he possesses these admirable qualities. The R&D environment is substantially different from traditional basic or laboratory research. As we stated previously, R&D typically takes place within an organizational structure, is normally a group effort, and aims at bringing specific, practical products into being within a limited time period. All this must be done while coping with a variety of interests, differing goals, and not infrequently conflicting personal commitments. Considerable uncertainty and risk surround the tasks, and the specter of failure looms ever present over the effort. It is not surprising, therefore, that in such an environment, egos are bruised, patience at times wears thin, tempers flare, and tears flow.

In the CIP, supervision and monitoring were exhausting for all concerned: for the headquarters staff, for the supervisors, and for the field staff itself. There was a great deal of pressure felt as the result of the firm control necessary to maintain the boundaries of the R&D system. The nature of the research often required field staff members to change their customary way of functioning to include social engineering elements. A great deal of strain and tension was thus involved as the practitioners were prodded to perform consciously in a conversion role and to record their experience systematically. In as seemingly simple a matter as adequately defining how each element of the guideline was to be operationalized, for example, problems arose almost immediately as the practitioners attempted to carry the guideline forward. The review procedure for achieving a level of conceptual accuracy and specificity with all practitioners that had been agreed upon by the headquarters staff clearly required differing amounts of time and intensity of follow-up with different practitioners. This was a result of the variance in the conceptual ability and styles of approaching guideline operationalization among the different practitioners, and occasionally raised the specter of favoritism or neglect and represented an implied threat to the harmony of the field staff.

The volume of materials input into the central office created extra burdens on the project secretary, the research assistants, and the project directors, burdens which had not been fully anticipated. There was considerable going back and forth among field staff, making sure that materials were submitted on time and in the proper form. Use of techniques such as PERT charting helped, but the burdens caused by the sheer quantity of paper that must be handled in a social R&D program of this magnitude must be experienced to be truly appreciated. For example, three different types of logs were received for each of the several practitioners in the five units for each of four different guidelines ultimately implemented. Information had to be checked by different staff for routine content and conceptual matters. Copies had to be made for the headquarters staff for a review procedure of the Initial and Final Summary Logs. Charting procedures had to be carried by the Field Operations Director. Often, one or more telephone calls had to be made to a practitioner or unit coordinator, or both, before a log could be checked through, readied for review, or completed following review. We had to be certain that logs and baseline instruments were complete and accurate. Cleared-through logs of various types had to be duplicated for routing to two different files, for return to the appropriate practitioner, and to the appropriate unit coordinator. All things considered, there were some very hectic days.

Keeping the field staff motivated while nudging them to perform their assigned tasks was a delicate and on-going problem. So too was the handling of "political" or other extremely sensitive information that practitioners brought to the attention of the headquarters staff concerning their agencies and work situations. There were, in addition, a myriad of problems that centered upon the necessity for the field staff to handle what was essentially an unfamiliar conversion task—theoretical concept to practice behavior—and to record this in an accurate and timely fashion.

This introduces the "systems engineering" elements of R&D work. One school of R&D thought propounded by both academics and practitioners approaches the subject from the standpoint of the scientific management of complex technical processes, or "organized creative technology." The position is articulated by Mervin K. Kelly (1950), a pioneering leader of the Bell Labs system:

One of the principal responsibilities of systems engineering is technical planning and control. In the planning an appraisal is made of the various technical paths that can be followed in employing the new knowledge obtained . . . in the development of new designs and facilities . . . It makes exhaustive studies that appraise and program development projects for new systems and facilities. Each study outlines the broad technical plan for a development, its objectives and its economic and service worth . . . As the development organization proceeds with a project, systems engineering maintains close contact, continuously appraises the results, and amends the objectives and plans as required. (pp. 293–294)

As an aid to programmatic control, two important instrumentalities have come forth from the R&D experience. One is the PERT system, used to visualize an entire program over a period of time. The other is the Gantt chart system, based on the concept of functional decentralization. The Gantt chart system allocates tasks of individuals in graphic presentation. PERT (Program Evaluation Review Technique) was first introduced in 1958 with the Navy Polaris program. According to Villers (1974), it can be best described in terms of five key components and steps:

1. Preparation of a model of the fully developed plan of action to achieve a program objective. A network diagram is sketched.
2. Timing for each component of the network is determined. This is based on estimates of the time needed to perform each activity between two events.
3. A critical path to implementation is identified together with a specific completion date.
4. Cost estimates are made by translating each activity in the network into manpower hours with related wage aspects.
5. Follow-up and monitoring are conducted with revisions along the way as long as anticipated projections do not match actual performance.

PERT charting may be used with highly complex projects involving hundreds or even thousands of events in a network. Computer programming is a means of facilitating the procedure. PERT may be used with simpler undertakings and without computer assistance as a way of closely monitoring progress toward project objectives.

The Gantt procedure can be used as a supplement to PERT. The advantage of PERT is that it can give a clear picture of the entire program as a series of events over time. Each activity in the network, however, typically involves more than one individual or department. Gantt provides a way of assigning and monitoring responsibilities of individuals within the flow of a series of events.

PERT has been found to be particularly effective as a systems control device because it focuses attention on goals and the means to their completion within given time boundaries. One of the outgrowths of this approach is the use of milestones; i.e., sub-objectives along the way that provide feedback on pacing toward long-range goals. Milestone have been used and are considered beneficial in both physical and social R&D programs. A National Academy of Sciences manpower lab review panel (1974) strongly recommended regular employment of this device:

Management plans should include clearly defined objectives to be used as reference points in the assessment of laboratory progress. Project milestones should be tied to fiscal decision points and used as benchmarks for measuring progress in the research process. Scheduling, reporting requirements, and budgetary controls should constitute an integral part of the plans. . . . (p. 6)

While it is possible to interpret this type of structuring as a potentially inhibiting and constraining influence on the creative aspects of R&D, people in the field have found it to offer support for productive professional work. Milestones provide feedback with regard to progress on intentions and can be used to redirect and adjust goals constantly. In other words, they can be used flexibly as a compass rather than rigidly as a one-way street. In the tangled world of R&D, confusion and inappropriate criteria can come to dominate, acting as an impediment to creative or satisfying work unless held firmly in check. Milestones permit such control.

From educational R&D comes this observation by Butman and Fletcher (1974):

Where the development team has a clear conception of what they are doing and why, and they are saddled with a narrow view of evaluation, they need protection. Where the development team, including evaluators, have a clear conception of the scientific R&D process and they are working within an organization that does not recognize or reward such behavior or adheres to a different set of priorities, they again need protection. The most effective protection, in either case, is to create and live by a set of decision-making processes that support and enhance the scientific R&D process, rather than inhibit it . . .
The best approach is for the organization to establish policies calling for periodic, i.e., milestone, reviews of the work of the evaluator/developer R&D teams and demand that the team justify what it has done with logic and evidence . . . To be effective, each member of the organization must be convinced that such a process, including the increased time and energy commitment to look at and understand what is going on and why, served the best interest of the product and the organization. (pp. 50–51)

Such procedures are a check on the turbulent setting, but they are certainly not a "cure" for it.

OPERATIONAL MANAGEMENT AND INTELLECTUAL LEADERSHIP

One might be led to ask what the role of the R&D lab director is, given the functional requirements of this type of organizational setting. To the director fall such overarching tasks as general intellectual and professional leadership, top staff development, coordination of the disparate elements of the lab, and setting and maintaining the basic goals and tone of the lab community. The lab director, in addition, has a vital role in determining the composition of the staff and recruiting and selecting appropriate candidates for major positions. To him falls, also, the maintaining of external relationships and the interpreting of lab objectives to the constituent groups, to funding sources, and to professional and scientific groups.

The character of managerial leadership is indicated by Gibson (1964) in the following:

The idea expressed by this heading is brought out very clearly by the following quotation taken from a speech by Lee Du Bridge: "And whenever you find a highly successful group, I suggest you seek the causes for its success not in the organizational chart, not in the budget book, not by counting uniforms or rank, but by finding a man or a small group of men who have created the spirit of the place and who know how to preserve that spirit. . . ." (p. 50)

Gibson describes the qualities of this nucleus group as including competency in science and/or engineering, direct experience in the field, a commitment to high standards of research, imaginative thinking, a capability to inspire skillful and creative action by other staff members, and the inclination and authority to reward such behavior.

While the lab director is concerned about systems control and takes responsibility for helping to arrange the procedures and to select the persons who carry them out, it is a misdirection of his effort to get into the day-by-day minutiae of management details or systems operations. Without the encompassing outlook of the director and his human relations skills in dealing with the politics of a heterogeneous mosaic of an organization, disintegrative tendencies may quickly take over. Sayles and Chandler (1971) highlight the interpersonal skill requisites with regard to project managers:

Unfortunately, most discussions of the functions of project management stress the painstakingly logical activities; making sure that specifications are clear, and that no step is omitted, that only authorized changes are made, that responsibility is clearly allocated and compartmentalized, and that appropriate measures are constructed to monitor every significant aspect of the program (costs, performance, schedules, weight, etc.). In many ways these are computerlike functions . . .
It is easy to be deceived about the functions of the project manager because these computerized controls appear to play such a crucial role. In fact, their operation is largely the responsibility of staff personnel within the project office. The project manager is more likely to want to see raw data, original correspondence, and the actual people who must make and carry out the development decisions. It will be his personal energy, powers of influence and quickness that will be crucial in keeping things moving, avoiding holdups, and resolving seemingly unresolvable problems.
As one observes these managers, they seem to be engaged in a ceaseless round of "political" give-and-take. They appear to be seeking, by weight of a variety of influence techniques, to counter the frictional forces and fatal drift in the human systems. (p. 213)

Thus, while the systems engineering control mechanisms and staff serve to ensure that the disparate elements have order, the director stands apart from system details to make sure it remains holistic and meaningful.

THE SIGNIFICANCE OF SOCIAL ENGINEERING ROLES

In concluding this discussion of development, we want to reinforce the significance we attach to the establishment of social engineering roles. One way to highlight the deficiencies of the vacuum currently existing in this connection is to look back to that time, not long ago, when the same situation prevailed in the physical sciences. MacLaurin (1961) discusses the subject in the following:

The growth of the engineering profession has made a radical difference in the speed with which new scientific discoveries are translated into commercial practice. The principal emphasis during the nineteenth century, both in this country and abroad, was in training a limited group of *scientists* rather than a large number of professional *engineers*. Germany was an exception to this rule and was the first country to pioneer in engineering education. The American engineering school began to expand rapidly after the Civil War; but until the twentieth century, our schools were inadequately financed and considerably less scientific than their German counterparts.
The principal contributors to electrical invention in the United States in the 1870's and 1880's were men like Thomas A. Edison and Alexander Graham Bell, who were largely self-taught. By 1900, however, electrical engineering departments had been established in a considerable number of universities, and streams of young men were beginning to flow into industry—workers who combined some basic training in science with an intense interest in practical applications. This meant that several of the leading electrical concerns were acquiring a sufficient supply of trained engineers to be capable of shortening the time lag between the scientific discovery of wireless and its commercial applications. (p. 72)

The physical and natural sciences went through a process of evolution wherein specific linking roles between the scientific and practical worlds were established and institutionalized. The R&D function was part of this evolution.

Looking forward, now, Urban (1976), one of the few social scientists to engage in a serious analysis of R&D, describes its values and contrasts it with the program evaluation approach currently in vogue:

Complex human service programs cannot be expected to change successfully if we continue to evolve them in haphazard fashion without adequate attention to their initial design. We must acquire the practice of conducting careful feasibility studies before we elect to proceed; we must organize ourselves so as to carry out effective R&D projects before we install services and begin to process clients. We must discontinue our practice of installing a program first, and then mounting an evaluation effort to see whether what has been built proves to have any merit. Finally, efficient development of innovative programs is more likely to occur when resources are marshalled and directed toward change within a well-organized and concerted effort.
... Thus, continued pursuit of contemporary procedures of program evaluation will not only prove to be excessively costly in the long-run, but are also unlikely to produce operational services and systems with the efficiency and economy which are sought. A shift of the field of human services program development should be made toward R&D strategy instead. (p. 11)

Such a strategy is keyed to the creation of products that are useful, effective, and user-ready. In industry the packaging of such products commonly receives enormous amounts of time, attention, and money. In the social fields only scant consideration has been given to the problems and possibilities of packaging. Approaches to product packaging in social R&D will be the focus of concern in the next chapter.

BIBLIOGRAPHY

BUTMAN, JEAN W., and JERRY L. FLETCHER, "The Role of Evaluator and Developer in Educational Research and Development," *Evaluating Educational Programs and Products*, ed. Gary D. Borich. Englewood Cliffs, N.J.: Educational Technology Products, 1974.

FAIRWEATHER, GEORGE W., *Methods for Experimental Social Innovation.* New York: John Wiley & Sons, 1967.

GIBSON, R. E., "A Systems Approach to Research Management," *Research, Development, and Technological Innovation: An Introduction*, ed. James R. Bright, pp. 34–57. Homewood, Ill.: Richard D. Irwin, Inc., 1964.

KELLY, MERVIN J., "The Bell Telephone Laboratories—An Example of an Institute of Creative Technology," *Proceedings of the Royal Society*, Series A, Mathematical and Physical Sciences, 203, no. 1074 (October 10, 1950), 287–301.

KLAUSMEIER, HERBERT J., "The Wisconsin Research and Development Center for Cognitive Learning," *Research and Development Toward the Improvement of Education*, Herbert J. Klausmeier and George T. O'Hearn eds. pp. 146–156. Madison, Wisc.: Dembar Educational Research Services, Inc., 1968.

KLINE, B., and W. MECKLING, "Application of Operations Research to Development Decisions," *Operations Research*, 6, 1958, 352–363.

LORSCH, JAY W., and PAUL R. LAWRENCE, "Organizing for Product Innovation,"*Harvard Business Review*, 43, no. 1 (January–February 1965), 109–122.

LOW, WARD C., "Identifying and Evaluating the Barrier Problems in Technology," *Technological Planning on the Corporate Level*, Proceedings of a conference sponsored by the Associates of the Harvard Business School, September 8–9, 1961, ed. James R. Bright. Cambridge, Mass.: 1961, pp. 104–113.

MACLAURIN, W. RUPERT, "The Process of Technological Innovation: The Launching of a New Scientific Industry," *Technological Planning on the Corporate Level*, Proceedings of a conference sponsored by the Associates of the Harvard Business School, September 8–9, 1961, ed. James R. Bright. Cambridge, Mass.: 1961, pp. 69–72.

MORTON, JACK A., "From Research to Technology," *The R&D Game: Technical Management and Research Productivity*, ed. David Allison, pp. 213–235. Cambridge, Mass.: The MIT Press, 1969.

NATIONAL ACADEMY OF SCIENCES, National Research Council, "The Experimental Manpower Laboratory as an R&D Capability," Washington, D.C., February 1974.

PELZ, DONALD, "Creative Tensions in the Research and Development Climate," *Science*, 157, no. 3785 (July 14, 1967), 160–165.

ROBERTS, EDWARD B., *The Dynamics of Research and Development.* New York: Harper & Row Publishers, 1964.

ROTHMAN, JACK, JOSEPH G. TERESA and JOHN ERLICH, "Developing Effective Strategies for Social Intervention: A Research and Development Methodology," PB-272 454/TR-1-RD, National Technical Information Service, Springfield, Virginia, 1977.

SAYLES, LEONARD R., and MARGARET K. CHANDLER, *Managing Large Systems.* New York: Harper & Row Publishers, 1971.

SCHUTZ, RICHARD E., "The Conduct of Development in Education," Unpublished internal report of Southwest Regional Laboratory for Educational Research and Development, (undated).

SCHUTZ, RICHARD E., "The Nature of Educational Development," *Journal of Research and Development in Education,* Report, University of Georgia, (Winter 1970), pp. 39–64.

SHEPARD, HERBERT A., "Nine Dilemmas in Industrial Research," *The Sociology of Science,* Bernard Barber and Walter Hirsch, eds. pp. 344–355, New York: The Free Press of Glencoe, 1963.

SMITH, DAVID B., "Critical Decision Points in Technological Innovation," Proceedings of a conference sponsored by the Associates of the Harvard Business School, September 8–9, 1961, ed. James R. Bright. Cambridge, Mass.: 1961, pp. 72–99.

URBAN, HUGH B., "The R&D Strategy as an Alternative to Program Evaluation Methodology," Draft of paper prepared for Symposium: *Correctional Treatment Evaluation: Present Dilemmas and Future Directions,* American Psychological Association Meeting, Washington, D.C., September, 1976.

VILLERS, RAYMOND, *Research and Development: Planning and Control.* New York: Financial Executives Research Foundation, 1974.

The Product
of
Development

We are the boys who are always forgotten
When praises are passed for the stuff that you use,
R&D men, engineers who design,
Who develop and modify, mold and refine
Every thingus and product the mind can conceive
(We make real all the things that were
    once make believe);
Yet when prizes are handed out (money and such)
It's the R&D boys who have never got much,
Though you readily use all the junk we produce.
We find your disdain simply rotten.

Donald E. Barnhorst
NASA Parodies & Paradoxes

In industry, development is likely to materialize in products of a rather hard nature—machines, equipment, appliances, and the like. In the social sciences the product is more likely to be in such software forms as procedures, techniques, operational guides, etc., that work and have been encapsulated in some written or audio-visual form. Typically, these would include handbooks, videotapes, training or procedural kits, and so forth. Radnor (1976) and his associates at the Center for the Interdisciplinary

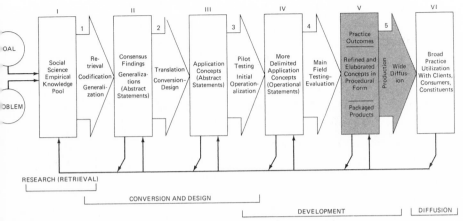

Study of Science and Technology, explicitly acknowledge the existence and validity of such varied development creations:

The term "products" is meant here to convey the *full* array of Development outputs—programs, processes, models, strategies, approaches, etc., as well as the narrower range of outputs we usually think of as "products." [emphasis in original] (p. 72)

Havelock (1968) specifically supports the need to develop handbooks and operational manuals addressed to the change process and to change agents in the field. When the results of development field testing have been brought together, both qualitative data and quantitative specifications, they need to be consolidated—"packaged"—in a form that is clear, communicable, and easy to replicate by potential users. This package needs to take into account certain psychological and intellectual characteristics of the user, and to treat a broad range of problems related to implementing what may be rather complex practice procedures. Whether we call such a package a handbook, a manual, a guidebook, or whatever, the package will need to have a practical, "how-to" character.

In this presentation we will offer a set of communication principles geared to bridging the gap between theory and application, between the researcher and the practitioner—that gap that we discussed in the second chapter. These principles constitute rules for constructing the development package. The package should attempt to effect the necessary bridge by showing specifically how application concepts were made operational by staff practitioners functioning in typical user settings during development. We will illustrate these communication principles and the forms they may take through excerpts from a handbook that deals with promoting an innovative service or program. (Rothman, Teresa and Erlich, 1978). The

171

handbook included both qualitative and quantitative data from the development phase. Much of the discussion that follows immediately embraces qualitative data. The development of specifications from quantitative data has already been demonstrated.

Let us begin with a simple listing of the broad principles of communication—principles that were conceived to convey the results of development work and foster product use.[1] Some of these principles act in concert with others. Some are operative in their own right. All are expeditors of the implementation process as incorporated within the package.

Principle 1: Provide the research basis for the application concept.

Principle 2: Convert the research generalization into its specific applied form.

Principle 3: Provide narrative examples showing the implementation of the application concept with regard to a problem situation or a practice context familiar to the practitioner-users.

Principle 4: The examples should be as close as possible to the user's real world perspective, using practice language, or, if possible, the actual words of similar practitioners.

Principle 5: The underlying dynamic of the application concept should be clearly and simply delineated. This may be aided through visual explication.

Principle 6: State the relevancy of the application concept to the general practice outlook of the user: his objectives, tasks, problems, needs.

Principle 7: Provide definitions, qualifications, and elaborations as appropriate to clarify or amplify use of the application concept.

Principle 8: Provide concrete practice examples of all elements of the concept having empirical referents.

Principle 9: Show various possible patterns of implementation of a given application concept. These patterns represent different general modes of action within a common intervention strategy.

Principle 10: Present statistical findings in a clear, simple application-relevant fashion.

Principle 11: As an aid to the practitioner-user, possible problems ("pitfalls") in implementing the concept should be presented.

Principle 12: Useful avenues of attack ("tips") should be offered.

Principle 13: In order to promote and facilitate use of application concepts and a package of operational guides, it is necessary to convey a reasonable amount of encouragement, reinforcement, and optimism in order to give the practitioner a push-off toward utilization. If possible, such encouragement should include legitimation from peer colleagues.

---

[1]These communication principles and the material illustrating them appeared originally in somewhat different form in Jack Rothman, *Organizing and Planning for Social Change: Action Principles from Social Science Research,* New York: Columbia University Press, 1974, chapter 11. Adopted with permission.

Principle 14: Provide guidance on how to take the initial steps toward active implementation of the application concept in a practice situation.

Principle 15: Structure an opportunity to take initial steps toward implementation.

Principle 16: Present information in brief, direct, attractive, and easily readable form.

These principles of communication emerged from the author's practical experience in preparing packages for practitioners. At the same time they are supported by both theoretical and empirical literature in the field. Let us now examine the rationale underlying these communication principles and illustrate how they may be materialized in composing the CIP handbook. Literature support will be indicated wherever appropriate.

1. Provide the research basis for the application concept.

2. Convert the research generalization into its specific applied form.

It has been our experience that practitioners are, on the whole, concerned with and interested in the basis for a research generalization that underlies a proposed practice technique. There is enlightened self-interest operating here, for they want reasonable assurance that the generalization has valid scientific support. Most, however, do not wish to be encumbered with a great deal of verbiage concerning the research itself. This is particularly true where such a presentation involves highly technical language or a number of statistical tables. Studies conducted in the specific circumstances of the practitioner's situation—setting or problem area or clientele—are reassuring and tend to reduce doubt over transferability of findings from one context to another.

Weiss (1977) found in her investigation that research used by human service administrators was subjected by them to a "truth test"—was the research trustworthy, can it be relied on, was it produced through appropriate scientific procedures? Paisley (1968) indicates that the technical quality of the information source is of importance to engineering professionals in determining whether they will employ new findings. It is pointed out by Smith et al. (1969), however, that the details of research do not need to be presented *per se*. Applicability to a specific local area, according to Klein (1968) is highly conducive to research utilization. Van de Vall et al, (1976) found data primarily from the application setting to be facilitative.

In addition to a truth test, according to Weiss, administrators employ a second major criterion—a "utility test." Does the research provide a direction for change? Does it show how to go about making feasible changes? Based on observing utilization of social welfare research, Klein (1968) indicates the process is facilitated when implications are stated in clear cause and effect statements. Also basing his observations on the social welfare context, Benjamin (1972) states that the research worker "has got to be prepared to fill out the picture behind the figures, including all the deficiencies and reservations. He has got to be able to indicate where the figures appear to lead in terms of policy implications, and he has got to be able to do this in a simple and direct manner" (pp. 19–20).

For example, in our handbook the following generalization introduced the concept of "partialization":

Innovations that can be tried on a partial basis are more likely to succeed than innovations that require total adoption without a preliminary trial.

Then, in addition to providing generous but unobtrusive bibliographic support, there was an illustration of the concept that shows how "new math" joined the curriculum of schools in Allegheny County, Pennsylvania:

A group of five superintendents who had close association with one another introduced the new approach in 1959. As a result of their example, and their contacts with other superintendents, another ten schools adopted the new math in 1960. Still another twelve schools were added in 1961; and by the end of 1963, thirty-eight schools were employing this altogether different method of teaching mathematics. This snowball effect can be found in the spreading of many innovations.

Related to the concept of partialization, and vital to it, is the concept of "proximate" goals—moderate, tangible objectives attainable in a short time. In the new math example, the initial five schools represented a partial target group of schools and the additional ten schools adopting the following year presented a proximate target. After defining this concept the next step was to proceed with the conversion of the research generalization into its specific, applied form—the application concept, also referred to as an action guideline.

To promote an innovation in a general target system, first develop the innovation in a limited portion of the target system.

Clearly, the practitioner seeks—and needs—a clear, direct conversion with specific implementation implications such as that given above. Lacking it, it often happens that practitioners are left with a vague or confused sense concerning the practice or policy implications of research findings. Those with more sophisticated backgrounds may tend to dwell on limitations or qualifications in a finding. They may also tend to consider to a greater degree the relevance of that finding for future research rather than its use for present application. For this reason a straightforward statement concerning practice or policy directions is vital if research products are to stand a good chance of being put to work in the real world of human service agencies.

To be sure, there are practitioners—perhaps many—capable of working directly with the generalization, drawing an appropriate action concept

for themselves. To require that they do so, however, may place an unnecessary burden upon them; and, for those who would experience difficulty in such matters, it would do little to ease the tensions of the
research-practice conflict.

3. Provide narrative examples showing the implementation of the application
   concept with regard to a problem situation or practice context familiar to
   the practitioner.
4. The example should be as close as possible to the practitioner's perspective,
   using practice language or, if possible, the actual words of similar practitioners.

Practitioners, quite understandably, tend to think more in terms of
problems and skills than theories. They develop an inductive, cognitive
style, often evolving general principles from specific common sense and
clinical reasoning based on exposure to direct experience. It is, therefore,
reasonable to expect that they will respond most readily to such direct
experience.

In reviewing their experience in a vocational rehabilitation Research
Utilization Laboratory, Soloff et al. (1976) state that practitioners were
deeply concerned with whether a research-derived prescription "will
work," and that their tendency to use it was increased by "awareness of
other people's positive experience" with it. The beneficial effects of quantitative data and presentations is pointed up in a study of research utilization in industrial settings (Van de Vall et. al., 1976). Managers were found
to be more likely to apply research in their work if a qualitative rather than
a tabular form of presentation was made and if the methodological mix of
research methods favored the qualitative ones. Using the experience and
language of other practitioners is a way to deal with a factor discerned to
be important by Davis and Salasin (1975), namely the need for the re-
searcher-communicator to indicate his identification with the practitioner-
user.

Consider the following material from the handbook. The narrative
episode it contains illustrates principles 3 and 4, and could usefully be
among the first items of textual material presented:

The report below was written by a community practitioner based in a family
service agency in a conservative, middle-sized community in Michigan. The practitioner was new to the agency, that had over the years conducted a traditional
casework program, geared to serving essentially middle-class clients who went to
the agency offices for assistance. This worker, the first staff member with a community orientation to be hired by the organization, viewed the job as an opportunity
to introduce innovative programs with a community focus and to service neglected
client populations. She employed this (Innovation) Guideline as one way of formulating a strategy geared to promoting an innovative program:
   The Innovation Guideline works very well! In fact, I would recommend it
   highly to any worker wanting to get a new program or new practice accepted.

I tried it with two different kinds of "innovations" in very different situations, and it worked well in both. The first was a program designed for mentally retarded adults to prove that such a program could be done with volunteer help, and that response from volunteers would be forthcoming. Two small groups of adults were selected initially by using some Department of Social Services community care homes and their residents. To promote acceptance I wrote up the project carefully and presented it to the Executive and the Board, the Department of Social Services staff, and the Association for Retarded Children staff. We recruited and trained volunteers; we selected the initial group with some care; and we tried to monitor everything constantly.

Through demonstration with a small portion of the target population, we could then open up the program to the larger population—which we did. If we had not limited the group initially, we would have had disaster, because we did not have the volunteers, the space, the equipment, or the know-how to handle a large group. In addition, we did not have the acceptance of the agency board that this was a viable way to proceed in this program. This particular test of the guideline was a rather large scale programmatic effort requiring a considerable amount of time to test it; but it was a basic need in program development for the agency . . .

This example of the innovation application concept in action leads us directly to the next communication principle:

5. The underlying dynamic of the application concept should be clearly and simply delineated. This may be aided through visual explication.

We have already indicated literature support for giving direct action implications. Davis and Salasin (1975) suggest as a means of achieving this the use of "pictorial and other illustrative material" (p. 641).

For example, consider the following diagram:

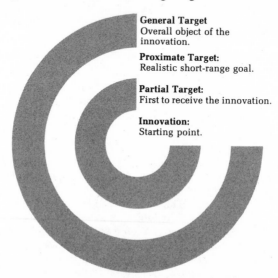

General Target
Overall object of the innovation.

Proximate Target:
Realistic short-range goal.

Partial Target:
First to receive the innovation.

Innovation:
Starting point.

Figure 9–1   Steps in the Partialization Strategy of the Innovation Guideline

Such a visual presentation provides instant awareness of the serial nature of the total implementation process involving the innovation guideline.

6. State the relevancy of the application concept to the general practice outlook of the practitioner: his objectives, tasks, problems, needs.

An action guideline must be related to the practitioner's perspective, and its value to him in doing his job must be demonstrated. To accomplish this, it was our experience, it is necessary to show the significance of the guideline and to illustrate how it fits into the spectrum of concerns of the typical practitioner.

In studying professional use of vocational technical information, Magisos (1971) found practice application to be associated with "relevance to perceived problems." As noted earlier, Klein (1968) indicates relevance to the local situation in which the practitioner is operating to be of importance.

An example of this principle is:

Innovation and Community Practice The human service professions generally, and the area of community organization in particular, have sometimes been characterized as *change-oriented* fields. For this reason the process of diffusion and adoption of innovations is of special importance. Practitioners are constantly involved in promoting new programs, new techniques, new tactics, and new ideas, which they wish to propagate in working with target and client systems of various kinds.

7. Provide definitions, qualifications and elaborations as appropriate to clarify or amplify use of the application concept.

Applied statements should be written in nontechnical language. That does not mean that it may not be necessary to define terms or to clarify concepts. Even before operationalization, obvious limitations and qualifications implicit in the guideline should be indicated. Where appropriate, special theoretical or conceptual notions associated with the guideline may be offered. These notions seem self-evident. We found the following definition of, and elaboration on, the term *innovation* both useful and necessary:

Innovation: generally speaking, an innovation may be viewed as any program, technique, or activity perceived as new by a population group organization—in our terms, a target system. An innovation as most often operationalized in research literature refers to technical-professional and commercial novel ideas and practices such as the use of contraceptive devices for population planning, new medical products, and farming techniques. These are typically legitimate, conventional, and within the normative consensus of a community and its elites. In general, the promotion of broad and radical political change is not encompassed by the diffusion literature, though it seems likely that some applications can be made in this area.

Not all definitions need be this elaborate, of course, but the necessity for getting all users of the package to understand the basic conceptual language involved in an interventive action should be self-evident.

8. Provide concrete practice examples of all elements of the concept having empirical referents.

As we have already indicated, an application concept can be divided into a number of analytical elements. It is useful to give specific examples of how these various elements are concretized in several different practice situations in the field test. Consider, once again, the example of guideline implementation offered above—that of the practitioner who attempted to introduce a volunteer program for the adult mentally retarded:

In the example given, a means of operationalizing this guideline was depicted: a program was provided to a small segment of the mental retardate population within a city. It might be noted that this example also involved certain transfer mechanisms for facilitating diffusion from the smaller to the larger population. The board of directors of the Family Service Agency, a key decision-making unit with authority to act, voted to extend outreach services to the mental retarded after having witnessed the small demonstration project.

It may be useful to illustrate some instances of field test implementation in order both to show a range of types of innovation to which this guideline has been applied by practitioners and to demonstrate how other practitioners have concretized the concepts of a general and partial target system. The Table 9-1 summarizes these and also indicates mechanisms by which the transfer from the smaller to the larger target system was affected.

9. Show various possible patterns of implementation of a given application concept. These patterns represent different general modes of action within a common intervention strategy.

There are problems in moving from a theoretical formulation to a complex practice arena. Practitioners may find difficulty in pinning down pertinent points of application. They may discover one possible mode of action and settle on it without considering other alternatives. It is useful, therefore, to provide a range of alternative implementation patterns from the field test that the practitioner may consider for use. Van den Ban (1963) alludes to the existence of "practitioner ruts"—the tendency to find a particular solution to a practice task or problem and to use it in a repetitive fashion. Lack of time to experiment and reflect, she says, accounts for this in part. By offering alternative routes for applying an application concept along the lines suggested, the practitioner may be opened up to a greater range of action possibilities.

TABLE 9–1
OUTLINE OF FOUR ACTUAL INNOVATION PROMOTIONS

setting:	innovation:	general target:	proximate (short-run) target:	partial target:	transfer mechanism:
A community mental health center in a semi-rural county.	Stimulate local unions to accept the function of community care giver for their members.	All 200 local unions in the county.	Fifty unions from around the county.	A limited number of union members and leaders participated in a workshop on community care giving — including ten unions.	The county-wide (all-inclusive) AFL-CIO Labor Education Committee voted sponsorship of a follow-up workshop to be offered to all county locals.
Traditional settlement house serving a largely black population.	Introducing an intensive educational focus into a program that had been essentially recreational.	Entire school-age membership of the settlement house.	The same as general target.	A group of 20 teen members were involved in two educational counseling sessions.	Board of directors voted an allocation for hiring an educational director to serve the membership.
A regional planning council serving several counties.	Have the planning council gain responsibility for advising HUD on housing applications from all regional municipalities.	All 30 municipalities in the region.	12 municipalities with whom practitioners have had positive previous contact.	With HUD approval, reviewed and assessed trial applications from four municipalities.	HUD approved review procedure for all municipality applications.
A social welfare employees union in a metropolitan community.	Decentralize program implementation through building level unit committees.	All 25 building level units in the union: the total membership.	Six units in a contiguous area.	Shop stewards at a single building location were involved successfully in union program implementation functions.	The union executive board instituted a policy of building level program implementation.

Patterns of Implementation

Two basic patterns have been observed in the actual application of the [Innovation] Guideline. The first pattern, a "Direct Flow" model, works as follows:

PRACTITIONER→PARTIAL TARGET→PROXIMATE TARGET

Here the action flows from the practitioner to the partial target system to the proximate target system. This pattern is typical of agricultural extension approaches in which the farmer is motivated by the worker to use a new seed. He is successful, his neighbors see the results, and they plant the same seed. In the direct flow model, the proximate target population accepts the innovation directly. The second pattern is the "Decision-Making Unit" model:

PRACTITIONER→PARTIAL TARGET→
DECISION-MAKING UNIT→PROXIMATE TARGET

In this pattern, the action moves from the practitioner to the partial target system to a relevant decision-making unit (e.g., a board of directors or policy committee), and only then to the proximate target system. This process typically is used in organizational situations. In the decision-making unit arrangement, a transfer mechanism authorized the passage from the smaller to a larger group.
There are many variations on this model. Sometimes the practitioner needs initial approval from a supervisor. In some cases there are two decision-making units involved. Some practitioners arrange to have the decision-makers experience the demonstration directly, as in holding a conference for board members at which a new technique is employed.

To further assist the practitioner, each of the implementation patterns may be amply illustrated with practical examples from the field. For example, one member of the field staff was president of a social workers' union. He desired to set up a training program for his executive board, to teach them a new method in which case examples and the sharing of personal experiences would be used to deal with grievances more effectively. He obtained approval from the board to begin the process, and described the experience as follows:

I then selected four board members to participate in the committee. They each agreed to present a case example for the meeting.
I chaired the committee meeting, suggested the rationale for the model to be used, and assumed responsibility for following up on specific tasks. The committee decided to conduct the training session before the board, following the format of the committee meeting. Individual contacts were made to publicize the event. The model was used at the training session, and the response was very favorable. The board had directly seen and experienced what I was trying to get across.
The proximate target system, the executive board, participated in the training session with positive evaluative comments: "We were able to share problems in a new way"; "It was helpful to know that other people had some of the same problems."
The key suggestion at the training session was that the next target system could be the general membership, with the same model being applied.

This is a rather clear example of one common pattern of implementation.

10. Present statistical findings in a clear, simple, and ideally, application-relevant way.

There is little practical relevance to a practitioner's needs to explain to him that X% of a sample responded in a certain way or that something is true at the Y level of confidence, information that is the bread and butter of researchers. Quantitative research findings are more useful to the practitioner when presented in an application-relevant way.

Soloff and his associates (1975) found that it was useful to soften the technical character of their products. "Written material should play down the research aspect of the total presentation" (p. 419). The chances of impact are increased, according to Glaser et al. (1967), if the findings are presented in brief and nontechnical form. And Smith et al. (1969) point to the value of selecting and interpreting the research with an application focus and mainly within the context of clarification and illustration.

For example, trend findings concerning the salience of the practitioner's personal resources in guideline implementation were presented prescriptively as follows:

1. develop and rely upon good relationships within the agency;
2. select a program to which you are committed and which is logically related to your position in the agency;
3. take advantage of your prior experience—select a program and setting in which your experience will be an asset. If the program is consistent with your other assignment, this can serve to legitimize the activity and allow a concentration of energy.

The "feel" and practice relevance of a quantitative research finding may also be effectively presented through related qualitative data by using direct quotations from the practitioners themselves. For example, in discussing practitioner responses concerning the need to manage time and energy effectively, the following direct quotes were used to make the point:

I had little time to implement the guideline.
One problem was having to be patient before things started happening. Constant assessment had to take place, along with an incredible amount of public relations. The guideline is valid, but one should remember to think clearly and to limit the goal sufficiently.
I would not advise another person to work on as many communities as I have attempted. Responsibilities should be delegated to other leaders and organizations.

As a further assist, a series of checklists can be provided, guiding the practitioner to those personal, agency, client, and community factors that, based on the field study, have a high probability of helping or hindering the attempted implementation.

These points can be made without the necessity of having to resort to the sometimes mystical numerology of statistics. Such a direct approach is not always appropriate, but where it is, it should be used. Whenever possible the R&D staff should absorb and work through burdens of interpretation and uncertainty rather than passing them along automatically to the practitioner. This may not always be possible but it should constitute a standard task to be worked at.

11. As an aid to the practitioner, possible problems ("pitfalls") in implementing the concept should be presented.

12. Useful avenues of attack ("tips") should be offered.

Overselling the virtues of an action principle may leave the practitioner unprepared for the difficulties he may face, or the frustration he may feel, when things don't work out as well as he had anticipated. By presenting some of the possible problems that have been encountered by others in the field study, he may be more prepared to cope with them. Also, when successful techniques, based on the field test experience, are available, these should be shared to ease the way. Whenever possible, it is desirable that these "nitty-gritty" practice matters be presented in the actual words of the field staff who had the specific prior experience.

According to the literature, the presentation of "pitfalls" may accomplish two things (Van den Ban, 1963). One is to alert practitioners to the possible consequences of taking recommended actions. A moral obligation may be involved here. The second is to win the confidence of practitioners. Acknowledging deficiencies and difficulties avoids an oversell posture which can evoke suspicion. A tactical consideration may be implicated in this instance. Offering "tips" also contributes to the "utility test" identified by Weiss as important.

To illustrate:

Problems and Prospects in Implementation

Pitfalls. Practitioners, although they have had most favorable experiences with this guideline, also allude to certain problems in using it. Here are some of their comments:

a. "Hard to conceptualize what 'promote acceptance of an innovation' actually means; what is acceptance, how is it measured, how many have to accept?"

b. "Identification of what is meant by a 'partial target' was problematic."

Tips. . . . Selection of an appropriate, facilitative partial target system is crucial in carrying out the approach. This selection must be done strategically, so that the probability of success on a limited scale is enhanced. The practitioner who attempted to foster a building-level-program-implementation arrangement, discusses the factors he took into account in selecting an initial target as follows:

The basic consideration for the successful application of this guideline, at least in my case, was the selection of the partial target subpopulation. I was able to employ the following factors: geographic location (proximity of buildings to one another); history of organizational activity leading to cohesiveness (time period over which folks had been relating to each other organizationally); leadership availability (both actual and potential) within the partial target population; existence of a reasonable level of skill and experience within the target population.

13. In order to promote and facilitate use of application concepts and a package of operational guides, it is necessary to convey a reasonable amount of encouragement, reinforcement, and optimism in order to give the user a pushoff toward utilization. If possible, such encouragement should include legitimation from colleagues.

We assume that to facilitate use of research-based, fairly abstract written material, it is necessary to offer special encouragement or impetus to proceed, in part based on the experience and advice of fellow professionals who had participated in the field test.

Van den Ban (1963) states that practitioners will only use research findings to solve problems if they believe the findings will be of direct help to them and if they have confidence in the researcher. In addition, such use may entail additional work as one goes about having to learn a new way to do things. For this reason, she indicates, the researcher must take the role of "persuader," convincing the practitioners to try new concepts and approaches. Conveying positive experiences of other practitioners was found by Soloff et al. (1975) to be an important way of providing such persuasion and encouragement.

For example,

It might be said that among pilot-year practitioners there was a general consensus that this guideline would be useful to others. Several practitioners felt it would be useful in terms of long- and medium-range planning, at least to point out operational problems on a small scale before the innovation was attempted on a large scale. Specific comments . . . include the following:
a. "Helpful when a situation is unclear or when a relationship is being built."
b. "Provides a simple and fairly uniform, concrete way of introducing new ideas."
c. "Helpful in a number of ways: attempting to change the attitudes of the board, clearer identification of method of meeting client needs."

14. Provide guidance on how to take the initial steps toward active implementation of the application concept in a practice situation.

15. Structure an opportunity to take initial steps toward implementation.

Encouragement and persuasion can be aided by moving practitioners toward a first step in implementation. Toward these ends, it is advisable to include a section in the package on "getting started." It should give some basic steps to consider during planning stages. This may be followed by an initial log or planning form in which the practitioner is asked to set down in writing his preliminary notions concerning operationalizing the elements of the guideline: initial comments in an interview, the physical setting, the main individuals and groups to contact in a community intervention, reasons for contact, and what might be some of the major facilitating or limiting conditions that would impinge upon the use of the guideline.

A "getting started" section may be formulated along the following lines:

1. Think of some new program, technique or other activity that you have been planning to carry out.
2. Attempt to set this down as a goal, but of moderate scope and dimension.
3. Conceptualize the general or "total" target system at which this innovation is directed: who are the people who would be benefiting from, utilizing, or participating in this innovation?
4. Think through a smaller segment of that target system, a more delimited subgroup who:
   a. might easily be drawn into a trial or demonstration;
   b. might very likely succeed in an initial trial;
   c. by succeeding would likely, through its linkages, have an impact on the larger target system, or on a relevant decision-making unit.
5. When you have worked the issue through in your mind to this point, begin to fill out the initial log.

An initial planning form need be neither complicated nor forbidding looking. Working with it should present very little difficulty. An example from the handbook is given in Figure 9–2.

16. Present information in brief, direct, attractive, and easily readable form.

Most practitioners operate under multiple demands and pressures from clients, administrators, other professionals, etc. A flood of printed materials, both administrative and professional, is likely to pass before them in any given time period. To compete for the attention of the typical practitioner, materials need to be to the point, compelling, attention getting, and hopefully, agreeable.

A large number of researchers and observers have commented on the need to present research implications in a way which is accommodating to the mindset and situation of practitioners. Brevity, accessibility, and the packaging of relatively small units of information are called for by Magisos (1971) and Paisley (1968). Soloff et al. (1975) speak to the utility of "highly readable prose" presented in a form which is "visually attractive and clearly written." In concurrence, Davis and Salasin (1975) declare for "ease of presentation" which is facilitated by "readability, coherence and understanding" from the standpoint of the intended audience. Van den Ban (1963) devotes considerable space to a discussion of writing style, diagrams and tables and other visual aids.

INITIAL LOG

1. Date of preparation: _____

2. What is your goal (i.e., the innovation) in using the guideline? Be as specific as possible. Keep a short-term time perspective (five to twelve weeks).

3. Describe the circumstances (conditions, assignments, events, requests, etc.) which led you to use this guideline to achieve the above goal.

4. Look back at the Action Guideline. How would you begin to define *each* element of the guideline in your immediate situation? (How might you operationalize these components?) Keep in mind the innovation goal stated in #2.

   a) What is the general target system?

      The proximate target?

   b) What is the specific partial target system?

   c) What decision-making unit, if any, is involved? How will its members be encouraged to accept the innovation?

   d) How will you foster diffusion (forms of linkage, communication, promotion, etc.) from the partial to the general target?

5. List the *major* steps you anticipate taking in employing this guideline.
   _____
   _____
   _____

Figure 9–2

The need for media specialists as consultants and staff collaborators, something heretofore given too little consideration, is pointed up by these considerations.

DISCERNMENT IN USE

An operational guide ordinarily cannot take into account all the factors which may appear in a particular *implementation* situation. It cannot be a blueprint or cookbook. It can point out some basic factors that have been considered important and influential by other implementers in the field test. Despite a careful study plan, some degree of slack remains. The package constitutes a way to proceed. However, other salient factors that appear relevant in a given implementation experience cannot be overlooked or ignored in deference to those that are dealt with in the package. A certain amount of professional judgement, the art of practice, must be contributed by the user.

These kinds of precautions may be built into a package in prominent places. This forewarns the user and gives a helpful while cautious perspective to application. The following words were used to convey this experimental outlook:

This handbook is not a technical blueprint. It offers a general strategic direction to achieve an objective which you define. You cannot expect to proceed step by step in cookbook fashion, as in baking a pie. Sensitivity, judgement, creativity, and moral choice on the part of the user are essential. Furthermore, the handbook is not intended as an all-inclusive, diagnostic and problem-solving tool. It must be supplemented by other approaches and materials. For the purposes of systems diagnosis, a variety of supplementary sources may be tapped. See the bibliography for some especially helpful references.

. . . While the guidelines have been derived from social science research, and the field experience with them has given the authors confidence in their utility, they are not presented as a panacea or a routine prescription for solving all mental health problems. The reader will have to rely on personal judgement in the application:

Does this initiative fit my situation?
Am I comfortable with it organizationally? Philosophically?
Does it seem as good or better than alternative approaches that come to mind?

The "product" of development work provides specific direction and thought processes to facilitate the implementation of application concepts under development. At the same time, it should leave room for discretion and discernment by the user. It is probable that in most human service operational guides a degree of slack may be necessary in presenting materials to practitioners. For some simpler, more routine tasks and circumstances, tighter, more closely programmed guide materials may be possible.

Such materials, as we have pointed out earlier, can range from a single chart, through slides and films, to an elaborately produced multimedia presentation. Through experimentation with a range of such forms, answers may be obtained about the most appropriate format, presentation, and so on for a specific use.

When a development product has been appropriately packaged, it is ready to be test marketed and diffused actively and widely to potential users and beneficiaries. It is to this diffusion task that we will now turn our attention.

BIBLIOGRAPHY

BENJAMIN, BERNARD, "Research Strategies in Social Service Departments of Local Authorities in Great Britain," *Journal of Social Policy*, 2, no. 1 (1972), 13–26.

DAVIS, HOWARD, and SUSAN SALASIN, "The Utilization of Evaluation," *Handbook of Evaluation Research*, Elmer Struening and Marcia Guttentag, eds., vol. 1, 621–666. Beverly Hills, Calif.: Sage Publications, 1975.

GLASER, E. M., H. S. COFFEY, J. B. MARKS, and I. B. SARASON, *Utilization of Applicable Research and Demonstration Results*. Los Angeles: Human Interaction Research Institute, 1967.

HAVELOCK, RONALD G., "New Developments in Translating Theory and Research into Practice," Paper presented at the 96th Annual Meeting of the American Public Health Association, Detroit, Michigan, November 1968.

KLEIN, HELEN D., "The Missouri Story: A Chronicle of Research Utilization and Program Planning," a Paper presented at the National Conference of Social Welfare, May 1968.

MAGISOS, J. H., *Interpretation of Target Audience Needs in the Design of Information Dissemination Systems for Vocational-Technical Education*, Columbus: The Center for Vocational and Technical Education, The Ohio State University, 1971.

PAISLEY, WILLIAM J., "Information Needs and Uses," in *Annual Review of Information Science and Technology*, ed. C. A. Cuadra, vol. 3, 1–30. New York: Interscience, 1968.

RADNOR, MICHAEL, et. al., "Agency/Field Relationships in the Educational R/D &I System: A Policy Analysis for the National Institute of Education," *A Policy Analysis for the National Institute of Education*, Evanston, Ill.: Northwestern University, October 1976.

ROTHMAN, JACK, *Planning and Organizing for Social Change: Action Principles from Social Science Research*, pp. 556–71, New York: Columbia University Press, 1974.

ROTHMAN, JACK, JOSEPH G. TERESA and JOHN L. ERLICH, *Fostering Participation and Innovation,* Handbook for Human Service Professionals, Itasca, Ill.: F. E. Peacock Publishers, Inc., 1978.

SMITH, R. L., F. HAWKENSHIRE, and R. O. LIPPITT, "Work Orientations of Teenagers," Ann Arbor, Mich.: Institute for Social Research, University of Michigan, 1969. (Report for Contract No. OE-5-85-067 for Project No. 5-0118.)

SOLOFF, ASHER, et. al., "Running a Research Utilization Laboratory," *Rehabilitation Counseling Bulletin,* Special Issue: Research Utilization in Rehabilitation, 19, no. 2 (December 1976), 416–424.

VAN DEN BAN, ANNE W., "Utilization and Publication of Findings," in *Survey Research Methods in Developing Nations,* C. H. Backstrom and G. D. Hursh, eds. Chicago: Northwestern University Press, 1963.

VAN DE VALL, MARK, CHERYL BOLAS MARK, and TAI S. KANG, "Applied Social Research in Industrial Organizations: An Evaluation of Functions, Theory, and Method," *The Journal of Applied Behavioral Science,* 12, no. 2 (April, May, June, 1976), 158–177.

WEISS, CAROL H., *Evaluation Research in the Political Context,* pp. 13–25. Beverly Hills, Calif.: Sage Publications, 1975.

———, "What Makes Social Research Usable: Data from Mental Health," paper prepared for annual meeting of American Association for the Advancement of Science, Denver, Colorado, February 24, 1977.

10

Diffusion
and
Social Marketing

Social marketing provides a rich conceptual system for thinking through the problems of bringing about changes in the ideas or practices of a target public . . . The adoption of an idea, like the adoption of any product, requires a deep understanding of the needs, perceptions, preferences, reference groups, and behavioral patterns of the target audience, and the tailoring of messages, media, "costs" and facilities to maximize the ease of adopting the idea.

Philip Kotler
Marketing for Non-Profit Organizations

DIFFUSION

Introduction

The term "product advocacy" conveys the essence of what we shall attempt to communicate in this chapter. This concept, as articulated by Radnor and his associates (1976) embodies an aggressive, energetic stance toward following through on development outcomes. It reflects a professionally responsible attitude toward the results of one's action-research efforts. In other words, once a product has been created in which the development team has confidence (based on hard evaluation of performance outcomes), it follows that careful and sustained effort will be di-

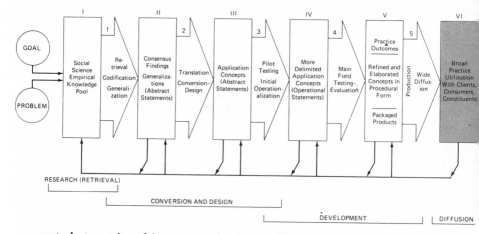

rected at putting this construction into wide use on behalf of consumers and clients—the intended beneficiaries of human service organizations. "Social marketing" intersects with the product advocacy concept as will be seen shortly.

DEVELOPMENT AND DIFFUSION

The integral relationship between development and diffusion has been expressed by Boyan (1968), at the time director of the Division of Educational Laboratories of the United States Office of Education:

Emphasis on the importance of development as an activity of great consequence in no way deprecates the importance of other building blocks in the relationship between the production and utilization of knowledge. These other blocks, such as credible demonstration and sophisticated dissemination, constitute critical elements in the total set that makes for sufficiency in promoting and improving the relationship. (p. 36)

Boyan goes on immediately to add: "The burden of the argument here is that development is the keystone" (p. 36). We concur. Without a substantive development phase there is no assurance of the bringing forth of a reliable, effective product worthy of distribution. Further, awareness of, and technical proficiency in, development are at a stage of early emergence in the human services. Therefore, this area requires major attention. Nevertheless, its close interrelationship with the next phase should neither be ignored nor underplayed.

In the business world the importance of diffusion is well recognized. A variety of code words signify its saliency: marketing, promotion, sales, distribution. Ansoff (1961) points out that all research and development work in a business firm is based on "market-product strategy," a central purpose of which is to "maximize profits over the long run" (p. 209). A number of different roles have been institutionalized in order to implement this aspect: salesmen, detail men, publishers' representatives, etc. Indeed, one is quite able to conclude that in the commercial sphere this is the tail that wags the entire operation.

For this reason and others, the place of diffusion has often been deprecated in the social sciences and the human service professions. It is associated with the crass commercialism of business. In describing their attitudes toward disseminating a mental health innovation, Tornatzky and Fairweather (1976) state:

> Unfortunately the role demands of this type of research are quite incongruous with many of the role demands of the traditional academic researcher. In many ways the role that we play is more akin to that of a Willy Loman with a Ph.D. (pp. 11-12)

Guba (1968) makes the same point:

> Diffusion is an activity regarded with some distaste by many members of the educational establishment, particularly the research community. It is often equated with hucksterism . . . (p. 53)

The norms of these professionals dictate a more staid, detached posture toward one's products. Study findings are to be published in some respectable outlet—a scientific journal, for example, as opposed to the more popular media. Normal processes associated with intellectual merit are, thereby, set in motion, allowing contributions to receive the reception they deserve. It is considered undignified to agitate this diffusion process too actively; it is unworthy to popularize one's work so as to make it intelligible and available to non-elite audiences. Because of neglect or ineptitude, the outputs of social science effort often fail to have an impact on real world problems and service programs. In a large scale evaluation of the diffusion effort of the National Institute of Education (1977), the Dissemination Analysis Group indicates:

> the study found that few of the existing dissemination activities encourage the kinds of combination of existing networks and capabilities needed to improve educational dissemination in a major way. (p. i)

This study team went on to identify twelve different operational problems that currently stand in the way of effective educational diffusion. These include failure to delineate target groups properly, failure to use two-way communication, and failure to provide adequate incentives to potential users.

In concluding an investigation of manpower labs supported by the Department of Labor, an advisory study committee of the National Academy of Sciences (1974) concluded:

There is agreement between [Labor Department] and laboratory officials that efforts to promote use of laboratory findings have not been successful. (p. 8)

No special effort is required to discover numerous, similar published comments concerning the discouraging state of utilization of social science research. Our failures in this area are generally well known.

In the field of business, economic factors constitute the chief spur to diffusion. Distribution and profits are explicitly and functionally intertwined. There is an absence of such an operational incentive in favor of diffusion in the social area. Recent concern by the public for accountability, however, may serve as a stimulus to more active diffusion. In addition, expectations by government and private funding organizations for inclusion of dissemination components in grant proposals may also provide an economic push in that direction. Nevertheless, the development of internalized professional norms, rather than economic levers may constitute the main driving force for diffusion in the human service fields.

DIFFUSION AND SOCIAL MARKETING

In its most simplified form, Research and Development has functioned as a process by which business and industry meet some societal need or want. When a relevant product or service has materialized to a suitable level, some activity must direct the effective flow—the dissemination or diffusion—of the product or service from the producer to the appropriate customer, consumer, or user. This activity is called "marketing."

A recent development of interest is an attempt to apply the methods of marketing to nonprofit organizations. Kotler (1975) introduces the notion of "social marketing" and describes it as follows:

Social marketing is the design, implementation, and control of programs seeking to increase the acceptability of a social idea or practice in a target group(s). It utilizes concepts of market segregation, consumer research, idea configuration, communication, facilitation, incentives, and exchange theory to maximize target group response. (p. 283)

The complex social marketing planning system is depicted in Figure 10–1, reproduced from Kotler's presentation (p. 297).

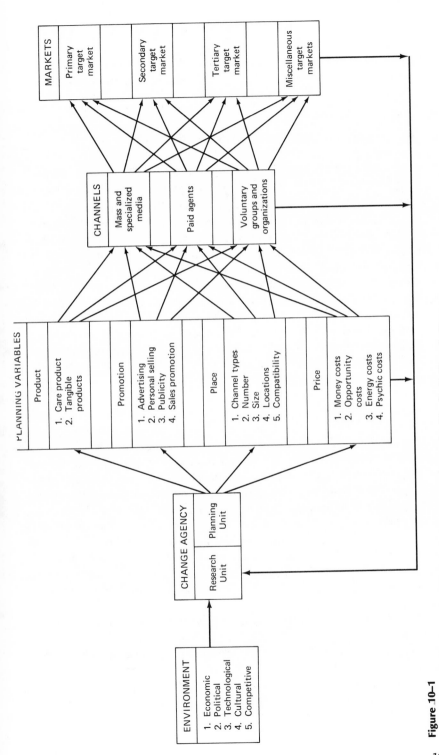

Figure 10–1

Reproduced with permission from Philip Kotler, *Marketing for Non-Profit Organizations,* Englewood Cliffs, N.J.: Prentice-Hall, Inc., 1975, p. 297.

193

The Radnor group (1976) visualizes diffusion essentially as a linking process. In their view the functions of this linkage are three-fold:

a. To inform users of the results of Research and Development which are relevant to and usable by them.

b. To enable users to effectively utilize the results of research and development.

c. To enable developers and producers to develop and produce products which fit user needs. (p. 120)

These comments point to the place of user input into the R&D process, and, in particular, to the relevancy of such input to the effectiveness of the diffusion phase. Traditionally, commercial diffusion programs have included a marketing research component that aims at assessing the extent of consumer interests, desires, and responses.

Tinnesand (1975) correctly points out that there are a variety of different types of marketing research that may be related to different functions and stages of the R&D process. One way of making distinctions is to discriminate between market research and test marketing. Market research is said by Tinnesand to refer to "market environment of the organization." This type of research takes place at the inception stage of R&D. It signals whether a need exists for a given potential R&D product, and it indicates whether a particular R&D endeavor should be initiated at all. It asks whether a pool of potential users is standing by to engage a given output. Test marketing, on the other hand, takes place on the opposite end of the R&D continuum, after a product has been brought to full development. It is a form of operations research that seeks to discover where potential users are located and through what means they might best be reached. Users, thus, may be viewed as playing an important part, at least at these two critical points. It is possible to go further and visualize users participating as full partners throughout the entire R&D process. In their study of R&D enterprises, Sayles and Chandler (1971) discovered three different patterns of user involvement: *separate* (little systematic user participation), *sequential* (periodic involvement, as described above), and *integrated* (user organizations or representatives are conjoint participants in the R&D system) (p. 141).

It is interesting to note that, while Kotler transfers business marketing techniques to the social field, King (1966) describes the carry-over of research and theory from the diffusion literature of social sciences to the field of marketing. He feels that the "diffusion research tradition can make a unique contribution to more efficient new product marketing and to understanding the diffusion process in the mass consumer market context" (p. 684). Apparently, there is a convergence of activity in these disparate fields.

DIFFUSION IN THE SOCIAL SCIENCES

Of the various phases of R&D, perhaps the most substantial accumulation of theory development and research (as far as the social sciences are concerned) is in the area of diffusion. This considerable outpouring of research has been gathered and synthesized in major volumes of scholars such as Rogers and Shoemaker (1971), Glaser (1967), Zaltman, Duncan, and Holbeck (1973), Havelock (1968), and Rothman (1974). Well-authenticated generalizations have been formulated with regard to factors such as stages in the innovation process, different innovation roles and actors, characteristics of innovators, and the place of "opinion leaders" in the two-step flow of communication. More recent developments have included the delineation of organizational variables associated with the adoption of innovations, and of collective and authority decisions as part of the diffusion process. Rogers and Shoemaker indicate that the diffusion tradition in the social sciences has been fed by such diverse fields as rural sociology and agricultural extension, anthropology, education, medical sociology, and communications—and, of course, marketing.

One is led to conclude that the knowledge component of diffusion is under much more control in the social fields than is its applied expression. Some sustained action-research diffusion undertakings, however, have been ventured and reported upon. One such study by Fairweather and his associates (1974) has attracted wide professional notice. The study team engaged in a protracted campaign to diffuse a new mental health service program, the "lodge model," that consists of a largely self-directed halfway house for patients discharged from mental hospitals. The lodge concept originally emerged from a form of development effort called "experimental social innovation." This effort involved the collaboration of researchers and mental health practitioners. When the "demonstration" lodge failed to be adopted, even by the hospital that cooperated in the experiment, the Fairweather group decided to initiate a national dissemination effort among mental health hospitals. Three different strategies of dissemination were employed: a brochure, workshops, and on-site demonstrations. It was found that the demonstration modality was most effective in stimulating adoption, and that other factors also contributed to utilization, such as action consultation and user participation.

Another example is the vocational rehabilitation project by Glaser (1967) to obtain widespread use of a new program for placing mentally retarded young men into gainful employment. This program, based on the work of the Tacoma Goodwill Industries, was disseminated through three distinct diffusion strategies as well: a booklet, a conference at the demonstration site, and a consultation visit to potential adopter sites. It was found that the combination of booklet and demonstration conference had the greatest diffusion payoff.

In a later experience Glaser and Ross (1971) undertook the dissemination of a new mental health technique called "saturation group therapy," a prolonged series of weekend group treatment sessions. Varied diffusion strategies were employed, including: a descriptive pamphlet, a consultation visit to the user site, a visit by users to the central demonstration site, and a consultation visit to the user site following the demonstration observation. These investigators found that an insignificant number of adoptions or adaptations of the program were made. They attributed this to the nature of the innovation itself. They indicate that careful screening must take place regarding innovations to be disseminated to ensure that these have relevance for the target organizations and that they can be adopted readily within the user's normal environment. The authors conclude that the character of the product itself, and the means of diffusing it are critical considerations in bringing about utilization. This is consistent with our view.

Here, then, are three different examples of attempts to channel a developed product or service to "consumers" who will use it. Had we been describing events in the commercial sphere, we would say, simply, here were three marketing efforts. These three particular efforts, however, were directed to the channeling of three social problem-solving application concepts. These, then, were efforts at *social marketing*.

The lesson of these and other studies that might be described is that utilization depends on a "product advocacy" or "campaign" outlook, carefully articulated with social marketing methods and procedures conducive to user adoption. In other words, the same attention, drive, and competency that goes into formulating a research study or into doing development work must also be given to the design of a plan of diffusion.

Broader and firmer conclusions concerning the processes and effects of diffusion are available in the works of Rogers and others described earlier, who based their studies on the diffusion efforts of others. Because of a more limited experience, action-research or field experiment diffusion studies have offered fewer generalizations to this point, but they may in the long run provide a particularly rich source of knowledge concerning the phenomenon.

In order to discern some of the elements of a dissemination campaign, let us return for a moment to the discussion of diffusion presented in the second chapter. There we stated that the diffusion phase of the R&D model was comprised of activities such as:

a) Isolating a universe of practitioners or organizations who are potential target users.

b) Determining key attributes, attitudes, and needs of users.

c) Packaging appropriate materials and appeals in an attractive, responsive way.

d) Reaching and motivating potential users.

e) Locating functional gatekeepers, authority figures, opinion leaders, or informal networks as entry points and diffusion channels.

f) Providing intitial training and ongoing support and reinforcement to users.

g) Developing procedures for scanning results of diffusion strategies, etc.

No responsible social scientist or human services practitioner would argue that the present tools of our trade are adequate to deal with the huge social and personal problems that come before struggling practitioners and/or administrators in human service agencies. Even when new, excellent technologies are invented or developed, these diffuse through the professional infrastructure in a slow and halting fashion. We already know that the lag between the creation of an innovative idea or technique and its widespread application may involve years—even decades—and there are good reasons for that lag. There is comfort and security in using familiar, accepted methods. Extra energy and nagging risk come with trying something new. Ideological barriers, enveloped in traditional thinking, also stand in the way. Furthermore, new methods and procedures are not always guaranteed to work. Changing over to behavior modification forms of mental health treatment, for example, means discarding a half century of Freudian precepts about the nature of human beings and how they may be given psychological assistance.

Our own R&D efforts in the Community Intervention Project involved meeting and dealing with a two-level problem of acceptance. First, we were developing a methodology for the invention of new, need-specific practice strategies. This methodology, because of its antecedents in the business and industrial worlds, was—and quite properly should have been —suspect with respect to its relevance to social problem solving. Second, having demonstrated with reasonable success the utility of social R&D by developing new and useful practice tools, it was necessary to determine effective ways of disseminating these in a timely fashion to those who could use them to advantage in problem solving. This involved developing and executing a dissemination plan (i.e., a social marketing effort) that would place a product of our R&D effort (our intervention strategies handbook) in the hands of the appropriate "consumers" (i.e., practitioners —our market) who might benefit from the product.

A company launching a new product it believes may meet a societal need often engages in a test marketing of that product. It will "try out" the product on a limited scale and experiment with various ways of presenting the product to the potential consumers. The company may direct-mail free samples or store coupons; it may erect large point-of-purchase displays; it may hold consumer workshops; it may engage heavily in print or electronic media advertising campaigns. The purpose of attempting these varied approaches is to determine the best (i.e., the most cost-effective) way of disseminating the new product.

The same procedure obtains in the social marketing effort, as our own experience illustrates. That experience included the types of action components outlined in our social R&D model. It also affords an opportunity to examine some of the methods, theoretical issues, and operational problems that may be encountered in this sort of approach.

AN EXAMPLE OF "SOCIAL MARKETING" DIFFUSION

In the previous chapter we described the packaging of a product: our handbook that was to be directed at professionals in the mental health field (community mental health centers and family service agencies). Following the inherent logic of the R&D process, a diffusion plan had to be devised to put the materials in the hands of potential users.

While the social science diffusion literature and the commercial/industrial experience provided us with a general road map of the major problems we could expect to encounter along the way (such as the turbulent, often confusing, and frequently frustrating environment of R&D itself), it could not flag for us the potholes, barriers, stumbling blocks, resistance, turmoil, and detours we would meet as we proceeded toward our goal. Furthermore, much of the ground we would cover was not well-traveled; many of the conceptual tools and specific procedures we would need did not exist in the social sciences. For example, the counterpart of the industrial engineer is the practicing social engineer. These did not exist, so we had to invent them. Always, there were surprises and on occasion a result that challenged traditional social science notions.

Following the models of professional marketing specialists, we designed a two-step approach to our dissemination effort. Step one was test marketing, systematically examining and comparing a variety of different diffusion strategies. Step two would consist of our principal marketing effort, derived from an examination of the test marketing data.[1]

[1]Our interest here is the presentation of a general approach to our test marketing effort. The specific details of our low and high intensity studies, including sample selection, experimental designs, data analysis and specific results will be reported elsewhere. See, for example, Jack Rothman, Joseph G. Teresa, Terrance L. Kay, and Gershom Clark Morningstar. *Social Marketing: Strategies for Disseminating New Mental Health Practice Methods* (tentative title), Community Intervention Project, University of Michigan, Ann Arbor, Michigan, 1978 (in preparation). The contribution of many collaborators to this discussion is warmly acknowledged.

The scale of the test marketing effort was larger than might be true for a typical R&D undertaking, for our purpose was in part to arrive at a reasonably validated set of generalizations about diffusion, following the action-research character of the project. This action-research program constituted a large scale diffusion undertaking in its own right. At the same time, these initial activities were intended to obtain data that would facilitate even wider diffusion efforts.

Diffusion methods have been discussed by Rogers and Shoemaker (1971), Zaltman and others; and there are a multitude of such approaches. These can be conceptualized in two broad categories of "high intensity" (personal contact approaches) and "low intensity" (mass communication approaches). High intensity approaches offer a greater degree of personal interaction, immediate feedback, and focused expertise. Such approaches require a large investment in staff time and financial resources, however, and ordinarily cover a smaller number of potential users. In comparison, low intensity techniques reach larger numbers of people and ordinarily require less resources per contact. Their drawback is that they allow less initiative and flexibility in influencing potential users. Litwak (1959) provides us with a cogent discussion of these theoretical perspectives.

As high intensity approaches are considerably more expensive in terms of manpower, time, travel, facilities, and other costs, not all agencies have the resources to engage in this type of diffusion. Further, such procedures ordinarily sacrifice communication with a larger pool of potential users. Utilizing this larger pool might well result in greater aggregate utilization. In the event that what is communicated is simple or the audience is favorable or highly motivated, low intensity might be the preferred approach.

From a pragmatic point of view human service agencies will continue to use both approaches, based on available resources, ideological preferences, and complexity of innovations. Accepting this as an organizational "fact of life" in the human services field, the project employed alternative diffusion procedures within both high and low intensity approaches.

We asked: "Given that you are able to, or prefer to, use a mass communication approach or a personal contact approach in diffusing a new practice technique, what are more effective ways within each type of approach to achieve a high adoption rate among target practitioners?" We wished, also, to assess cost-effective variation between the two basic approaches.

In both cases target users were defined as the professional staff complement of community mental health center, federally funded through NIMH, and of family service agencies, affiliated with the Family Service Association of America. A follow-up evaluation for market testing purposes was conducted three months after the diffusion treatment (workshop or mailing) in which users were asked to specify their experience with the handbook. A specially devised instrument, the "Depth of Utilization Scale" (DUS) was used to measure behavioral aspects of handbook use. Specific increments in using a package may be and were visualized as follows:

	I did not receive a handbook.
LOW LEVEL OF UTILIZATION	I examined the handbook.
	I read it.
MEDIUM LEVEL OF UTILIZATION	After examining the handbook, I later thought about it or referred back to it.
	After examining the handbook, I seriously considered applying it to my practice.
	I applied some of the concepts from the handbook, either in a formal or informal manner.
HIGH LEVEL OF UTILIZATION	I partially implemented a specific action guideline (stopped before completing tasks of implementation).
	I fully implemented a specific action guideline (completed tasks of implementation). Moderately attained the goal (less than 75% goal attainment). Largely attained the goal (75–100% goal attainment)

The DUS constituted the chief dependent variable used for appraising diffusion results in this dispersion effort.

In the low intensity program a "Dissemination Rate" measure was also employed. Dissemination refers to the amount of mass distribution brought about as a result of mailings. The rate was calculated from the number of orders placed for handbooks by agencies subjected to different treatments. It was an unobtrusive measure, drawn from bookkeeping records of orders received and filled. It is an indicator of distribution (entry into the organization) rather than utilization (the process activated once entry is achieved). Social marketing may be concerned with either or both of these aspects of diffusion.

LOW INTENSITY MASS COMMUNICATION DIFFUSION

According to Rosenau (undated), low intensity or impersonal approaches provide information in a simple and inexpensive way. These approaches are of various kinds: direct mailings to agencies or individual professionals; printed matter delivered by hand through such devices as hang-bags on the recipient's doorknob, a stack of copies at a booth in a convention, delivery in faculty mailboxes, and so on; periodicals distributed by professional associations through newsletters, journals, special issues, etc. Each method has its advantages and special purposes. Direct mailings, for example, are viewed by Rosenau as suited especially for installing or replacing visible or low risk innovations. Mass media may provide awareness and arousal while printed matter may offer awareness and interest. Professional periodicals can offer more detailed information on previous trials.

In the CIP low intensity program, mass mailings to agencies were used as an intermediate-level mass communication technique. (Mailings directed at particular agencies are obviously less diffuse than radio broadcasts or newspaper ads, but not as concentrated as printed matter delivered by hand.) Two factors may be important in such mass-mailing dissemination: point of entry into the organization, and type of reference group appeal to potential users. In other words, in a direct mailing to an organization one must decide to which level in the hierarchy the communication should be addressed—the director, middle management, or line staff. It is also necessary to decide what type of appeal will catch the attention and motivate members of that organization. For example, should the appeal engage loyalties to the agency itself, to professional norms, or to the interests and requirements of clients?

POINTS OF ENTRY

Within the diffusion literature, findings regarding the chief administrator as a facilitator of innovations are conflicting (Mohr, 1969; Rosenthal and Crain, 1968; Walter, 1966; Hage and Aiken, 1970). The chief organizational officer is in a key position (potentially) to legitimate and enforce procedures and practices. However, because of maintenance needs and a multiplicity of pressures, his concern is often more with stability than change. The attitude of an administrator toward innovation in general, or toward a particular innovation will affect the degree to which he is a facilitating factor in instituting new practices.

Collegial and decentralized decision-making processes have been viewed by some as facilitating with regard to innovations. Program people are seen by some theorists as more open to innovation and/or more inventive than top level personnel. Collegial discussion and mutual support are considered to enhance this natural positiveness toward new practices. At the same time, other studies have shown that resistance by such personnel can be a major obstacle to the adoption of new ideas and practices (Wood and Zald, 1966).

Some theoretical and research writings, particularly those of Litwak, et. al. (1970) and Fairweather (1974), have suggested that diffusion rates would be approximately equal, regardless of point of entry; but the evidence of this is scant. In our own diffusion program we selected two *levels* and three *points* of entry into the hierarchial structure of the organization for experimentation. The first level was at the top of the structure, the executive. The second level was in the middle of the structure, and here we used two different locations for entry: training specialist and a special interest person (i.e., Consultation and Education). Each entry was viewed as follows:

Executive: Though having the most formal authority in an agency, it was also possible that the executive might have the greatest time restriction.

Training: While a training staff person might not have much authority or influence in an agency, this person could potentially be highly interested in using training materials.

Special Interest: The special interest person (e.g., Consultation and Education Director or Director of Family Advocacy) was also assumed to lack formal authority but to have a strong interest in obtaining materials concerned with community outreach and social action.

These considerations point out elements of strategic planning to take into account in a diffusion effort.

REFERENCE GROUP APPEALS

In considering an appeal to professionals, role orientation is a useful point of departure. Three basic role orientations have been suggested in studies concerning professional workers: *bureaucratic* (or *agency*), *professional,* and *community/client* orientations. We have observed elsewhere (Rothman, 1974):

In this formulation, professional orientation implies a high concern with professional values and standards, a bureaucratic orientation refers to a preoccupation with policies and norms of the employing agency, and client orientation connotes a primary attention to the needs of those served by the agency. (p. 83)

Client and *community* orientation may be combined, as observed in the work of Epstein (1968, 1970, 1970). Epstein also suggests, as do Billingsley

(1965) and Wilensky (1967) that the *community/client* appeal is not likely to be as strong as the other two. There is variation among the studies that predict which of the remaining two role orientations would be more powerful within the heterogeneous professional population serving together in the community mental health field.

In order to incorporate alternative approaches, an appropriate and "appealing" brochure is necessary. Our brochure was designed to "sell" the product and was uniform, except the sections on the front page and inside front page where appeals were specified. The project staff believed that the greatest expertise and experience in social marketing resides in commercial advertising firms. We chose to work with such a firm, reserving for ourselves final authority to decide on the content, form and style of the brochure. Its composition represented an amalgam of professional interest and styles and advertising field interests and styles, a prototypical blend for social marketing.

An appeal must be formulated in language appropriate to the intent. The following are examples in this instance:

BUREAUCRATIC OR *AGENCY* APPEAL: (Mental Health agencies as the reference group)
RESPONSIBILITIES PROMOTED BY MENTAL HEALTH AGENCIES The National Institute of Mental Health, the Family Service Association of America, and other important mental health agencies have urged increased responsibility for work with community groups and institutions.
These mental health agencies have increased their concerns in the areas of community psychology, community psychiatry, and community organization. Policies and programs of these agencies encourage preventative programs.

PROFESSIONAL APPEAL: (Mental Health professions as the reference group)
RESPONSIBILITIES PROMOTED BY THE MENTAL HEALTH PROFESSIONS The mental health professions have urged increased responsibility for active work with community groups and institutions.
Professional associations have increased their concerns in the areas of community psychology, community psychiatry, and community organization. Current professional literature encourages preventative programs.

COMMUNITY/CLIENT APPEAL: (Community & Client groups as the reference group)
The National Association for Mental Health, the Child Welfare League, and other important voluntary community organizations have urged increased responsibility by professionals for active work with community groups and institutions.
Together with key political leaders, concerned community people support developments in the areas of community psychology, community psychiatry, and community organization. And, they encourage preventative programs.

The format of this low-intensity diffusion program can be depicted as follows:

REFERENCE GROUP APPEAL

	Bureau- cratic	Profes- sional	Community/ Client
Executive			
Training Specialist			
Special Interest Specialist			

POINT OF ENTRY

There were about 600 agencies involved in the low intensity program: a few less than 350 community mental health agencies and a few more than 250 family service agencies. (Approximately 65 agencies were included in each of the nine treatment cells.) This included, basically, the universe of the target agencies. Because of economic constraints and for purposes of market testing, however, a limited number of handbooks (a maximum of 12) were made available to any responding agency. The level of response by agencies to the mailed brochure was higher than we had anticipated. Overall, the number of agencies responding affirmatively (i.e., handbooks were ordered) was better than 40% of those contacted. The community mental health agencies were more responsive in that almost half of these agencies ordered handbooks. The family service agencies' response was more modest, about 35%. In all, about 2,700 handbooks were ordered, with mental health centers asking for nearly twice as many as family service agencies. This was within the range of expectation for the diffusion campaign, but somewhat in the high direction.

There are two points of particular interest that emerged. First, the handbook attained substantial application—slightly more than one fifth of the respondents reported a "high" level of utilization. Second, while we saw earlier that dissemination was higher in community mental health centers, the smaller number of individuals in family service agencies who received a handbook tended to put it to greater use. Perhaps there was more precise selection of potential users in the family service system by the individual doing the ordering.

In examining the question of point of entry, no pathway into the organization proved to be significantly better than any other. This was consistent with the theoretical position of Litwak and the findings of Fairweather.

With regard to appeal, the *bureaucratic* or *agency* appeal appeared to be the most effective in promoting dissemination. For community mental health centers, the bureaucratic appeal was significantly more effective than the other two. For family service agencies, the direction of findings was similar but there was not a great enough difference to be significant.

The dissemination and utilization findings were not identical. For community mental health center professionals, the *bureaucratic* or *agency* and *professional* appeals both contributed to utilization approximately equally, and at a level significantly higher than the *community/client* appeal. No one appeal was significantly more compelling for family service agency personnel, although the tendency was for the *bureaucratic* or *agency* appeal, again, to be stronger than the other two appeals for this group. The community mental health system was found to be more differentially responsive to different appeals.

None of the nine treatment cells was found to be a significantly better *combined* initiative (type of entry *and* type of appeal) than any other cell.

The low intensity program revealed one additional useful piece of information concerning the response to the handbook. A great deal of effort, as we saw in the previous chapters, had gone into packaging the handbook, both in regard to content and to format. In the evaluation form, respondents were asked to indicate their positive or negative reactions to this project product. The percentage of respondents checking "favorable" or "very favorable" to handbook attributes was as follows:

item	percent checking "very favorable" or "favorable"
Applicable to my agency	94.6
Applicable to my job	84.3
Clear, concise, easy to read	89.9
Not too technical	89.1
Overall reaction	75.6

The staff interpreted these results to be generally supportive of the rationale behind the handbook, particularly the principles for communicating with practitioners that were discussed in the previous chapter.

HIGH INTENSITY PERSONAL CONTACT DIFFUSION

High intensity or personal methods of diffusion involve direct contact and interaction between the diffusion agent and the receiver of the communication. According to the Rosenau analysis previously introduced, this approach may include such methods as visitation by potential users to a demonstration site, workshops or training sessions, and educational or sales "pitches," direct visits to individual potential users such as those carried out by publishers' representatives or detail men associated with drug firms. Rosenau again points to differential use, and relative advantages among each of these methods. If the package is highly complex a demonstration may be useful. A workshop can assist in gaining peer support to try out something that is risky. The one-to-one personal visit allows considerable feedback and clarification with regard to an innovation requiring the working through of attitudes or the providing of much information.

In the particular diffusion program to be described the workshop format was employed. It involved personal contact intensity, but at the same time allowed such contact to influence fifteen or twenty individuals at one time. In other words, it appears to be a cost-effective means of applying this method. It is also a common and familiar procedure by which professionals learn new techniques in the field.

With regard to a workshop format, one is immediately confronted with the question of what type of workshop leadership is conducive to adoption of new ideas. Two factors may be considered.

The first concerns the location of the diffusion agent inside or outside the target agency. Should the agent be an individual regularly employed by the agency, or should he be an external person, sent in for the purpose of dissemination? Previous studies of the question, such as those of Havelock (1970) and Watson and Glaser (1965) have "split down the middle," offering no guidance. The second question has to do with the status level of the diffusion agent: should he be an authority figure with high status, or should he be a peer of moderate status? Again, the research evidence offered by Havelock and Havelock (1973), Zaltman and his associates (1973), and others is highly contradictory.

In deciding on the diffusion plan, a standardized workshop format was employed, and different types of diffusion agents were trained to conduct it in a uniform fashion. The four types of agents are indicated below:

diffusion agent status

	Authority	Peer
Internal to Agency	Agency Executive Level Staff Member	Agency Program Level Staff Member
External to Agency	University Research Project "Expert"	Practitioner who engaged in the development field study

The *internal authority* is an individual at the executive level within the participating agencies. The *internal peer* is a member of the program staff of the agency, someone without executive duties or titles. The *external authority* is a member of the headquarters research staff of the project, based at the university, who comes into the agency situation with the posture of an expert. The *external peer* is a practitioner who has taken part in the developmental phase of field work. This person enters the agency as a colleague with experience in implementing the strategies of the handbook and is on the scene to share that experience. The internal diffusion agents in the CIP program were invited to take part in a preliminary workshop at the university at which time they were trained in use of the handbook and were instructed with regard to conducting a follow-up workshop in their own organizations.

Workshops were conducted in about forty community mental health and family service agencies in eight urban centers in the eastern and midwestern United States (Boston, New York, Philadelphia, Cleveland, Detroit, Chicago, Minneapolis, and Kansas City, Missouri). It was decided to diffuse in large cities because of the complexity and urgency of social and mental health problems in these areas. The particular cities were selected on the basis of relative proximity to the project headquarters for essentially economic reasons. More than 700 individuals participated in the diffusion program. Three months later, about half completed the follow-up market testing evaluation form dealing with utilization. Because there were a larger number of community mental health centers than family service agencies in the target cities, responses from the mental health centers number about 270, compared to about 100 for the family service agencies.

Analysis of DUS scores revealed no basic differences with regard to the authority/peer variable. As utilization scores were practically identical for these two types of agents, the status level of the diffusion agent apparently makes no difference. With regard to the internal/external variable, the findings consistently favored the internal agent. DUS score differential for internal/external was significant at the .05 level within community mental health centers. This differential was not significant within family service agencies, but the direction of the differential favored internal. In addition, on a large number of attitudinal items included in the evaluation instrument, participants who had experienced internal leadership scored significantly higher. These items included:

The handbook helped the agency.

The workshop was adequate.

The workshop experience encouraged utilization of the handbook.

The workshop was informative.

The workshop fulfilled my expectations.

On the remainder of the attitudinal items, the direction of response without exception favored the internal agent. The level of difference, however, was not statistically significant in those instances.

The staff concluded that in disseminating a product or technique of this nature, there was sufficient evidence to suggest that an internal, rather than external, diffusion agent be relied upon. A question remains as to whether this generalization holds for agencies in small cities as well as it appears to for those in large urban centers.

Several additional marketing findings were of interest. Immediately after the workshop was concluded, for example, participants were asked to fill out a reactionnaire giving their immediate impressions and feelings about the experience. The analysis of this immediate data revealed significantly more favorable responses by those who had an external leader, in particular the expert. This suggests that the external agent may generate more excitement and enthusiasm in the short run. For a product or technique of some complexity that requires working through over a period of time, the internal person who remains in the situation may provide the best stimulus and support. It might be inferred that a combined internal/external team would offer the most ideal, balanced leadership—assuming such an arrangement is feasible and team members can work well in collaboration with one another.

The staff attempted to correlate a range of additional variables collected in the high intensity study with the utilization scores. The factor that was found to be most salient in its association with utilization was the handbook itself. The respondents indicated that the character of the *product* was of highest moment in engaging their propensities toward utilization behavior. This response lends support to the importance we have placed on the development phase and on the creation of a suitable product that is perceived as appealing and useful by the target population.

COMPARISON OF HIGH
AND LOW INTENSITY DIFFUSION APPROACHES

Is a high or a low intensity approach more effective and efficient? Our comparative analysis of the cost effectiveness of the two approaches resulted in a more favorable assessment of the low intensity program. Excluding fixed costs (the central facility, core personnel, etc.), high intensity program expenses were approximately double the cost of the low intensity program ($8,000 vs. $4,000). These extra costs were used for transportation, per diem for traveling staff, salary for extra staff that needed to be engaged, special facilities for workshops, etc.

How much more utilization was brought about by this greater intensity of diffusion? Since the same utilization scale items were used, it is possible to state this with some definiteness. Based on the same three levels of utilization employed previously, we find the following patterns of use for all respondents:

		low utilization	medium utilization	high utilization	
High	#	127	134	113	
Intensity	%	34.0	36.0	30.0	100%
Low	#	466	334	223	
Intensity	%	45.0	33.0	22.0	100%

It is clear that, overall, the high intensity approach brings about a greater proportion of utilization at the high level (30% vs. 22%). With those participants with whom it makes contact, it can be said to have a better effectiveness record. However, looking at absolute numbers, it is seen that the low intensity approach resulted in almost twice as many individuals (223 vs. 113) employing the handbook guidelines at high levels of utilization. In other words, for half the cost the low intensity approach resulted in twice the amount of high utilization. Despite its lower cost, the low intensity approach created 110 more instances of high utilization than did the other approach. (It is interesting to note that the family service sub-sample showed similar percentages of high utilizers for both approaches, with a slightly greater proportion of high utilizers stimulated under the low intensity approach.)

SECOND STAGE DIFFUSION PROGRAM

Market testing should provide the basis for a wider and more finely tuned diffusion program. Using the two diffusion approaches and a variety of product advocacy methods, handbooks had been placed with almost 3,500 practitioners. Based upon these tests among users, a plan for wider diffusion of our materials becomes fairly obvious. This plan bears some elaboration, for its elements may be readily extrapolated and applied to other social R&D efforts.

Since the low intensity approach was more cost effective, our plan emphasizes this mode of diffusion, incorporating within it, in a subsidiary way, the things we learned about high intensity diffusion. We will begin with announcements of the handbook's availability. As no special entry position was shown to be most effective in our research, the announcements will not be channeled through a single gatekeeper but will, instead, be sent through a variety of channels, using, for example, newsletters or brochures. In our advertising media for dissemination, we will give particular emphasis to the agency appeal.

Relevant information will be located within the handbook itself, suggesting that readers consider developing an agency workshop as a means of encouraging staff use of the handbook. There will be a description of the format of the workshop that we employed in the earlier program. The insert will suggest that an internal agency staff member conduct such a workshop, using the descriptive materials as an aid. It will be noted that the workshop can be conducted by either a member of the executive staff or by someone from the program staff. We will point out that the workshop leader should be someone who has the interest, ability, and confidence of agency personnel, since official rank in itself was not found to be of great importance in our work. Finally, it will also be suggested that, if possible, an outside individual with appropriate expertise should be invited to share in the presentation of the workshop. This design indicates ways in which the marketing analysis can be integrated into the plan for wider diffusion and, hopefully, more extensive utilization.

A CONCLUDING NOTE ON DIFFUSION

We hope three elements of diffusion and social marketing have been amplified: a proactive posture in carrying the fruits of development out into the world of the user; a well-thought-out, strategic plan for diffusion; and a conscious, empirically based evaluation of means of reaching users by testing user reactions. These are the conventional methods of R&D in the industrial sphere. Adapting them to the social sphere—selectively, and with proper attention to the different operational and value considerations in the two fields—may offer much potential for making social science more relevant and influential.

Questions may be raised concerning various aspects of the particular diffusion program. These might include whether the variables of workshop leadership that were examined are the most pertinent, whether the types of appeals used and tested were the most salient, whether direct mailing is the most appropriate means of announcing an innovative package, whether the measurement tools were adequate, and so forth. These matters can indeed be debated and subjected to further research. This should be done, we feel, in the context of and toward advancing social marketing concepts and methods.

The discussion of diffusion brings us to the end of a process that we have tracked stepwise and in depth through this section of the book. The intention has been to flesh out and substantiate conceptually the model of social R&D that was propounded at the outset. The conceptual presentation, however, may not convey to some readers an ample sense of how social R&D really works in the doing: the kinds of specific problems encountered, exact instrumentalities and procedures devised and employed, the interconnected flow of activities from one phase of a particular development undertaking to its next phase. That omission we shall accommodate in Part IV with a concrete illustration of how social R&D was implemented in the field across its various phases. At this time, however, a final theoretical (as well as practical) consideration will be dealt with in order to round out R&D conceptually—the type of organizational structure needed for R&D implementation in the human services field, and basic resources that have to be marshalled to accomplish this task.

BIBLIOGRAPHY

BILLINGSLEY, ANDREW, "Bureaucratic and Professional Orientation Patterns in Social Casework," *Social Service Review*, 10, no. 2 (January 1965), 33–40.

BOYAN, NORMAN J., "Problems and Issues of Knowledge Production and Utilization," *Knowledge Production and Utilization*, Terry L. Eiddell and Joanne M. Kitchel, eds., University Council for Educational Administration (Columbus, Ohio) and Center for the Advanced Study of Educational Administration (University of Oregon), 2 (1968), 21–37.

EPSTEIN, IRWIN, "Professional Role Orientation and Conflict Strategies," *Social Work*, 15 (October 1970), 87–92.

EPSTEIN, IRWIN, "Professionalization, Professionalism, and Social Worker Radicalism," *Journal of Health and Social Behavior*, 11 (March 1970), 67–77.

EPSTEIN, IRWIN, "Social Workers and Social Action: Attitudes Toward Social Action Strategies," *Social Work*, 3, no. 2 (April 1968), 101–108.

FAIRWEATHER, GEORGE W., DAVID H. SANDERS, and LOUIS G. TORNATZKY, *Creating Change in Mental Health Organizations.* New York: Pergamon Press, 1974.

GLASER, EDWARD M., "Utilization of Applicable Research and Demonstration Results," final report to Vocational Rehabilitation Administration, Department of Health, Education and Welfare, March 1967.

GLASER, EDWARD M., and H. L. ROSS, "Increasing the Utilization of Applied Research Results," final report to the National Institute of Mental Health, Los Angeles: Human Interaction Institute, 1971.

GUBA, EGON G., "Development, Diffusion and Evaluation," *Knowledge Production and Utilization*, Terry L. Eiddell and Joanne M. Kitchel, eds., University Council for Educational Administration (Columbus, Ohio) and Center for the Advanced Study of Educational Administration (University of Oregon), 2 (1968), 37–63.

HAGE, JERALD, and MICHAEL AIKEN, *Social Change in Complex Organizations.* New York: Random House, 1970.

HAVELOCK, R. G., "Dissemination and Translation Roles," *Knowledge Pro-*

duction and Utilization, Terry L. Eiddell and Joanne M. Kitchel, eds., University Council for Educational Administration (Columbus, Ohio) and Center for the Advanced Study of Educational Administration (University of Oregon), 2 (1968), 64–119.

HAVELOCK, R. G., and MARY C. HAVELOCK, *Training for Change Agents,* Institute for Social Research, The University of Michigan, Ann Arbor, Michigan, 1973.

KING, CHARLES W., "Adoption and Diffusion Research in Marketing: An Overview," reprinted from *Science, Technology and Marketing,* Fall 1966, Reprint Series No. 188, Herman C. Krannert Graduate School of Industrial Administration, Purdue University, Lafayette, Indiana.

KOTLER, PHILIP, *Marketing for Non-Profit Organizations.* Englewood Cliffs, N.J.: Prentice-Hall, 1975.

LITWAK, EUGENE, "Some Policy Implications in Communications Theory with Emphasis on Group Factors," in *Education for Social Work,* Proceedings of Seventh Annual Program Meeting, New York: Council on Social Work Education, 1959, pp. 96–109.

MOHR, LAWRENCE B., "Determinants of Innovation in Organizations," *American Political Science Review,* 63, no. 1 (March 1969), 111–126.

NATIONAL ACADEMY OF SCIENCES, National Research Council, "The Experimental Manpower Laboratory as an R&D Capability," Washington, D.C., February 1974.

RADNOR, MICHAEL, et al., *Agency/Field Relationships in the Educational R/D&I System: A Policy Analysis for the National Institute of Education,* Evanston, Ill.: Center for the Interdisciplinary Study of Science and Technology, Northwestern University, October 1976.

ROGERS, EVERETT M., and F. FLOYD SHOEMAKER, *Communication of Innovations,* 2nd ed. New York: The Free Press, 1971.

ROSENTHAL, DONALD E., and ROBERT L. CRAIN, "Executive Leaders and Community Innovation: Fluoridation," *Urban Affairs Quarterly,* 1, no. 3 (March 1968), 614–625.

ROSENAU, FRED S., "Tactics for the Educational Change Agent: A Preliminary Analysis," San Francisco, Far West Laboratory for Educational Research and Development, no date.

ROTHMAN, JACK, *Planning and Organizing for Social Change: Action Principles from Social Research.* New York: Columbia University Press, 1974.

TINNESAND, BJORNAR, "The Importance of Market Research and Intelligence in the Innovation Process," *Product Innovation: Models and Methods,* ed. Knut Holt, III/8–III/15. Trodheim, Norway: The Norwegian Institute of Technology, Section of Industrial Management, 1975.

TORNATZKY, LOUIS G., and GEORGE FAIRWEATHER, "The Role of Experimental Research in a Social Change Process," paper presented at the

Annual Meeting of the American Psychological Association, Washington, D.C., September 1976.

WALTER, BENJAMIN, "Internal Control Relations in Administrative Hierarchies," *Administrative Science Quarterly*, 11, no. 2 (September 1966), 179–206.

WATSON, G., and E. M. GLASER, "What We Have Learned about Planning for Change," *Management Review*, 54, no. 11 (November 1965), 34–46.

WILENSKY, HAROLD L., *Organizational Intelligence*. New York: Basic Books, 1967.

WOOD, JAMES R. and MAYER N. ZALD, "Aspects of Racial Integration in the Methodist Church: Sources of Resistance to Organizational Policy," *Social Forces*, 45 (1966), 255–265.

ZALTMAN, GERALD, ROBERT DUNCAN, and JONNY HOLBECK, *Innovations and Organizations*. New York: John Wiley and Sons, 1973.

Interlibrary Loan Workform

WIDENER UNIVERSITY
WOLFGRAM MEMORIAL LIBRARY

Book Request

IL: 210F729

Date 6-25-94

Not Needed After 9—25

(Please Print)

Name _Linda Youngstrom_

Mailing _____

Address _____

☐ Faculty/Staff ☑ Graduate ☐ Undergrad

Dept. _NY_

Soc. Sec.# _210-36-0235_

Is this title listed in Wolfgram Holdings?

Telephone:

☐ Campus —

Home _532-5470_

Best time to call:

Author(s) _Rothman, J._ (Last name first)

Title _Social R&D_

Place, Publ, Date _Englewood Cliffs, NJ Prentice-Hall 1980_

Source of Information

Locations: _P21-PVU-BMC-ELZ-CMZ_

(For Office Use)

Edition _1980 Ed Only_

Verified:

OCLC# _5029316_

ISBN#

(For Patron)

Date Due _8—02-94_

No Renewals

Renl Req. Date

New Due Date

Signature _Linda Youngstrom_

Messages

Date Rec'd. _7-7-54_

(For Staff)

Date Rec'd. _7-06-94_

Lender _P2L_

Date Renewed

Date: ....

Notified _7-06-94_

Left Message

part three

ORGANIZATIONAL STRUCTURE FOR SOCIAL R & D

11

Structures and Resources for Centers of Social R & D

We seem to erect walls around our university departments of pure and applied science, our colleges of technology, our industrial research centers and our government research establishments. Many are the kinds of bricks of which walls are made: A Treasury liking for tidiness, secrecy, industrial jealousies, academic snobbery and, not least, too much thought of personal comfort and convenience. Interchange of research staff between various users should be far more common than it is. The nation would benefit thereby and so would the research workers concerned . . .
University departments of pure and applied science, colleges of advanced technology, government research establishments and industry need to be considered together as one scientific complex, with plenty of open gaps in their walls . . .

A. P. Rowe

Carrying out the multiple functions and activities of social R&D within an organized system requires a unique structural form. In this chapter we will discuss aspects of that form and present a model of a relatively small-scale R&D laboratory or center. The model we will suggest is based on the relevant literature and our experiences with the Community Intervention Project in carrying out each of the social R&D functions on a linear basis over time. It is important to recognize, however, that while this model has grown out of both experience and theory, it has not been operated as a total integrated system. It thus represents the design of an experimental prototype that still needs to be operationalized, tested, and refined. Several structural and resource requisites for adequate R&D lab operations will be indicated. Finally, we will discuss the need for research on the research and development process itself.

AN EXPERIMENTAL HUMAN SERVICES RESEARCH AND DEVELOPMENT LAB

A model R&D Human Services Laboratory would be related to a given service delivery system and geared to solving operational problems from the field. It would be based in a university setting, but it would have strong and interactive links with the field. The lab might have either a regional or a national basis of operation with regard to a given service delivery system. Such a lab would be composed of an interdisciplinary team competent to attack human service problems using a basic R&D methodology. The major components of the method include:

1. Retrieving of pertinent research on the problem
2. Designing derived solution strategies
3. Testing and initial operationalizing of these strategies in pilot agencies in the field
4. Developing of operational strategies that have been evaluated and "proven out" in field agencies
5. Packaging these evaluated strategies in the form of appropriate user-ready media (such as a handbook, videotapes, etc.)
6. Using lab training staff and dissemination specialists to diffuse the media in a broad cross-section of agencies experiencing the particular problem
7. Evaluating the broad impact of lab products in solving problems

Critical problems from the field would be actively solicited and filtered through a screening committee. These would then be processed in a systematic, uniform way through the lab structure and fed out again into the field in the form of user-ready problem-solving intervention tools.

Figure 11-1 presents an organizational chart for one possible structure of the lab. This is followed by a process chart (Figure 11-2) showing the normal flow of activities within it. It will be evident quickly that this organizational model precisely incorporates the model of R&D process we presented in Chapter 2. It also includes the various kinds of roles and competencies that have been discussed throughout the book.

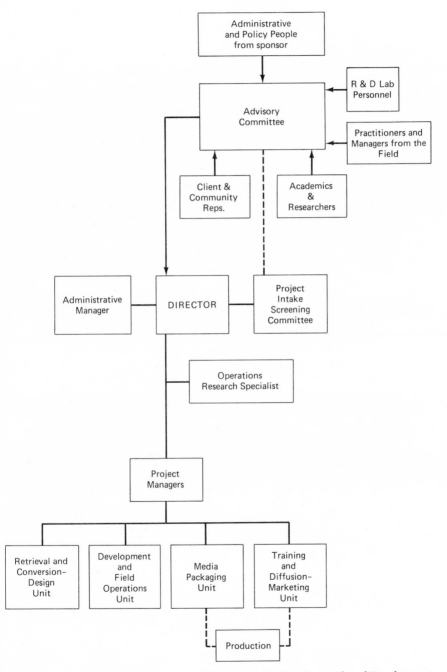

Figure 11–1   Organizational Structure of the Human Services Research and Development Laboratory

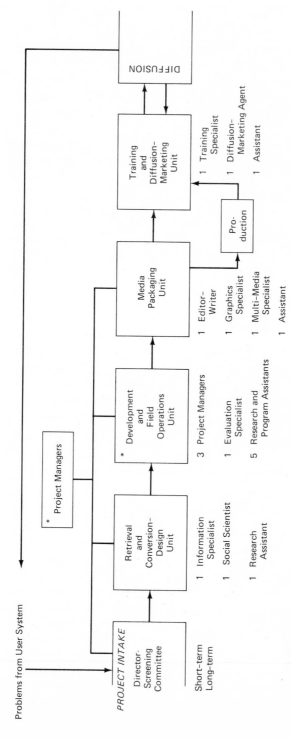

Problems from User System

PROJECT INTAKE

Director-
Screening
Committee

Short-term
Long-term

Retrieval
and
Conversion-
Design
Unit

1 Information
  Specialist
1 Social Scientist

1 Research
  Assistant

* Project Managers

Development
and
Field
Operations
Unit

*

3 Project Managers
1 Evaluation
  Specialist
5 Research and
  Program Assistants

Media
Packaging
Unit

1 Editor-
  Writer
1 Graphics
  Specialist
1 Multi-Media
  Specialist
1 Assistant

Pro-
duction

Training
and
Diffusion-
Marketing
Unit

1 Training
  Specialist
1 Diffusion-
  Marketing Agent
1 Assistant

DIFFUSION

*Could fill both positions

220

R&D LAB STRUCTURE AND OPERATION–KEY DIMENSIONS

After a problem or practice need has cleared the screening committee, it would be assigned to one of the project managers. This person would then play an active role in coordinating all subsequent phases of work and maintaining at least monitoring responsibility through the diffusion stage.

The problem would first be assigned to the Information Retrieval Unit. Here, an information specialist, working with an applied social scientist, would scan a wide range of pertinent research and professional practice literature for data and theories that bear on the problem. Working as a team with the project manager, they would then devise application concepts that appear to be promising solution strategies. These would likely be discussed with contacts from the field (perhaps relevant individuals serving on the advisory committee) to assess on a face validity basis the appropriateness of these design concepts. The retrieval staff might then conduct a further literature search to clarify and reshape the application concepts.

From this point, the application concept would be passed on to the development and field operations unit. Since the project manager has his main direct responsibility in this area, unit staff would have been involved and prepared to begin field testing of the application concept. The first step would be to select a relatively small number of agencies in the service delivery system for pilot testing. Selection of pilot agencies should include at least the following criteria:

1. existence of the problem in the setting
2. availability of agency staff with the willingness and capability to try out fairly abstract practice innovations (social engineering traits)
3. a supportive agency director

Pilot work may be perceived by some as a drain on staff time, so immediate and long-term payoffs must be adequately spelled out. In addition, rewards of various kinds, material as well as prestigious, would need to be made available by the involved service delivery system in order to encourage participation in the pilot work.

Assuming the pilot phase has demonstrated the practicality of the intervention design and signalled what it takes to carry it through, the next step within the development unit would be to arrange for a main field test. A larger number of agencies manifesting the problem would need to be selected. In this instance, the application concept would ostensibly have been viewed as useful by peer pilot practitioners and administrators within the service delivery system; and initial working tools for implementation (such as a preliminary draft of a handbook) would have to come into being. The obtaining of additional sites for further development work should not prove to be difficult. The evaluation researcher located within the development unit would be responsible for constructing quick, adaptable, but reasonably reliable evaluation procedures for assessing the efficacy of the intervention design. The development staff would be composed of persons with mixed practice and research backgrounds or abilities.

From here the project moves on to the media and packaging unit for fabrication into a communicable, attractive, user-relevant and user-ready form into which specifications for successful implementation have been incorporated. This form might be a handbook, film strip, audio tape, film, poster, check list sheet, instruction sheet, etc., depending on the type and complexity of the problem involved.

Once packaged, the product needs to be reproduced in sufficient quantity for use in the system. This production phase is roughly equivalent to manufacturing in industrial R&D. Few service delivery systems possess the organizational capability to carry through the bulk printing, TV production, poster work, etc., that might be required. Production, therefore, is likely to take place through outside organizations on a contract basis. The project manager and the media specialist assigned would continue to take an active part throughout this stage to make sure that the production is consistent with the basic purposes and uses of the product. In some instances, for simpler products, reproduction could take place internally; for example, if mimeographing or photocopying were all that was necessary, or if the host service system had its own print shop.

After this production phase has been completed, the product would go to the training and diffusion-marketing staff. They would take "product advocacy" responsibility for seeing that the packaged solution intervention became known in the field and came into use within agencies and by appropriate practitioners and/or managers. For some types of social marketing, impersonal mass communication through the mails might be sufficient. For others (those of greater complexity or in which staff resistance might be encountered), more personal high intensity approaches would be conducted through workshops, conferences, etc. One of the staff should be available to travel to field agencies demonstrating materials in on-the-spot visits. This person would be analogous to the detail man in pharmaceuticals or the area representative salesperson in the textbook publishing field. If the host agency has publications, or staff development personnel, the lab staff would link with them, interpreting products and facilitating diffusion through existing system structures. The project manager would continue to monitor this phase, less actively, to assure that the product is indeed receiving dissemination, and in an appropriate and valid way.

The diffusion staff should be aware that a part of their function is assessing the utility of the products and problem finding. In other words, as they involve themselves in the operating environment of the service system, they are likely to be told, or to observe, problems that the product does not address at all or misses in its application. These problems should be fed back into the R&D lab system to the problem intake unit for new problems, or to the media staff if a fault in presentation is uncovered.

The operations research staff person, in addition to assisting with the scheduling and organizing of work processes, would be expected to gather data for evaluating the lab outputs: the dissemination rate, degree of use, and impact of lab products.

The lab would work on projects of limited scope, middle-range and short-range in character, since more long-range or more complex problems may need basic research attention. The lab screening committee would need to be careful and sensitive in selecting problems that would lend themselves to R&D treatment. It is our view that it might be possible to choose some simpler problems that could be processed in a five to seven month period (such as devising a form that might help certain families control their budgeting in a more reliable way). Middle-range problems would be those that might be processed in a period of eight to fifteen months. Each of the three project managers might be expected to carry concurrently one short-range and one middle-range problem. Thus, the lab could take on (up to) six projects at one time, comprised of the right mixture of short-term and long-term undertakings.

Having presented an overview of social R&D lab operations, we will now concentrate in a more specialized way on particular elements of the lab.

PROJECT SELECTION AND INTERACTION WITH THE FIELD

If lab products are to have utility, they must be related to the needs and desires of potential users. In the discussion of diffusion we indicated that, while this takes place at the end of the R&D process, the perceptions and needs of those to whom products will be diffused must be accounted for systematically even before any product development work ensues. Without this type of "market research" or "needs assessment," products can turn out to be elegant white elephants, gathering dust in storage rooms and on book shelves. Referring to his R&D experience in naval civil engineering operations, Early (1975) states:

For effective research utilization, the client or potential client should have an open communication channel to the researcher. The client or potential user should have some influence on the selection and approval of products. (pp. 83–84)

The same general point is made by a team who studied manpower R&D labs for the Department of Labor (National Academy of Sciences, 1974). In their view the use of an advisory committee is a key structural device for channeling user input with regard to lab activities. The team recommended that the department:

encourage each laboratory to form an advisory committee composed of representatives with interest and competence in the particular areas of concern to aid in the development of project activities . . . [Have] the proposed R&D Manpower Advisory group involve present and potential users of the laboratory products and processes in the research planning of laboratory work. (pp. 7, 9)

In evaluating applied research projects for NIMH, Glaser and Taylor (1973) indicate that successful projects are characterized by frequent and close communication between lab staff and external sponsors, users, and experts. The advisory committee is an instrumentality through which such communication can be built into the program.

The importance of multiple interrelations between the lab and its outside publics has been stressed in industrial R&D (Gibson, 1964):

The *external* links involving interactions with the technological, economic, social, and political environments are the channels through which the raw material for policy making flows into an organization. They provide the basis for estimating the compatibility of the products of R&D with the potential and demands of the environment, and of assessing the probability that a development will not only be excellent technically, but that it can be reduced to public practice with "profitable" results, using the term in its broadest sense. (pp. 48–49)

In industrial R&D, field links to the user are direct, and feedback is often swift and decisive. Profits and sales are the most immediate indicator of meeting user expectations and needs. In the absence of this kind of natural mechanism of feedback and adjustment in the human services, user input mechanisms, such as the advisory committee, seem necessary. Otherwise, human service agencies and social science institutes can go on with the same ineffectual programs for many years while receiving stable funding from the government, private philanthropy, or universities. Since these funding sources are likewise often removed from users and clients, they do not serve as instruments of accountability and redirection, even given the best intentions by all concerned.

In the lab model we have included an advisory committee that can serve as a general link to the field and to related scientific and professional areas. We also suggest a project intake committee, drawn in part from the advisory committee, that would be responsible for the actual selection of specific development programs. This would be a smaller group, fairly sophisticated and one with which the director should have more intensive, ongoing interaction.

The size and composition of the advisory committee is an important consideration in terms of insuring an optimum level of communication and a number of different types of input. In studying the NASA program, for example, Sayles and Chandler (1971) observe that many difficulties arose from having advisory committees that were dominated by scholars and experts from the basic sciences. It is difficult to arrive at a rule of thumb concerning the precise make-up of R&D advisory committees. Being clear on the function of such committees, it should be possible to experiment with approximate arrangements geared to achieving these.

The same point can be made with regard to the relative influence of an advisory committee on the lab staff. While the staff needs to know the attitudes and views of users and other relevant parties, it needs also a measure of autonomy and protection in coping with an already extremely complex, turbulent, and multifaceted process. A "delicate balance" needs to be struck in this connection, one that will at this stage reflect more the art than the science of R&D work.

ORGANIZATIONAL RESOURCES AND SUPPORTS

Carter (1968) states that "certain critical conditions are essential" for effective R&D. These conditions by and large attach to the organizational stability and sustenance within which R&D takes place. Among these, according to Carter, are:

a trained, motivated and experienced staff available for long-term application to the problem. Generally, the problem will not be solved in any short period of time, and those responsible must recognize that the same staff must be maintained over a number of years if the problem is to receive real attention and solution ... Funding must be available not only to support the staff but often to make many physical and organizational changes within the setting in which the problem exists. (p. 16)

Carter writes as a systems expert who has been associated with R&D undertakings over a number of years. Almost the identical set of conditions is cited by Klausmeier (1970), speaking from his experience as an administrator of an educational R&D center:

From the beginning, four conditions were regarded as essential to achieve the goal: first, educational researchers and developers with ideas and skills who were willing to work cooperatively in achieving the goal; second, time to plan and carry out research and development activities; third, monetary support assured over an extended period of time, mainly for people's time and for supplies and equipment; and fourth, facilitative (applied) environments in which to carry out research and development activities and to demonstrate successful practices. (p. 45)

We have previously made note of the tumultuous professional and technical climate in which R&D occurs. Given this inherent restlessness, observers who have studied the phenomenon suggest that a counter-balancing, secure organizational base is necessary in order to achieve a reasonable level of operational stability in the situation. Three aspects of that organizational base will be considered here: long-term perspectives, sufficiency in staff, and adequate funding.

Long-Term Perspectives

As was suggested by Carter (1968), R&D problems ordinarily take sustained and somewhat extensive effort to work through. R&D essentially attempts to contract drastically the time lag between scientific discoveries and the implementation of derivative innovative technologies. Scholars on the subject ordinarily describe this time lag in terms of decades or substantial portions of a century. While R&D can make inroads on this time dimension, it cannot wipe it out with a technical "magic wand."

R&D specialists in industry have long been cognizant of this time consideration, and also sensitive to the impatience expressed by management concerning it. Shepard (1963) states:

Companies operate on annual budgets, but research and development projects are likely to go on for years without producing useful results. It may take a long time to investigate a research problem even to the point of estimating the probabilities of eventual solution, and this is a source of strain between scientist and businessman. Management is frustrated by its inability to determine whether progress on a project is as good as could be expected; the research staff is frustrated by management's inability to understand the nature of the technical problem. (p. 347)

Villers (1974) approaches the problem from a budgetary point of view, and suggests a fiscal device for gaining a time perspective:

Accountingwise, R&D expenditures are a current expense and for obvious need of tax deduction the accounting methods cannot be changed. But for effective appraisal of the financial picture, the R&D expenditures should be considered an investment since it may take many years before the benefits from research expenditures are received. When this is not done, misunderstandings may occur between corporate and division management or between research management and other executives. (p. 8)

The expected variance range of estimates related to R&D operations is bound to be greater than the variance range for estimates related to other activities. The time it takes to produce a part of the sales forecast of current projects for the next year cannot be estimated with 100 percent accuracy and a much larger range of variance must be expected for estimates related to the volume of sales of a product that will be on the market three years from now, or estimates as to the time it will take to conduct the necessary research work. (p. 10)

A variety of programmatic difficulties and pressures on staff are evidenced when the time perspective is given insufficient recognition. In surveying manpower labs supported by the Department of Labor, this issue was singled out as an important impediment to the effective functioning of the units. The National Academy of Sciences review committee, referred to earlier, reported their observations as follows:

Uncertainty concerning continuation of activities and the new level of funding from one contract period to the next has also had the effect of reducing the long-range view that project personnel are expected to cultivate. Laboratory directors have had problems in retaining staff who desire the security associated with long-term employment. An additional problem involves the annual or 18-month funding cycle, which forces laboratory staff to engage in documenting and justifying the organization's program activities to DOL [Department of Labor]. For laboratory staff, this contract-renewal effort is an unnecessary interruption, cutting into the time available for accomplishing contractual commitments. It appears, then, that ORD's desire to build program flexibility into the laboratories (i.e., its definition of long-term efforts) is frustrated by constraints on projects with respect to both time and financial support. (p. 51)

The same observations can be made with regard to educational R&D laboratories and centers.

Sufficient Staffing

The variety of different tasks involved in R&D, both those in the central technical areas and those necessary for supplementary activities, results in a staff complement of considerable size. Staff roles and the internal structural arrangements which facilitate their functioning have been discussed in detail in Chapter 8. There is no way to build the necessary broad-based R&D staff while maintaining a diminutive personnel group. Even in the rather small-scale lab proposed in the model, the total number of professional staff members amounts to almost a dozen, while auxiliary technical aides and clericals come to another dozen. In terms of ordinary thinking in the social sciences concerning the size dimensions of projects, this may appear to be enormous. Viewed from the standpoint of counterpart labs in the physical sciences, however, it is a meager operation. For example, in describing the program of the Naval Civil Engineering Laboratory, Port Hueneme, California, Early (1975) reports that it is staffed by nine naval officers, seven navy enlisted personnel, and three hundred civilians. The scope of applied and scientific competencies encompassed within the lab is indicated by the following listing: (p. 65).

Engineers:	Chemical	Structural
	Civil	Hydraulic
	Electrical	Mechanical
	Electronic	Sanitary
Scientists:	Biologist	Physicist
	Geologist	Oceanographer
	Chemist	Operations Analyst
	Metallurgist	Mathematician

It is not being suggested that social R&D facilities should compete for this type of staff composition. The suggestion would be politically and economically impractical, and in the absence of existing knowledge and experience in social R&D, professionally and scientifically premature. But these figures expose the limited resources which have been allotted thus far to social R&D, the obsequious and self-effacing posture exhibited by human services R&D in making its claims, and a sense of the human and economic resources that need to be put into play in order for social R&D to be given a meaningful and full-fledged chance to demonstrate its potential contribution to the solving of social problems.

Adequate Funding

Adequacy of funding pertains to two factors touched on earlier: amount and stability of available finances. The amount has been intimated in the previous section when staffing was discussed. Further light is shed on the need for increased funding in the social field in another article describing the Civil Engineering Lab (Tempest and Van Rooy, Jr., 1975). After pointing out that the lab maintains a staff of over 300, the authors discuss the Department of Defense Technology Transfer Consortium, which had gained the participation of 31 army, navy, and air force R&D laboratories. This represents only a small proportion of possible participants. The authors state that there are 37 different navy programs, alone, involved in R&D throughout the United States. In 1974 the membership in the original consortium group was expanded beyond military-only R&D facilities when the Federal Technology Transfer Consortium was formed to include government sponsored labs outside of the military.

The intent of the preceding discussion is to demonstrate that high levels of funding are currently being allotted to military and other aspects of physical R&D. Indeed, billions of dollars are involved. We project that a model lab such as we have described would require funding of perhaps three quarters of a million dollars per year. Only experience can demonstrate whether this would be adequate in order to attain high level R&D operations and products. In addition, such funding should be appropriated on a stable basis for a sustained time period of perhaps five or six years. The importance of steady and predictable support has already been introduced. Klausmeier's discussion (1968) of funding of the Wisconsin Research and Development Center for Cognitive Learning provides a frame of reference for considering the funding aspect:

Any organization requires stable funding over a period of years in order to secure excellent staff at reasonable salary levels. Stability of funding was an important consideration in starting the Center. This Center, in line with the general USOE policy, was awarded a 5-year grant, starting September 1, 1964, by the USOE with three important provisions: First, that the contract would be amended annually; second, that, if, for any reason, it became necessary to discontinue the Center the phasing out process would be accomplished over a period of time mutually satisfactory to the University of Wisconsin and USOE; and third, in the fourth year, the achievements and operations of the center would be evaluated comprehensively in order to arrive at a decision regarding a second 5-year period. The Center was awarded approximately $500,000 for the first year of operation. Each amended contract for the next three years showed a modest increase in the level of support. (p. 155)

Federal funding in this situation was supplemented by state funds through the university.

The necessity of a much greater governmental commitment if social R&D is to become a vital factor has been underscored in the previous discussion. In his study of the federal roles in technology transfer, Doctors (1969) illustrates the dominant and growing position of governmental backing:

. . . The process of technology transfer is not new. What is new is the increasingly large part the federal government is playing in the production of new technology. . . . Also important is that quantitative estimates of R&D spending by NSF and the federal agencies do not reveal the full magnitude for a significant portion of this federal contribution is buried in overhead funding . . . (p. 10)

Social R&D has received little of that fiscal outpouring, despite the persistence and severity of a wide range of social and human problems that have been manifested during the 1960s and 1970s in this country. Slowness in developing and demonstrating an R&D technology on the part of social scientists and human service professionals in part accounts for this disparity.

Host Organizational Setting

In considering the establishment of an R&D lab, an important question is the kind of larger host organization within which to locate it. Three obvious organizational locations come to mind: (1) within a large human service organization (i.e., an organization concerned primarily on an on-going basis with providing services, etc.); (2) within a university setting; and (3) within an independent community-based R&D organization or consulting firm.

As Soloff et al. (1975) have observed, industrial R&D labs typically have production-service organization type of sponsorship. In addition, governmental labs are similarly supported; for example, the naval labs discussed earlier. In the human services field, the Rehabilitation Services Administration has financed a vocational rehabilitation research utilization lab within the Chicago Jewish Vocational Services agency, and in other locations. As described by the Soloff team, these labs exhibit R&D tendencies.

Universities are common settings for certain types of R&D efforts. The Educational Research and Development Centers established by the Office of Education, for example, had such a type of organizational arrangement.

The Regional Laboratories supported by the Office of Education were placed within independent community-based organizations, autonomous and separate from either the area educational systems or from a university in the region. A voluntary community board constituted the governing bodies. Contract work let out by governmental bureaus to independent consulting firms having R&D programs (such as ABT Associates, and the RAND Corporation) take this form. In this instance, there is a quasi-corporate structure with profit making objectives for rendering R&D services.

Clearly, R&D work can and does take place under any of these arrangements. Even in industrial R&D labs, mixed arrangements can occur with some of the work given over to external labs to a larger or smaller degree. An industrial R&D specialist, Villers (1974), states that lab management must constantly ask:

Should we hire specialists on a salary basis, on a consulting basis, or have the particular job done in an outside laboratory? Should we rather pay royalties for research completed by others?
. . . Should we organize a new department, with specialists and equipment, or have the work done in an outside laboratory?
. . . As to a particular piece of equipment wanted—
1. Should we purchase, rent, or use equipment in a nearby laboratory?
2. If we need particular equipment, should we make it, or have it built for us?
. . . Is there a need for a pilot plant building, near the research center, to house

various pilot plants? Should a full-scale pilot plant, which presumably will continue to operate when the process and product has been proved, be housed near the laboratory or in its ultimate final location? (p. 129)

While there is no definitive answer to the question of what organizational location is best, certain criteria concerning optimal conditions may be advanced. For example, wherever the lab is located, it needs both a measure of independence and operative linkages. The Manpower Lab Review Committee of the National Academy of Sciences concluded that the setting in which a laboratory is located has important consequences for its success. Certain optimal conditions are suggested:

> Laboratories located within organizations that share their research orientation, sympathize with their purpose, and provide support for their project activities are more likely to make progress toward the attainment of their objectives than those that do not. The freedom of laboratories to establish and work toward the attainment of their goals, to select their staffs, to design their research programs, and to report administratively to the Labor Department, rather than the host-agency is emphasized for its importance in decisions on their locations. (pp. 2–3)

From the spacecraft experience, Sayles and Chandler (1971) extrapolate:

> A kind of "sovereignty," not for the individual components, but for the project as a whole is needed. Autonomy appears to be a significant requirement for the international project intent on excellence. And financial autonomy is perhaps most important of all. (p. 128)

While these observers emphasize lab protection from ongoing and inappropriate production pressures, in a previous discussion we pointed out that it is also necessary not to be insulated from these pressures, but rather to have some connection to them and some involvement in them. The lab staff in a social R&D undertaking needs to know the problems, to suffer some of the travails of the system it is attempting to assist and enhance. That staff has to be in touch with the real world it is attempting to affect. Morton's notion of "barriers and bonds" applies to a certain degree here. The host setting should ideally offer the opportunity for both of these conditions to be at play.

We have suggested locating a model R&D structure within a professional school of a university. This option is supported in a special report of the National Science Foundation (1969) on the use of social science knowledge. The report states:

> The professions—law, medicine, engineering, social work, journalism, mental health work, and education—are among the main social institutions through which

social science knowledge can be translated into day-to-day practice . . . The professions have a distinctive role in the translation of knowledge into action. (p. 21)

We would specifically locate a human services R&D lab within the graduate schools in human-service professions. A sizable number of the faculty of such schools are made up of individuals from the world of practice who teach practice principles. Adjunct faculty members from other disciplines, or individuals with multiple department appointments are part of the teaching staff of such professional schools. This interdisciplinary attribute endows such schools with great potential for the utilization of social science research. That such potential is not always realized is of far less importance than the fact that it exists. Our own experience with the Community Intervention Project, located within a school of social work, demonstrated, at least to us, that such a setting can be conducive to productive R&D work.

The setting of a professional school permits effort to be focused on given social and human problems around which the contributions of several disciplines may be organized. A reality problem focus requires cutting across rigorous but static discipline categories, for complex and multifaceted phenomena are at work. This serves to soften the insularity of academic department categories. For these reasons, professional schools within universities are particularly suited to undertake knowledge-linkage roles.

Roberts (1964), a leading theorist in the field of industrial R&D, projects the professional school as a highly desirable R&D setting. Roberts' thoughtful views deserve somewhat extended expression here. First he deals with the benefits of an R&D approach to the school itself:

If graduate schools of management are to lead government and industry toward new, more rational, more empirically valid approaches, new institutional forms are required. Within and around our nation's schools of management we need to develop centers for action orientation. Such centers are needed for the management of research and development as well as in other areas requiring far-reaching managerial innovation. Each center should be created in a management area where the over-all university resources best permit attainment of linkage between traditional teaching-research interests and actual government-industry practice. They obviously should be developed only where the management school is willing to forsake (in part, at least) the comforts of the ivory tower for the orientation toward implementation of managerial change. (p. 17)

Roberts has very definite ideas about the structural and organizational requisites of his R&D and managerial innovation centers. Some of these parallel our earlier comments:

The proposed centers for management innovation need visibility, endurance, and courage. They should be large enough to be broadly productive in their areas of responsibility, not so narrowly defined by academic specialization that they drift back toward traditional academia. Their size should permit national and international accessibility, to managers as well as to university colleagues. They need longevity to endure to the point of major research accomplishments and through the slow, patience-demanding process of major change accomplishments. And they need the courage to attack key managerial problems, with boldness of approach if needed, and with a willingness to challenge the folklore-mongers both in private and in public. (p. 17)

He is aware that faculty members and staff from professional schools would need to approach this task with a new, particular and blended intellectual posture:

Such an instructional role shift requires a new orientation on the part of the associated university faculty and research staff. The required new self-image must be that of an agent of change who measures his achievements in terms of implemented results, not solely in measures of published papers or even in terms of well-trained students. The programs for developing such teachers-researchers-change agents must be geared to producing a new form of academic entrepreneur who believes that it is as proper to write for impact purposes in *Fortune* as to write for information purposes in *Management Science*. He also must be able to do both effectively. (p. 17)

There are some special advantages of a university base, if articulated correctly. One is the continuous circulation and influx of new faculty, students, and ideas. The contrast has been made with industrial R&D. One observer (Gibson, 1964) states that laboratories often start out enthusiastically but after several years

drop down to routine, mediocre, or worse. It is also held in many circles that a research institution especially needs a continuous throughput of investigators, usually graduate students, to preserve its freshness and creativity. The examples of successful universities are cited as confirmation of this view, and I think it is sound where applicable. However, a research and development laboratory in industry or government can effect a continuous renewal of its technical staff only to a very limited extent. (p. 54)

On a more practical basis, there is to be found a pool of graduate students and young faculty members, whose salary expectations are more modest than in many community based situations, who possess a range of technical competencies and skills, and who are available on flexible time schedules and for various durations that may be synchronized with particular project events and requirements. Klausmeier (1968) reports on services provided to one university based R&D center by its host setting:

The largest support lies in the availability of personnel to the Center—administrators, professors, graduate students, and classified personnel—and also other personnel in specialized fields such as computer science, opinion survey, TV production, and equipment development. The University also has leased a facility and provides the many services that are necessary to make an operation function well. (p. 155)

We have both exposed a range of host settings and expressed a preference for one of them. This preference is largely speculative, even if informed speculation. The National Academy of Science team concluded that there is little existing data concerning the organizational characteristics that lead to high or low R&D performance (p. 42). More rigorous evaluation is necessary in order to assess definitively what is the generalized ideal setting, or what settings are best with regard to what purposes and circumstances. Indeed, there is a vital need for basic research on the R&D process itself and its structural aspects.

The Need for Research on the R&D Process

Throughout this book we have talked of the place of evaluation in R&D, particularly with regard to assessing development products. The same scrutinizing stance pertains to evaluating different lab structures and operations, and the R&D process itself. The paucity of such research and the need for it has been expressed in several different quarters. Rowe (1964) observes that it is ironic so little research is done about research itself:

How odd it is that, at a time when expenditure on scientific research in government departments, universities, and industry is without parallel in our history, so little research should be done toward discovering the basic conditions for successful research work and for its eventual application. (p. 303)

Scholars in industrial R&D lament the lack of study of R&D along these lines. Roberts (1964) addresses the paucity of research:

Major corporations devote millions and even hundreds of millions to R&D on their projects and processes, yet most spend nothing on "research on research." Such backward attitudes result in the present situation; only a few organized groups in the United States are conducting broadly based studies relevant to the management of R&D. (p. 17)

Shepard (1963) points to the waste of available data:

There is a crying need for a more action-oriented approach to the study of research organizations . . . Every laboratory in the country unwittingly produces quantities of information bearing on organizational problems—and pours it all down the drain, through a lack of interest and skill in the design, conduct, and analysis of social experiments. (p. 355)

In the seventies there was movement toward improving the situation, but the knowledge gap is still large.

Educational R&D probably has the longest history and has been given the most abundant resource support among social R&D endeavors. Still, those who have studied the subject reach gloomy conclusions. Smith and Murray (1974) state: "There is no solid empirical evidence to justify the prescriptive use of development and evaluation models in instructional product development" (p. 12). Merrill and Boutwell (1973), after examining a range of instructional development procedures and their underlying assumptions, comment:

The paucity of research on these premises suggest that they are considered axiomatic. Numerous propositions have been suggested, but only a handful of rather poorly executed studies have tested them. (p. 95)

How might one explain this seeming discrepancy in a field tinged by the spirit of scientific inquiry? Several views have been advanced. One suggests that there is a sensitivity on the part of researchers to have their own work exposed to scrutiny. Rowe (1964) asks, "Is there a fear of what investigations would reveal, akin to that felt about time and motion studies on the shop floor?" (p. 36). Shepard (1963) suggests that there is a mechanistic attitude on the part of some people in the field:

Perhaps the same forces that result in a limitation of the laboratory's innovative potential by defining its contribution as "technical" inhibit systematic study of the impact of personal, social, and organizational factors on the conduct of research itself. (p. 355)

Still another argues that the problem is one of unclear and unstable goals brought about by the turbulent R&D environment (National Academy of Science, 1974):

If mission-oriented research is subjected to rapidly shifting demands, the task of formulating detailed and concrete objectives for an R&D program becomes very difficult. The parties involved may find it so difficult that they retreat into very general statements of goals or no goal statements at all, or tend to substitute and justify service functions for R&D activities. At the extreme, the investigators may merely begin to "do something" with no clear idea of what they are trying to accomplish. To the extent that specific concrete objectives are not made public it is difficult to know by what critieria an R&D program should be assessed. (p. 39)

Various lines of inquiry for fundamental research in R&D seem appropriate and useful. Some that have been suggested include:

Rigorous Case Studies of Development Projects and Processes

O'Brien (1961) indicates that the history of past projects provides a valuable basis for learning about R&D, especially from those projects which have failed for various reasons. "A large fraction of the much respected folklore of the subject is wrong," states O'Brien, "and current decisions are influenced by a distorted view of the past" (p. 91). Two types of project studies are offered to correct such distortions, one quantitative in nature and the other qualitative.

Regarding the first:

A simple quantitative summary of the objectives, the schedule achieved, the correspondence of results with objectives, the manpower, and money, all as a function of elapsed time would be helpful and can be compiled easily while the records are fresh.

The second approach is more open ended and involved use of:

an intellectual history of the conception and execution of a project in which the interplay of viewpoints, personalities, policies, and financial and marketing restraints are re-counted. Who were for and who were against the project, and what were the reasons? Were the forecasts of performance, markets, costs, and schedule correct and how were these forecasts really made and by whom? . . . The audit reports made during the course of a project will be valuable appendices to such a record. (pp. 91–92)

Studies of Technology Transfer—
How to Move from One Stage
to Another or from One Field to Another

Doctors (1969) indicates that "real field experiments have been rare, and it has been difficult to obtain measurable feedback on the process of transfer." He feels that such feedback is essential in order to formulate transfer policy in a way that is adaptive to a changing environment.

In short, there is a need for comprehensive experiments by social scientists which would investigate the acquisition, evaluation, and dissemination of technical information and the measurement of its use after dissemination. (p. 7)

Examination of Environments,
Political and Economic Influences
on the R&D Process

The National Academy of Science (1974) study comments on the lack of information on how R&D is guided by social, cultural, and governmental influences.

Researchers, particularly in social science and in various applied fields, are greatly influenced by the trends of their times and even by the way the larger culture thinks about problems. They are also influenced directly through governmental science policy particularly regarding the funding of R&D. Despite the fact that a majority of all R&D personnel are partly or wholly dependent on government, there are few research studies which shed much light on this influence process, either to assess it or to improve it. (pp. 15–16)

Rowe (1964) comes forward with an outpouring of researchable questions that would keep an army of doctoral students in dissertation topics for years to come:

Is necessity usually the mother of invention and of scientific progress or does success more often come directly from basic work having no known application? Whence and in what proportions stemmed the important ideas in pure and applied science of the war and postwar years? Some of the obvious sources are university teaching departments, university research institutes, government research establishments, headquarters of government departments, industry, and the general public. How often were they the product of rare and individual minds and how often the result of mass attacks by groups of workers having little claim to genius? In the latter case, were the groups usually homogeneous or were they groups of workers from different disciplines and specialties? Were the successful workers subject to rigid programmes of specific objectives or free from such restrictions? After conception of an idea, how long before there was a resulting practical application? What factors accelerated or retarded the transition . . . ? (p. 303)

We have propounded a model of process and one of structure in this volume. They are advanced in the spirit of the R&D process, itself. Designs need to be piloted, operationalized, and tested. On the basis of this feedback from the empirical world, theories and procedures can be confirmed, refined, modified, or rejected. Also, in the spirit of R&D we urge a proactive posture rather than a neutral pose. Work should go forward vigorously while knowledge is expanded in the action-research mode of professional activity reflected in this book. The potentialities of R&D toward a rigorous means of coping with social problems, and for enhancing the methodology of applied social science, are too rich in human and intellectual potentialities to be retarded by an awareness of imperfect knowledge.

The social scientist, Karl Deutsch, was once heard to remark that man's intellectual capability for coping with problems pertaining to the human condition was a splendid possibility but lacking in some essential tools. We do not offer social R&D, and particularly human services R&D as a panacea for human problem solving. We present it as a splendid possibility. We are also persuaded that in time it may prove to be an essential tool. It is a tool, however, that requires the hands of many different craftsmen to wield. The possibilities will be realized only as the social disciplines and professions come to articulate with one another using a common, basic methodology, forged through organizational structures that encourage creativity and collaboration. There is much to be accomplished and much to be learned in this endeavor.

BIBLIOGRAPHY

CARTER, LAUNOR F., "Knowledge Production and Utilization in Contemporary Organizations," *Knowledge Production and Utilization*, Terry L. Eiddell and Joanne M. Kitchel, eds., University Council for Educational Administration (Columbus, Ohio) and Center for the Advanced Study of Educational Administration (University of Oregon), 1 (1968), 1–20.

DOCTORS, SAMUEL I., *The Role of Federal Agencies in Technology Transfer.* Cambridge, Mass.: The M.I.T. Press, 1969.

EARLY, E. H., "Measuring the Effectiveness of a Rapid Response Technology Transfer Program," *Technology Transfer in Research and Development*, J. A. Jolly and J. W. Creighton, eds., pp. 61–80. Monterey, Calif.: Naval Postgraduate School, 1975.

GIBSON, R. E., "A Systems Approach to Research Management," *Research, Development and Technological Innovation: An Introduction,* ed. James R. Bright, pp. 34–57. Homewood, Ill.: Richard D. Irwin, Inc., 1964.

GLASER, E. M., and S. H. TAYLOR, "Factors Influencing the Success of Applied Research," *American Psychologist,* 28 (1973), 140–146.

KLAUSMEIER, HERBERT J., "The Wisconsin Research and Development Center for Cognitive Learning," *Research and Development Toward the Improvement of Education,* Herbert J. Klausmeier and George T. O'Hearn, eds., pp. 146–156. Madison, Wis.: Dembar Educational Research Services, Inc., 1968.

KLAUSMEIER, HERBERT J., "Organizing the School for Research and Development Activities," *Research, Development and the Classroom Teacher/Producer/Consumer,* ed., M. Vere DeVault, pp. 48–60. Washington, D.C.: The Association for Childhood Education International, 1970.

MERRILL, DAVID M., and RICHARD L. BOUTWELL, "Instructional Development: Methodology and Research," *Review of Research in Education,* ed., Fred L. Derlinger. Itasca, Ill.: F. E. Peacock Publishers, Inc., 1973.

NATIONAL ACADEMY OF SCIENCES, National Research Council, "The Experimental Manpower Laboratory as an R&D Capability" Washington, D.C., February 1974.

NATIONAL SCIENCE FOUNDATION, *Knowledge into Action: Improving the Nation's Use of the Social Sciences,* Washington, D.C.: Government Printing Office, 1969.

O'BRIEN, M. P., "Technological Planning and Misplanning," *Technological Planning on the Corporate Level,* Proceedings of a conference sponsored by the Associates of the Harvard Business School, September 8–9, 1961, ed., James R. Bright. Cambridge, Mass.: 1961, pp. 72–99.

ROBERTS, EDWARD B., *The Dynamics of Research and Development.* New York: Harper and Row Publishers, 1964.

ROWE, A. P., "From Scientific Idea to Practical Use," *Minerva*, 2, no. 3 (Spring 1964), 301–320.

SAYLES, LEONARD R., and MARGARET K. CHANDLER, *Managing Large Systems.* New York: Harper & Row Publishers, 1971.

SHEPARD, HERBERT A., "Nine Dilemmas in Industrial Research," *The Sociology of Science,* Bernard Barber and Walter Hirsch, eds., pp. 344–355. The Free Press of Glencoe, New York 1963.

SMITH, NICK I., and STEPHEN L. MURRAY, "The Status of Research on Models of Product Development and Evaluation." Portland, Oregon: Northwest Regional Laboratory, 1974.

SOLOFF, ASHER, et al., "Running a Research Utilization Laboratory," *Rehabilitation Counseling Bulletin,* 19, no. 2 (December 1975), 416–424.

TEMPEST, E. H., and L. A. VAN ROOY, Jr., "A Case Study of the Power Line Disturbance," *Technology Transfer in Research and Development,* J. A. Jolly and J. W. Creighton, eds., pp. 61–80. Monterey, Calif.: Naval Postgraduate School, 1975.

VILLERS, RAYMOND, *Research and Development: Planning and Control.* New York: Financial Executives Research Foundation, 1974.

part four

CONCLUSIONS AND PROSPECTUS

12

Social R & D
in Action:
The CIP Experience

The human services fields have much work to do if they become serious about
the adaptation of design [R&D] technologies developed in allied areas of application to the business of helping clients. . . . Skeptics concerning the merits in
utilizing such strategies will, of course, rightfully remain unconvinced by rhetoric alone; the test remains whether such an approach can succeed. . . .

> Hugh B. Urban
> "The R&D Strategy as an Alternative to
> Program Evaluation Methodology"

A CASE STUDY

Let us now shift from conceptual discourse to a concrete illustration of the
concepts we have propounded. The social R&D model we have advanced
may itself be viewed as an application concept, a hypothesized method or
strategy for producing useful human service programs and techniques. The
next question about application concept is: "Can it be made to work in
action?" In this sense the CIP experience can be seen as a pilot project in
model building and in operationalizing the basic R&D methodology with
reference to the social field.

In this section we will describe the Community Intervention Project
in some detail, tracing it through the sequential phases of the R&D model.

We trust that this case illustration will demonstrate the feasibility of the model, make the model more tangible and immediate, and point up its potentials. This illustration will also reveal some limitations of the model that require further work.

By way of general background, the CIP was based at the University of Michigan, located within the School of Social Work. It received funding through most of its existence from the National Institute of Mental Health. The project began preliminary activities in 1967–1968 and was engaged in final report writing through 1979. The CIP set out with a broad research utilization purpose at the outset and narrowed its focus to specific R&D product development goals as it progressed. The initial objective was to formulate a set of intervention strategies and techniques for community change agents, deriving these sytematically from existing social science research. In part the project sought to devise methods for such systematic retrieval and application of research.[1]

RETRIEVAL—CONVERSION/DESIGN

The first operational step in R&D presupposes the existence of a general body of knowledge, sufficiently large, relevant, and useful to warrant commencing R&D work at this step. We have identified this body of knowledge in our model as Materials Stage 1. Where no such body of knowledge exists, or where it is not of a size to permit the extraction of meaningful generalizations, that body must be constructed. We might call this the "pre-step" in the R&D process. More traditionally, we would call this "research." In part, the retrieval effort allowed us to test the supposition that the social research literature possesses content capable of yielding pragmatic intelligence for practice use. There was doubt among practitioners and leaders of practice on this point.

The body of knowledge is, ordinarily, of such magnitude that it is necessary first to delimit the area of search to define with some precision the scope of the R&D problem. In our search for workable social change strategies, it was necessary to relate to realistic problems faced by practitioners. This necessitated the definition of a number of "practice issue areas." These consisted of external field problems and professional implemental tasks confronting community change agents in the course of their work. As a starting point, an initial set of practice issue areas was devel-

[1]This presentation relies on the CIP technical report, and represents a condensation and adaptation of portions of that document. See Jack Rothman, Joseph G. Teresa and John E. Erlich, *Developing Effective Strategies for Social Invention: A Research and Development Methodology* PB-272 454/TR-1-RD, National Technical Information Service, Springfield, Virginia, 1977. Technical details and elaborations will be found there.

oped by the CIP project director. This initial set was arrived at inductively, based on extensive experience both as a practitioner and a teacher. This list was only tentative, intended to enable a pilot review of the research literature. Following this pilot exploration, several categories were dropped and others were added. The final list of practice issue areas that was carried forward included:

Diffusion and adoption of innovations
Legislative, political, and governmental processes
Movement and assimilation of populations
Organizational management
Participation
Practitioner roles

In the normal sequence of R&D a fairly delimited and practical problem or goal is defined at the outset—difficulties in using an existing device, for example, or the construction of a cheaper or more efficient appliance. In the CIP we were engaged in a more general exploration of the research utilization process, and thus defined a much broader basic set of problems. It was our assumption that in the field of community and organizational change practice, practitioners were functioning with less than optimal effectiveness and were not making systematic use of the intelligence available from social science. Rather than delineating a single problem area in a given agency setting, we described a set of typical problems encountered by most practitioners. These included among others gaining participation, diffusing innovative programs and services, and modifying organizational goals and structures. While this wider problem definition is not typical, the steps and activities which we employed in the R&D process were.

In addition to limiting the areas of search, we found that it was also useful to define a restricted time frame for the publication dates of the literature which we would consult. Selection of a workable time frame presented something of a problem for us in this R&D effort. The universe of fruitful social science work since the end of World War II is vast. Surveying all of this work was clearly beyond the resources of the CIP. We originally considered a ten year period, from 1958 to what was, at the start of our work, the "present" (1968). We quickly discovered that the most recent literature—within the three years previous to 1968—contained references to the more significant earlier research and generally represented "better" (more carefully controlled, more structurally elegant, statistically more sophisticated, etc.) research than that which had been reported in earlier years. Furthermore, social conditions were in rapid flux during that period. As it became clear that the quality of research was constantly improving and social conditions were rapidly changing, we adjusted our time frame to cover the most recent period of six years: 1964–1970.

The second parameter we had to deal with was the range of information resources we could cover. Defining this parameter proved a bit easier, if somewhat arbitrary. Our primary resource dimension consisted of thirty relevant scientific and practice journals that the staff, based on a review of sources, believed would contain a sufficiently large data base to meet our needs. The publications we selected were those found to contain specific kinds of pertinent data in relatively large proportions. Sociological journals received particular emphasis. However, journals in the fields of political science, applied anthropology, psychology and social psychology, and in several professional practice fields were also included.

The scale of retrieval effort was much more extensive, and the time provided for this effort was longer than would normally be allowable in typical R&D work. Our undertaking was exploratory and research oriented, however. It involved conducting R&D in "slow motion," under careful scrutiny.

The primary strategy in the retrieval process was to survey selected journals that contained materials relevant to CIP purposes. The preliminary review of journals led to an extensive, yet sufficiently circumscribed listing of relevant publications. These were in the following fields:

I. *The Disciplines*
   A. *Applied Anthropology*
   B. *Political Science*
   C. *Psychology and Social Psychology*
   D. *Sociology*
II. *The Professions*
   A. *Adult Education*
   B. *City Planning*
   C. *Community Mental Health*
   D. *Public Administration*
   E. *Public Health*
   F. *Social Work*

Each journal within our six-year time frame was examined article-by-article. The reviewer identified all relevant articles according to the specified criteria, and a standardized abstract was prepared for each article. In addition, the subject matter of each article was coded into each appropriate issue area category upon which it touched.

The research assistants who handled the retrieval task turned their reports in weekly. Their work was closely monitored and supervised in order to check for comprehension, clarity, and logical interconnections.

The main instrument of the investigation was the study report form. Information was recorded on this form for each study included in the data pool. The instrument first required the setting down of certain background information concerning the study. This was a kind of "vital statistics" overview (i.e., variables studied or themes covered, national and community context of the study, study design and methodology, etc.). This section also provided a mechanism for screening articles into the data pool (a check for variables related to community organization practice, and a check of whether empirical methods were used), or screening them out (eliminating studies that had major methodological defects).

Next, the reviewer prepared an abstract or summary of the study. This included: an elaboration of the theoretical perspective or problem investigated, including the conceptual framework or hypotheses; a reasonably well-developed description of the methodology; and a statement of the major findings. Reviewers were instructed to "stay close to the data;" that is, report in mainly quantitative form the outcome of the study, rather than accept as primary data the conclusions, implications, or conjectures of the author. When this was accomplished, the study was coded into relevant practice issue areas (participation, organizational behavior, practitioners' roles, etc.).[1]

We created a separate file for each of our defined practice issue areas. Typically, each study was coded in from one to five of these areas. A copy of the study was then placed in as many separate files as the number of separate practice issue areas into which it had been coded. Thus, a study that fell into five areas was distributed—one copy each—to the files of each of those areas. We then attempted to proceed in two directions. First, we went directly into the data and tried to discern inductively the kinds of categories into which the material naturally fell. Subsequently, we surveyed the literature of that area in order to determine the topology of the field as theoretically developed by scholars who had written in the area. We then sought the most useful way to assemble our data into subcategories, based both on an understanding of conventional treatments and our personal assessment of how our particular data tended to group together. In some instances, where there was a strongly established theoretical school, we leaned in that direction in devising subcategories (as with organizational theory and the diffusion of innovations). In other instances, where no commonly accepted overarching framework existed among scholars, we leaned in the direction of composing our own subcategories (as with practitioner roles and participation.)

The next stage was on the one hand an extremely tedious process, and on the other a highly imaginative undertaking. We sifted through large

---

[1]See, Jack Rothman, *Planning and Organizing for Social Change,* Columbia University Press, New York, 1974, Appendix A, for a complete discussion of the procedures employed in retrieval.

numbers of studies, sometimes running into the hundreds, in order to group similar elements; and we tried to visualize connections among different languages, concepts, and findings from diverse disciplines and contexts. Clusters of data comprising a consensus of findings were constructed, and appropriate statements constituting generalizations were composed. As might be expected, problems arose with regard to evaluating, interpreting and grouping retrieved data. In the first place, some measure of judgement was exercised in the selection of the investigations to be included in the data pool. Some rejected investigations, therefore, might have been included by some other reviewer. Thus, our selection of studies may not have been as broad as was theoretically possible.

In compiling consensus findings on given subjects, we brought together data that crossed social aggregate levels (such as small group, organization, and community), or that included interventions carried out by practitioners working with individuals, small groups, and communities. Some studies on the state and national level were also used. Judgement was employed concerning whether particular studies could be grouped together. It is possible to argue that traversing aggregate levels and contexts in this way may tend to diminish the strength of derived generalizations. We viewed the matter otherwise, arguing that consensus findings that converge, although drawn from a wide range of contexts, lend strength to generalizations. The tendency was to include disparate settings and subjects whenever such a mix seemed reasonable. A wide range of problems were encountered and dealt with. We acknowledge their existence, but will not treat them here.

Having acquired information from the knowledge base, it was necessary to manipulate that information in some meaningful fashion, to convert it to a form that would yield valuable application concepts. As a result of our retrieval effort, we gathered a vast pool of more than 200 generalizations and more than 500 subgeneralizations. The next step was conversion and design.

The real work of conversion/design began with the completion of the study report form. The data, as we indicated, was coded into practice issue areas, and policy or practice implications were drawn based on the data. This is where application was centered. As the reviewer coded the study within all the categories into which it fell, he was urged to consider matters of application and utilization of *each* of these categories. In making applications, the reviewer was cautioned to hold speculation within reasonable bounds—to make inferential statements based solidly on the data, not involving extensive leaps from the data. These applications were not to be so abstract that they failed to offer direct prescriptive behavioral initiatives for intervention. The exact instruction to the reviewer-coder read as follows:

For each item checked, indicate *major findings* from abstract and *practice implications.* Emphasize and develop implications. *Name below* those *issue areas* relevant to a given set of findings-implications. General guidelines—stay close to the *actual data;* push ahead from findings to practice implications. Be specific about directives suggested to the practitioner. What does this finding tell the [Community Organization] practitioner about what he should *do?*

This step in the process necessitated continuing training and mutual exchange between reviewers, or supervisor and the project director. In keeping with a multidiscipline approach, staff reviewers came from the disciplines of sociology, psychology, political science, anthropology, and from such professional practice areas as social work, education, community mental health, and public administration. This was the place where the project director was required to be most active in revising and expanding on materials produced through the retrieval procedures. Conversion is a function for which few students have been prepared with the requisite skills, either in the social sciences disciplines or in the professional schools of the human services.

This was the most difficult area for the reviewers. It required a synthesis-conversion capability, as between theory and practice. Even doctoral students tend to lack either the training, conceptual breadth, or dual experience in the theoretical and practical worlds to accomplish this task with facility.

We rated each of the guidelines we had drawn using three ten-point scales, geared to each of three design criteria: (commonality, implementability, and quantifiability.) The three ratings were weighted equally to give an aggregate score to each guideline. This process led to the distillation of twenty guidelines, which constituted entries for our final selection. It was our intention to carry out our developmental work during a typical human service agency program year; i.e., September to June. This meant that we would be able to field test only a a small number of guidelines. Our guess was that a practitioner could conveniently implement no more than eight or ten. Accordingly, we eliminated half of the tentative possibilities. Those eliminated were guidelines that tended to be somewhat duplicating in goals or strategies. Also eliminated were those whose original generalization had somewhat lower literature support ratings. Overall, our aim was to achieve some degree of balance and diversity in the final set of guidelines as an aspect of exploring R&D parameters.

PILOT PHASE

We began pilot work by establishing a basic headquarters staff. This staff consisted of a project director (analogous to a project manager in industrial R&D), a director of field operations (analogous to a production manager), and a director of research operations (who combined evaluation and operations research functions). We sought—and ultimately received—confirmation that this staffing format would be equal to R&D demands.

The criteria for practitioner field staff involvement in the pilot phase were simple. They were also unusual and innovative for an R&D "engineering" staff, and they reflect the level of developmental activity in the social sciences. Typically, an R&D engineering staff is employed within a particular company and under top management's direction to fulfill certain tasks seen as important for that particular company's future. In the case of the Community Intervention Project, the initiative originated *outside* of any operating human service system, and had experimental purposes related to a university.

Our approach, then, represented something of a "maverick" or marginal procedure, for our entire testing effort took place outside the physical boundaries of the CIP (rather than within them, as is generally the case with an industrial firm or organization). We were forced into such an approach because of the absence of R&D within existing social service systems. Consistent with R&D, however, the field staff were from, and conversant with, the real world of practice. Only those acquainted with the vagaries of application settings, we reasoned, could deal fluidly and well with the complexities of implementation.

Our field staff were to carry their regular job responsibilities. They would use the action guidelines strictly in connection with their regular assignments. Guideline implementation was within the normal work week and task expectations of the staff members' basic jobs. Outside of normal work time, they would record implementation experiences, meet with their supervisor, attend staff meetings, etc.

We believed it important that the headquarters staff be able to interact closely with the practitioner field staff on a close and regular basis. This position led to a relatively small field staff, located within easy commuting distance of the project office. It was not useful for our task to consider constructing a simulated pilot setting at project headquarters. Accordingly, eight practitioners were selected from Ann Arbor-Ypsilanti, Jackson, and Detroit. Eight was thought to be the maximum number that could be closely observed and supervised by the field operations director. It was impossible for a field staff of this size to include a full range of practitioner orientations and agencies in which community practitioners worked. No attempt was made, therefore, to secure a random sample. We did endeavor, however, to maximize the diversity of practitioners and agency situations.

For this pilot study, we needed special kinds of practitioners who could perform social engineering functions. They needed to be those who believed, at least minimally, that theory and conceptualization had something to offer to their practice. Furthermore, they had to possess a reasonable level of conceptual ability in order to work from abstract action statements, and to see the application potentials of those statements. They needed to be sufficiently capable as practitioners so that there was some reasonable chance of the guidelines being adequately operationalized in the field. They had to be dependable, both as practitioners committed to doing a creditable job, and as study participants who could be counted on to record their experiences accurately and in a timely and forthright fashion. Selection criteria were formulated around these requisites. The pilot work was intended to show whether we had used appropriate criteria for social engineering functions. Staff were hired to work one day a week for CIP.

Some limitations were encountered in relation to the use of already employed field staff. The practitioners were limited by the constraints of their jobs, and the multiple roles of practitioner-observer-recorder became very demanding of time and energy. Opportunities for guideline implementation had to be shaped to whatever job situations existed. These "limitations," however, were also positive in terms of R&D requirements, for the application by ultimate users would take place in contexts also characterized by constraints and pressures.

We made every effort to establish a balance between systematic and flexible observation by our field staff, by having them report and record their experiences in unstructured logs. These unstructured logs in the pilot study permitted observers to record many implemental or process factors of possible relevance. (The categorization of these factors into checklists would provide a systematic guide for common observations during the main developmental field study. Part of the log for the main field study would remain unstructured. This section would encourage, we believed, the observation and recording of any individually perceived, relevant information.)

The logs received continuing attention during the pilot study. This was appropriate, as the logs were the basic tool for reporting the process of guideline implementation and the outcome of use of the guidelines.

The pilot work pointed to the necessity for three types of logs that we believe might be useful in social R&D developmental field work generally:

1. an initial log, for completion before actually beginning intervention;
2. a periodic log, for completion on a regular basis (in our work that turned out to be bi-weekly) throughout the implementation process;
3. a final summary log, or retrospective, evaluative log, for completion after the intervention was terminated.

Although the three types of logs were similar in format, they elicited different types of data, according to their temporal relation to the implementation process.

Pilot work afforded an opportunity to experiment with means of evaluating success in guideline operationalization. We were able to work through formal recording devices that would facilitate evaluation of outcomes, and supervisory support procedures necessary to enable effective recording related to evaluation to take place.

Monitoring of Practitioner Practice

Our initial view of how closely it would be necessary to monitor practitioner practice in operationalization of application concepts was rather open. Between our general staff seminars, the regular individual meetings between the field operations director and the practitioners, and the opportunity to review practitioner recording on a regular basis, we thought that we would have the necessary monitoring controls. At the outset, we were inclined to be somewhat non-directive. We tried not to *force* practitioners to operationalize the guidelines accurately. It was clear almost from the beginning, however, that assistance would be needed in helping the practitioner to adopt the application concept of each guideline using his own "naturalistic," stylistic idiosyncracies and the complex potentials and limitations of each given situation. The necessity to be rather vigorous in guiding practitioners to function within the boundaries of the application concept became more clear as we went along. Practitioners often became enmeshed in the contingencies of the practice situation, and needed sustained assistance in keeping to the line of the application concept.

During the pilot study the field operations director, who supervised the eight practitioners, was personally acquainted with all of them. He found it useful to develop an informal, consultative type of relationship with them which considerably aided the guidance process.

Pilot Procedures to be Carried Forward

From the experience of those participating in the pilot study, as anticipated and planned for, several important procedural suggestions for the main field test emerged. These included:

1. Use the same administrative staff structure: project director, field operations director, and research operations director.
2. Employ a larger field staff for the main field test—as many as twenty or even more in order to achieve a larger number of instances of implementation.
3. Carry forward with the same social engineering criteria for field staff as those used in the pilot test.
4. Employ additional field supervision staff in order to keep a workable span of control or span of support. A small unit form of organization would approximate the intimate features of the pilot study.

5. Use more formal and precise evaluation instruments for outcome performance testing.

6. Use a shorter, more structured, closed-ended log, but one that also provides the opportunity for open-ended, descriptive, narrative reporting to give additional detail and "flavor" regarding implementation. Have these logs submitted biweekly. Reduce the number and length of instruments to be filled out. (Overly long reporting forms become a burden and an interfering element in social engineering functions.)

7. Establish a sequence of six guidelines to be implemented by each field staff member during the program year, in order of decreasing priority. Implement as many of the guidelines in this sequence as possible during the program year. (In fact, we were able to implement the first four in the sequence, indicating that our time estimate for implementation was not entirely out of line.)

8. Maintain support through group meetings with field supervisors and others of the headquarters staff. View the intended preliminary handbook as an additional orienting and directing device. Use this preliminary handbook to lower the needed intensity of support.

MAIN FIELD TESTING

Field Staff Qualifications for Social Engineering Roles

Since the "engineering" field staff were fundamental to fulfilling the social engineering roles of the project, we will discuss their qualifications and tasks initially. The role of these practitioners in the main field study was unique. On one hand they were observers and informants. In this respect, their behavior was recorded for treatment as data. On the other, they served as participants and social engineers, employed by the project to convert and operationalize application concepts into feasible practice techniques. The main field study began, essentially, with the selection of an appropriate sample of practitioners to make up such an engineering field staff. The project initially sought and hired twenty-four community-based professionals. All were regularly employed in a broad range of typical human service agencies in southeastern Michigan. As in the pilot study, the practitioners were hired and paid as part-time employees of the Project. They implemented the guidelines "piggy-back" within the parameters of their ordinary job responsibilities in their regular agencies. Outside the job, on a one-day-a-week basis, they recorded their experiences using standard log forms. They also participated in training meetings and took part in conferences with project supervisors. All held graduate degrees in social work (MSW). The agencies and organization settings for the main field study were as follows:

Area Health Planning Council
Area Service and Planning Council for Families
Catholic Youth Organization
Catholic Social Services
Community Psychiatry Department, State Mental Hospital
County Child Care Planning Federation
County Health Department
Department of Social Welfare, Regional Office
Elementary School (School Community Agent)
Family Service Agency
Human Relations Office, School District
Intermediate School District (School Social Worker)
Juvenile Court
Mental Health Association for Children
Model Cities Program
Neighborhood Community Center
Neighborhood Multi-Service Center
Regional Council for Urban Planning
Social Welfare Workers Union
Student Counseling Office, University
Y.M.C.A.
Youth Service Bureau, Regional Office for the State

For our field study, panels of "knowledgeables" rated the reputations of all identifiable practitioners in their local communities. They employed criteria confirmed and refined in the pilot study: practice competency, conceptual or theoretical capacity, and dependability-reliability in recording and reporting. Those who rated highest along these dimensions were recruited for the project.

We sought a "skewed" sample, tailored to a specific research purpose, requiring practitioners with specialized characteristics and training. We also sought practice situations with typical, and on an aggregate basis, broad characteristics.

The twenty-four practitioners ultimately employed at the start of the main field study were individuals of demonstrated practice competence. Nevertheless, they required continuous support from the theory-oriented headquarters staff. This support came in the form of a thorough orientation, initial and on-going training, and close supervision. In addition, the preliminary version of the practitioners' handbook for guiding them through the implementation experience was an added element of support that had not been available to the pilot study practitioners. The level of support was clearly less intensive during the main field test than during the pilot work, yet the need for continued close supervision had a definite constraining effect on the geographical selection of our field staff. This meant that the field staff had to be sufficiently close to project headquarters that the research staff could interact with them daily if it were necessary. It was for this reason that the field staff was drawn from either the Ann Arbor-Ypsilanti or Detroit areas of Southeast Michigan. Such geographical contiguity facilitated our on-going training efforts.

We selected three of the pilot study practitioners to act as supervisor-coordinators in recognition of the fact that a field staff of 24 was too large to be managed effectively by the core staff from project headquarters.

The size of the field staff was determined by the number of available, competent practitioners, the project capacity for training-supervisory functions, and also by monetary considerations. Roberts (1967) asks, "what determines the number of engineers that the firm desires to have on a project?" and he responds in a simplistically realistic fashion: "an obvious answer is that the financial support available to the firm determines the desired engineering level" (p. 129). The N of the main field study sample was also conditioned by this consideration. The existing budgeted funds did not permit us to consider a field staff larger than thirty, at the outside. The calculus of finances and project management brought that number down to twenty-four. Attrition during the process of development brought it down still further.

For our purposes, a staff of twenty-four appeared to be both manageable and appropriate to demonstrate the efficacy of applying R&D procedures to the particular social intervention techniques undergoing development. Furthermore, it was large enough to provide room for the normal attrition that we anticipated as a result of the long time frame of the main field test. (We lost six field staff members during the course of the year.)

In selecting our field staff, we made no attempt to achieve a sample that was "representative" of the human services. Our use of a purposive sample should cause the researcher no particular discomfort, though it may puzzle the practitioner who lacks a research orientation. For our purposes, what was necessary was a group of functionaries who could articulate the relationships being studied. It was not our intention to generalize attributes or attitudes of human service practitioners. The population is a population of behaviors. It is not a representative population of people. For this reason, in this design, a relatively small population, purposively selected for capability to produce the variables, relationships, and products of the project was composed. An attempt was made to select situations, behaviors, and settings similar to those of the ultimate practitioner-users of the handbook.

The CIP organization chart illustrates the structure we instituted to carry out the requisite functions. The study director served as project manager. He coordinated the work and maintained clear channels of communication to all levels of the organization. The organization was structurally divided into two major operating divisions: Research Operations and Field Operations. Each division had its own director.

The field staff, itself, was organized into five units of three to seven members each. Each unit was under the general supervision of the field operations director. Each unit had a supervisor-coordinator who assisted and oversaw the work of the unit members. To assure that all headquarters staff were in constant contact with the line operations and problems that might arise, one of the units had the field operations director as its direct supervisor-coordinator. A second unit was under the co-supervision of the project director and the research operations director. The three remaining units were under the supervision of persons who had served as pilot study practitioners, and who were thus familiar with the processes and goals of the main field test.

Diversity of orientation and competency are reflected in the make-up of the core headquarters staff. The project director had a background in both practice and research. He held a professional master's degree in social work and a Ph.D. in social psychology. He had been a practitioner, teacher of practice, and researcher. His commitment was a balanced one to both the scientific and practice aspects of the undertaking. As project manager, he served in part during this "pioneering" stage as an engineering theorist.

The field operations director had a master's degree in social work and had been a practitioner for seven years. He had subsequently been a professor of social work with the responsibility for conceptualizing and communicating the basic elements of practice, drawing liberally upon the social sciences in this connection. (His undergraduate major had been sociology, and he had begun doctoral studies in that field.) Within the project, his basic orientation was to be to the application and practice component, and, by agreement, he was to serve as an advocate of practitioner-related considerations. He had the general responsibility for overseeing and supervising the work of the practitioner field staff on a day-to-day basis.

The research operations director was a research methodologist who had completed a doctoral specialization in operations research. In addition, he held a bachelor's degree in education and had been a high-school science teacher for five years. His chief responsibility, by common agreement, was to safeguard the integrity of the evaluative and methodological aspects of the work. He had the major responsibility for operations research and performance testing within the project. This involved data collection, reduction, and analysis, and reporting periodic trends to the project director and to the headquarters staff.

COMMUNITY INTERVENTION PROJECT
ORGANIZATIONAL CHART

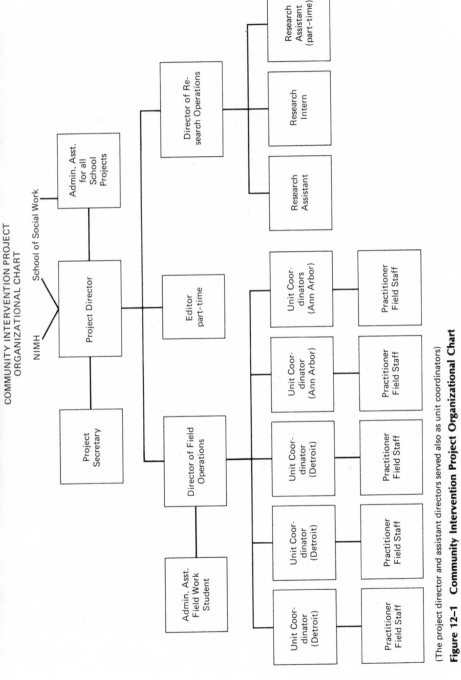

(The project director and assistant directors served also as unit coordinators)

Figure 12–1 Community Intervention Project Organizational Chart

In addition to their main assignments, the research operations director had responsibility for supervising several field staff members directly. The field operations director had assigned research responsibilities in instrument construction, data interpretation, etc. The project director had direct involvement in both areas.

All the key staff members had an admixture of training and skill. Decided role orientations, however, were fixed: toward research, toward practice, and toward optimal integration of the two. The project built-in and tolerated tension among the various roles and orientations, seeing this interplay as essential for creative R&D.

All important decisions were worked through all three main headquarters staff members (who met frequently with other staff members, as well). In this way, while representing some particular point of view, staff members were forced to deal with and to accommodate other considerations in making overall project decisions. The mixed backgrounds of the staff permitted this to occur without undue strain.

Pelz (1967) has written of some of the beneficial factors in the research and development climate. His conclusions coincide with the basic structural format of CIP:

Effective scientists . . . did not limit their efforts to either the world of pure science or to the world of application but were active in both.
The manager should beware of letting some individuals focus exclusively on research, others exclusively on development. He should encourage his staff to tackle some jobs in both areas. (pp. 161, 165)

In addition, a number of administrative aides, research assistants, student interns, and students on work-study assignments served as technical aides and technicians in a variety of capacities. A professional editor had the task of systematizing development outputs in fabricating the practitioner handbook that was the basic product of the development process.

Orienting the Field Staff

Before commencing field activities, the field staff was assembled and given an overview of the project format and procedures. Each was assigned to a unit, introduced to his coordinator-supervisor, and each received a definition of the intended field operations. They were told the sequencing and timing of the six guidelines to be implemented. They were also told that provision had been made in the research design to delete one or more guidelines if the time constraints of a program year prevented full implementation of all six.

Because the innovation guideline would be the first that each of the practitioners would implement, it was reviewed in considerable detail. The field staff was presented with several illustrations of how that guideline had been applied during the pilot study.

A practitioner appeared at the orientation session to describe and detail her use of the guidelines and to respond to questions about implementation. In addition, the field staff was taken step-by-step through the log recording process and through the process of completing the baseline instruments. Each was then given the preliminary handbook chapter on the innovation guideline. This was to serve as a guide in launching and carrying out the guideline. Subsequent chapters were provided as a prelude to initiating each new guideline.

A considerable portion of the success with which we were able to administer the various practitioner units was a result of the investment we made in time and effort in preparing the unit coordinators for their supervisory tasks. Previous to commencing field activities, agreement was reached among all the supervisors on the nature of their duties and responsibilities. Generally, these consisted of assisting the headquarters staff in the screening of the field staff, planning and participating in meetings, engaging in on-going monitoring of, and consulting with, the field staff, and collecting and forwarding data to the project headquarters.

Training of the supervisors was a matter of thoroughly preparing them to work with the practitioner units. In addition, they were shown how to prepare for the regular unit meetings and how to present each succeeding guideline. By the time the supervisors were to assume responsibility for their units, they were fully prepared to work with practitioners around completion of the project tasks and requirements. Unit meetings would be held every four or five weeks throughout the year.

The Context of the Main Field Test

With the availability of a preliminary handbook and the establishment of the requisite rules of procedure, we were ready to determine how and if the guidelines could be carried out in a wider field test. The six action guidelines selected for this main field test and the intended sequence of implementation were as follows:

1. *The Innovation Guideline:* practitioners wishing to promote acceptance of an innovation should attempt to formulate it in such a way that the total innovation can be experienced initially by a limited portion of the target system.

2. *The Role Effectiveness Guideline:* practitioners wishing to increase their effectiveness may approach this by establishing a relevant role or role aspect and by clearly specifying this role or role aspect and fostering mutual agreement among relevant superordinates concerning it.

3. *The Organizational Change Guideline:* practitioners who wish to change organizational goals may approach this by either (a) increasing the power of those groups within the organization holding goals compatible with the practitioner's, or (b) introducing new groups into the organization holding goals compatible with the practitioner's.

4. *The Fostering Participation Guideline:* practitioners wishing to increase participation in organizations, voluntary associations, or task groups should increase the number of benefits (instrumental, expressive, etc.) provided.

5. *The Client Involvement Guideline:* practitioners wishing to increase legitimized client involvement as decision makers within human service organizations should provide clients with appropriate technical assistance.

6. *The Uniform Task-Effectiveness Guideline:* practitioners wishing to increase their effectiveness may approach this by identifying uniform tasks within their work situation and using centralized decision making with formalized, standardized procedures to handle them.

All six of these guidelines had received attention during the pilot study phase. The indications were that none of them presented sufficient obstacles to implementation as to make them impractical for study during the limited program year available to us for our developmental work. The actual number of guidelines ultimately implemented by the participants of the main field study was more or less irrelevant for the purposes of this R&D demonstration, though there would have been little to report had our practitioner-social engineers been unable to implement any of them in the available time. The pilot work encouraged us that this would not be the case; and, indeed, our practitioners were able to achieve full implementation of the first four during the program year.

We sought to record in quantifiable terms, to as great an extent possible, the process of implementation. For the purposes of project evaluation, an ends-means concept evolved with a *single end goal* ("Y") seen as a product of each intervention treatment ("X"). For some guidelines, X involved more than one operation:

INNOVATION GUIDELINE

X: Formulate innovation to be experienced in a partial target system

Y: Acceptance or carrying out of an innovation in the larger or general target population

ROLE EFFECTIVENESS GUIDELINE

X_1: Establish relevant role
X_2: Clearly specify role
X_3: Foster superordinate agreement regarding the role

Y: Increase practitioner effectiveness

CHANGING AN ORGANIZATION'S GOALS

X_1: Alter the structure of influence within an organization

X_2: Introduce new groups into the organization

OR

X_{2A}: Increase the power of groups with compatible goals

Y: Change organizational goals

FOSTERING PARTICIPATION GUIDELINE

X: Increase benefits provided

Y: Increase participation in the organization

CLIENT INVOLVEMENT GUIDELINE

X: Provide clients with appropriate technical assistance

Y: Increase client involvement as decision makers

UNIFORM TASKS–EFFECTIVENESS GUIDELINE

X_1: Identify uniform tasks in the work situation

X_2: Use centralized decision making

Y: Increase practitioner effectiveness

The criteria for evaluating success of guideline implementation thus became:

1. *Innovation:* the degree to which the innovation was carried out in, or accepted by, the proximate general target system.

2. *Role Effectiveness:* the degree to which the intended effectiveness outcome was attained by exercising the role.

3. *Changing Organizational Goals:* the degree to which an organization's goals were changed.

4. *Fostering Participation:* the degree to which participation with the target group was increased (or modified).

5. *Client Involvement:* the degree to which client involvement in decision making increased.

6. *Uniform Task-Effectiveness:* the degree to which practitioners felt their effectiveness was increased.

Instruments

Each social R&D undertaking must select a preferred optimal data-gathering procedure. Our aim in this instance was to collect the highest quality process data possible in the most natural way available. This dictated our use of some sort of self-reporting method. We were interested not only in what our social engineering staff did, but why they did it and how they evaluated their actions and the reactions of others. We believed that through the imposition of carefully structured rules, constant and close monitoring, and on-going training in the reporting process, we would mitigate against a large measure of distortion and enhance social engineering competencies. After all, the field staff were not "subjects" in the usual sense; they were professional employees, engaged in a specialized task. We tested our assumptions during the pilot phase of our work. The results were sufficiently encouraging that we elected to use a set of three self-reporting forms for the developmental field study. This set of self-reporting forms (our logs) would constitute a sort of semi-structured field diary for capturing the essential facets of implementation-operationalization as it took place *in situ*. Structured response categories were used to offer a means of comparative analysis across different "cases" of implementation and operationalization. At the same time, there were open-ended, narrative items designed to encourage field staff to note in their own words any additional aspects of the process that seemed relevant. Combined with appropriate backup and supervision, these instruments gave the field staff a systematic way of observing and recording their experiences. For the purposes of our R&D demonstration, the logs seemed to provide a fruitful method for penetrating the process of field operationalization—a highly complex, multi-faceted phenomenon.

The initial log (IL), as we indicated earlier, was to be completed after a decision was made to use the guideline, but *before* actual implemental activities took place. In the IL the field staff member indicated specific goals in using the guideline. He was asked to present preliminary ideas on how the guideline elements would be operationalized, circumstances at the outset that led up to a decision to employ the guideline, and what steps and stages were anticipated in implementation. He was also asked to determine, as best he could, what groups and individuals were likely to be contacted and what facilitating and limiting conditions might be anticipated. In addition to giving baseline information about circumstances and outcome-assessment related information about goals, the IL also served as a planning tool for the field staff member.

The periodic logs (PL's) were completed on a concurrent, biweekly basis during guideline implementation. The PL's gave objective behavioral information, qualitative and quantitative, about such matters as number and types of community groups contacted and for what reasons, the number and types of individuals contacted and for what reasons, and factors that specifically facilitated or limited implementation during the course of operationalization. Specific steps taken and their order were to be clearly specified. The reporting schedule systematically embraced social-psychological sectors surrounding the implementation experience: the field staff member himself, the sponsoring agency, client factors, and community variables. In addition, each PL asked for an open narrative account of what transpired during the period of the report. Practitioners also indicated any changes from the IL in terms of goal statements or operationalization of guideline elements.

The final summary log (FSL) was for completion after implementing the guideline to the point where activities ceased in using the guideline to attain the specific goal. Only after the last PL, giving on-going behavioral information was completed, was the FSL filled out. The FSL was viewed as providing an overview of the implementation experience. That overview was given in retrospect, in terms of culmination, and with an evaluation of the most important aspects of the implementation process. The full log record of implementation was used as the backdrop for preparation of the FSL. The FSL covered the same basic implementation areas as the PL, but it asked for such summative, retrospective, and evaluative items as the field staff member's favorableness to the guideline, whether he or she would use it again, what the most problematic aspects of implementation were, and so forth.

This set of logs provided a detailed case study of each practitioner's implementation of each guideline. Tripodi, Fellin, and Epstein (1971), in their evaluation book, cite this case study approach, using a log type of process reporting, as particularly functional for studying practitioner intervention:

The case study technique has as its purpose the detailed description of a social program as it unfolds in its process of development. It employs both qualitative and quantitative data in an effort to develop hypotheses and new ideas for explaining the progress or lack of progress in program development. Among the methods used are participant observation, informal interviews, [etc.]. . . . Some of the methods employed in case studies, as indicated above, may be used by program staff. For example, each staff member may keep a diary of what activities he is engaged in, for what reasons, and with what success. Periodically, the content of these diaries are reviewed in order to locate possible strategies that could be used by all staff members. . . . Information from the case study is principally used for an evaluation of program efforts with respect to the nature and quality of staff activities and the extent to which staff efforts are related to program goals. (pp. 91, 93)

A standardized set of instructions was issued to the field staff in the field test in order to promote accurate recording and consistency among recorders.

While standardized reporting procedure facilitated reporting, data reduction, and subsequent data analysis, the inherent limitations of self-reporting instruments were always a potential source of problems. In the context of the field test we were not able to employ perfectly effective means of confirming the authenticity of reports. A number of procedures, however, were built into the design to promote accuracy and objectivity in reporting. The four most important were:

1. The *instructions* included such matters as reporting promptly after events took place, and stressed the criterion of accuracy rather than "success" as a project need, along with the need for full and legible information, etc.

2. On-going *training* reinforced the need for accuracy and objectivity, and the use of the aforementioned procedures to facilitate this.

3. *Field supervisors were located in the field,* close by the agencies in which field staff implemented guidelines. Supervisors were generally familiar with local situations and had only a small number of field staff members in their units. This facilitated their ability to "check out" any reports that seemed inaccurate, incomplete, or that were inconsistent with previous reports.

4. *Close monitoring of reports in the project headquarters* involved assessment of unusual occurrences or shifts, inconsistencies and other information that might indicate distortion and/or exaggeration.

In spite of their limitation, self-reporting instruments are an established feature of social science research. For our purposes they seemed to provide reasonable information concerning the process of guideline implementation in the field. It is important to keep in mind, however, the limitations of such data-gathering instruments when assessing the methods and outcomes of this particular project. It is likely that, for other social R&D tasks and contexts, particularly simpler or more contained ones, other process-recording techniques may be useful. These might include observation, service or administrative records, unobtrusive interviewing methods, etc. All these variations need to be experimented with.

Outcome Evaluation in the CIP

The fact that our primary data were derived from a set of logs kept by the practitioners who implemented the guidelines is a fact that will not have escaped the attention of the reader of the previous material. It is the final summary log, however, that is of particular interest to us at this point.

Outcome data were provided through the use of the FSL. These data were subjected to the judgement of knowledgeable experts who assessed the extent of attainment of intended goals.

It will be recalled that our general approach required the practitioner to specify his goal for a guideline in *both* the IL and the FSL. This had to be done in terms of clear, concrete, and short range ("proximate") objectives. Field supervisors had to give considerable attention to assisting practitioner in this task. Left to their own devices, the field staff demonstrated an awesome penchant for vague, confused, or multiple component goal statements. Frequently, too, they fell victim to that ailment, epidemic in human service professions, that impels one to list objectives in long range, platitudinous, and unmeasurable terms—lists that typically end with some variant of the expression, "the social good." Such goal statements were inimical to our research aims, and much effort was directed at reshaping them into an acceptable form.

The IL log item that elicited goal statement data read: "What is your overall goal (as you would generally characterize it) in using this guideline?" On the FSL the field staff were asked to provide concrete, behavioral, or factual indicators of the extent to which they reached their goal. Research staff worked closely with field staff to elicit a clear, direct, and (ideally) measurably empirical referent. For example, one field staff member, working with the innovation guideline, desired initially to institute a parent-tutorial project in three elementary buildings in a school district (partial target system) and, on the basis of a successful demonstration, diffuse the innovation to the other ten elementary schools in the district (proximate target system). This practitioner, in reporting, was expected to indicate whether the basic program was established in the partial target grouping of the three schools, and in how many of the additional ten schools was the basic innovation adopted. This included criteria of what constituted adoption. The fostering participation guideline lent itself to a similar numerical formulation (the specific increase in attendance or activity). The changing an organization's goals guideline and the increasing practitioner effectiveness guideline had less tangible referents. In these instances, also, however, concrete, evidential responses were asked for and elicited by the field supervisory and headquarters staff in the monitoring activities.

The FSL log item seeking data was worded: "Give some concrete, empirical indicators of goal attainment." We felt it was useful to also obtain the field staff member's opinion of the degree to which he was successful in implementing the guideline. This was not seen as *prima facie* data in the way the "empirical indicators" were, but it was descriptive information that might be taken into account in assessing the program's outcome.

Our approach to outcome evaluation was based on these sources of data. Three qualified raters with different orientations and backgrounds assessed these materials and arrived at a judgement of outcome success. The concrete, empirical indicators of outcome were their prime bases of judgement. At the same time they had at their disposal opinion-based information provided by the field staff member, to inform—though not to constrain—their judgement. They also had the total record of implementation available to them.

The final assessment of outcome was drawn by combining the judgements of the raters. In addition to the specific data indicated above, the raters had available to them the entire log file on the intervention to round out their understanding of the circumstances surrounding the episode of practice. Outcome assessment in such an extraordinarily complex and fluid setting is, without question, problematic. We relied heavily on the judgements of competent observers for this purpose, but we provided them with specific data and criteria to help focus and discipline that judgement. We used a rating packet composed of what was assessed to be the *minimum* amount of information in a standardized form that was *sufficient* to arrive at a *valid judgement* of goal attainment in the intervention case.

We developed an "assessment criteria frame" notion to assist us in our assessment objectives. This criteria framework for judging outcome was guideline specific; i.e., a separate frame was constructed for each guideline and contained within it components intrinsic to the guideline, relevant for making appropriate judgements. We considered developing one common frame for all guidelines but abandoned this as being too general and loose. We also experimented with an individual frame for each guideline for each practitioner but found this too fragmented an approach. The criteria frame by guideline appeared to be a useful level of assessment. An example of a criteria frame, that one developed for the innovation guideline, is given below.

Innovation carried out in (or accepted by) none of proximate general target system	Innovation carried out (or accepted by) a few members of proximate general target system	Innovation carried out (or accepted by) about half of proximate general target system	Innovation carried out (or accepted by) most of proximate general target system	Innovation carried out (or accepted by) all of proximate general target system

Figure 12–2 Innovation Guideline Criteria Frame

In the physical sciences it is possible to take direct measurements of the properties of materials—length in inches, weight in pounds, etc. In the social sciences, measurement is often more elusive; for example, feelings or attitudes. In the CIP situation indirect measures rather than direct ones were devised. While we had specific and factual information about outcomes, this, in itself, did not provide a direct indicator of the degree of success in the implementation of guidelines. It was the judgement of the raters that gave this. The rating frame, accordingly, is not a direct measuring tool laid on the implementation "case" but, rather, is an aid to "knowledgeable experts" who make judgements based on their examination of the standardized data concerning the case.

The five-point continuum by guideline offered a "yardstick" or framework for judgements by providing standard anchorage points specific to each guideline. The outcome scale specified the criteria for the rating as the degree to which the content-specific outcome goal had been attained for each guideline. Our experience in this instance suggests the kinds of difficulties to be encountered and some kinds of solutions that are possible in social R&D.

A general limitation of this approach is the self-reporting character of the methodology. This was offset to some extent by close supervision and monitoring. Field supervisors who were close to the practice situation were in a position to some degree to confirm or explore further information that was provided. In addition, logs were checked thoroughly in terms of consistency, appropriateness, completeness, all of which, we assume, contribute to the validity of the data provided.

No assumptions were made about the distance between intervals on the frame. It was primarily a guide to judgement on the part of the raters. The continuum was used primarily to classify cases into categories of success.

The FSL had one additional item related to evaluation. As the study was conducted in an open setting, close controls on variables were missing. We were concerned, therefore, that variables other than the intervention strategy—and variables in the log forms—might have influenced the outcome importantly. To deal with this, the field staff practitioners were instructed to scan the implementation experience for other factors that may have influenced the outcome. The practitioners were asked to attend to, and identify, intervening variables in the implementation setting. Training sessions gave special emphasis to preparation for this task.

The field supervisors vigorously reinforced this function as PL's were submitted during the course of the intervention and when the FSL was submitted at the conclusion. Their personal knowledge of the intervention situation was also helpful. The headquarters staff further scrutinized this aspect in processing FSL's. Any signs of intervening influences, or any inconsistencies in response patterns that suggested intervening factors, were vigorously pursued with the field staff and/or the unit supervisors.

Using this set of procedures, several practice episodes were eliminated from the data pool. As an example, in one instance a pre-existing conflict between an agency director and his board was so severe that his role and effectiveness were highly constrained. A short time later he was discharged from his position. The low attainment outcome in use of the guideline could not be ascribed clearly to the guideline itself, or to how it was implemented in that circumstance.

This procedure again illustrates some of the potential difficulties and possible solution strategies in social R&D. While rigorous controls were lacking, this procedure represented an approach to identifying and minimizing the effect of external influences in an open field setting.

Another element in our efforts to control goal specificity permitted practitioners to modify their goal statements during the course of the study if the logic for doing so was compelling. Normally, the practitioner was expected to stick with his original goal statement, as recorded in the IL. If he felt strongly that it would be detrimental or unproductive in his circumstances to hold to what later experience suggested as inappropriate or unrealistic, he could discuss this with his field supervisor. Goal shifts were permitted only when they could be justified in terms of the realities of the practice situation, were not capricious, and were not based on the motivation of allowing the practitioner to be more "successful" in the implementation.

Though permitting even such minor shifts in goal specification appears to clash with the canons of research generally, we felt justified on pragmatic grounds. The logic of practice calls for constant feedback and rediagnosis during the course of an intervention, leading to revision of intervention modalities, goal formulations, or both. We find support for such an approach from Weiss (1972):

A characteristic of evaluation research that differentiates it from most other kinds of research is that it takes place in an action setting. Something else besides research is going on: there is a program serving people. . . .
If there is some recognizable set of principles and procedures that can be called a program, I am not sure that it is necessary to hold it steady in the arbitrary and argumentative way in which most raisers-of-the-issue propose. Programs almost inevitably drift. If the program and the drift are classified and analyzed, it seems possible to attribute the ensuing effects to the program in terms of how it worked and will often work in this disorderly world. (pp. 92, 93)

As a practical matter, very few practitioners made changes in their goals over time. Those who did were given a means for providing for it. Generally, goal changes involved clarification and/or narrowing of goals that were initially too vague or ambiguous. In processing data the goal statement, as presented in the FSL, checked against the full implementation recording, was taken as the outcome goal. Clearly, this most accurately represented the practitioner's crystallized formulation of the intervention objective.

The tension between research standards and practice standards regarding goal shift is clearly a central methodology problem in social R&D. See Thomas (1978) for an incisive discussion of this issue.

In order to have confidence in the outcome evaluations, it was necessary to have confidence in the tripartite rating procedure. To assist in assessing the reliability of the procedures, we have summarized the ratings of each rater on each guideline in the accompanying chart.

TABLE 12-1
OUTCOME RATINGS: RATER × PRACTITIONER × GUIDELINE

Practitioner	guideline 1			guideline 2			guideline 3			guideline 4		
	Outside Rater	Evaluation Staff	Unit Coordinator	Outside Rater	Evaluation Staff	Unit Coordinator	Outside Rater	Evaluation Staff	Unit Coordinator	Outside Rater	Evaluation Staff	Unit Coordinator
01	3	3	3	5	4	5	4	5	4	5+	5+	5
02	3	4	4	5	5	5	—	—	—	5+	5+	—
03	5	5	5	4	5	4	4	4	4	—	—	—
04	5	5	5	4	4	4	5	5	3	5	5	5
06	5+	5+	5+	5	5	5	1	1	1	5+	5+	5
07	5	5	5	5	5	5	5	5	5	5	5+	5
08	1	1	1	2	2	2	1	1	1	—	—	—
09	4	4	5	5	5	5	5	5+	5	4	5	4
10	5	5+	5+	4	4	4	5	5	5	5	5+	5-
11	5+	5+	5+	5	5	5	4	5	4	5	5+	5
12	5	5	5	5	5	5	3	3	2	3	3	4
13	5+	5	5+	3	3	3	5	5	5+	5	5	5-
14	4	5+	4	3	4	3	5	5	5	2	5	5
15	1	1	1	4	4	4	4	4	4	5+	5	5+
16	5	5+	5	4	5+	3	1	1	1	4	5	5
17	5	5	5	—	—	—	4	4	4	5	5	5
18	5	5	5	4	5	3	5	5	5	5	5	5
19	4	5	4	4	4	5	2	2	2	5	5	5
21	1	1	3	4	4	4	3	4	4	4	4	4
22	5	5	4	4	4	4	5	5	5	3	3	4
24	2	2	2	3	4	4	—	—	—	—	—	—

We have substituted numbers 1 through 5 for the verbal labels ("none, little, some, much, all") with the higher number reflecting a more positive direction. It is clear from this chart that the ratings are heavily skewed in a positive direction. This positive skew is not altogether surprising. The field staff was directed to select proximate goals that could be realistically completed within the time frame of the field test, and that staff was selected according to competence. They had a support system of field supervision, staff seminars, a preliminary manual, etc., to assist them in operationalizing the guidelines properly. Further, the guidelines had support from basic research and were explicitly derived from such research findings. It might be said that, in a sense, the high success rate implied "validation" to the action principle of the guideline, although this was not tested in a formal experimental design in the study.

If we now present the percentage of rater agreement by guideline, it can be seen that rater agreement was generally high. Inter-rater reliability coefficients were, by guideline: Innovation: .98; Role Performance: .90; Goal Change: .98; and Participation: .73. These levels can be considered acceptable in this type of research.

TABLE 12-2
RATER AGREEMENT x GUIDELINE

	all agree		2/3 agree within 1		2/3 agree within 2		2/3 agree > 2		no agree	
	N	%	N	%	N	%	N	%	N	%
Guideline 1 N = 21	15	.71	5	.24	1	.05	0	0	0	0
Guideline 2 N = 20	13	.65	5	.25	0	0	0	0	2	.10
Guideline 3 N = 19	14	.74	4	.21	1	.05	0	0	0	0
Guideline 4 N = 18	11	.61	6	.33	0	0	1	.06	0	0
Total N = 78	53	.68	20	.26	2	.03	1	.01	2	.03

All three raters agreed on the outcome score in 68% of the cases in aggregate. This ranged from 61% on the Participation Guideline to 74% on the Goal Change Guideline. In an additional 26% of the cases, two of the raters agreed basically with the third, varying only by one interval (higher or lower). These two categories account for 94% of the total cases rated.

Rating Scale Validity

Another analysis was performed that had implications for both validity and reliability. An independent treatment was conducted that rated outcomes strictly on the basis of theoretical variables, their weights and relationships. Professor Josefina McDonough, a sociologist with training and practice experience in the field of community organization, was engaged expressly to carry out this analysis. She had available the basic rating packet, but worked primarily from the practitioner's narrative in the FSL. She did not have access to the full intervention file nor to the other rating scores. If outcomes predicted by calculations from this purely theoretical technique were similar to those based on rater judgements, some degree of cross-validation of the measuring instrument might be assumed.

Three theoretical variables were employed: goal difficulty, situational characteristics, and strategy characteristics. The main hypothesis guiding the analysis was that the less difficult the goal, the more favorable the situation; and the stronger the strategy, the higher (or more successful) the outcome; or vice versa. Two other factors entered the calculation: consistency between the strategy and the characteristics of the situation, and the position of the practitioner within the organization. The prevailing hypothesis was that the higher the consistency, the higher the field staff member's position within his/her organization, the higher the outcome.

Each of the dimensions of this formulation was coded from the FSL and given a weight according to inferences from the theory. This was an extremely complex type of analysis, involving a formulation with multiple predictions. The formulation holds only in relation to the cumulative effect on all dimensions. In regard to this particular analysis, Dr. McDonough in her report concludes:

We can verify that there was reasonable accuracy in the prediction of outcome. The predictive model was accurate in at least ordering the cases in these groups of different levels of success.

The high degree of rater agreement discussed earlier is of particular note in light of the fact that the independent ratings were made by persons of disparate backgrounds and relationships to the project. Since the raters were selected to provide diverse perspectives rather than to maximize inter-rater agreement, high inter-rater reliability reflects favorably on the scales and procedures in standardizing what was essentially a subjective judgmental process. The comparative analysis with the theoretical formulation adds force to this conclusion, supporting the validity and reliability of the method and of its potential utility in social R&D performance testing.

Process Evaluation

Our approach to process evaluation did not involve gradation or degree of process implementation as it did with outcome. The quality of the implementation was not assessed. In the design of the study, this was to be determined by relating implementation to outcome measures. The main factor being examined was whether or not the intervention strategy was actually operationalized by the field staff. This involved a categorical form of evaluation. Because we were proceeding with a treatment-outcome (X-Y) context, it was necessary to have a way of verifying the existence of X. As Messick (1969) has observed, the program, as practiced, is sometimes quite different from the program as planned. This makes it problematic to assume a causal relationship involving a given treatment.

The testing procedure did not include a study of the differences between those who did or did not achieve operationalization, what factors prevented operationalization, etc. Rather, we attempted to examine relationships and effects of variables, given the existence of treatment X. A separate qualitative analysis of different *forms* of implementation was also made.

The process evaluation procedure was clearly defined. The basic elements needed in order to operationalize the action principle were specified for each guideline: Some guidelines had only one element (as in participation: providing a *benefit*); some had several (as in role effectiveness: *clarifying role, reaching consensus,* with a *relevant superordinate*). In their ILs, the field staff was asked to indicate how they planned to operationalize each of the process elements involved in the given intervention. In the PLs they indicated changes in operationalization of the process. In the FSL, they indicated how the process elements were finally operationalized, taking a retrospective, cumulative view.

When the ILs were received, they were reviewed, examined, and evaluated by a designated staff team to determine whether the field staff member had properly conceptualized the intervention in terms of acceptable process criteria. If the process criteria were considered acceptable, no follow-up occurred. If not, the field staff member was asked to clarify or modify process elements until they were considered acceptable according to established criteria.

Once the initial process elements were approved, they were monitored in PLs on a regular basis. This was done in terms of changes, particularly changes that violated the action principle of the intervention. There was immediate follow-up when this occurred.

When the FSL was received, it underwent similar examination. If process elements were considered acceptable, the case was designated as "data" and filed for data processing. If problems were discovered at this stage, there was again immediate follow-up. Here, two possibilities occurred: (1) the statement was modified so as to indicate accurately what had occurred, but so worded as to meet the process criteria (thus designating it as data and permitting its further process), or (2) it was determined that X had not been achieved and the process criteria had not been met. This case was then removed from the main data processing route.

Two additional steps in process evaluation also took place. All approved FSLs were further reviewed by the project director. This occasionally resulted in a case being further clarified or removed from the main data analysis route. Finally, there was a terminal review in which all facets of the implementation were delimited in capsule form by a specialized evaluation aide on the staff. Here again, an occasional case needed to be further checked and clarified, or the case was removed as not adequately meeting process criteria. As a result of this constant monitoring, feed-back, quality control procedure, most of the cases were evaluated as meeting process criteria.

DATA ANALYSIS PLAN

What follows will be of particular interest to those with statistical leanings, but it is also of general importance. Multivariate statistical procedures—and the discriminant function in particular—are basic tools for the bag of those who would engage in social R&D. The approach we have taken to statistical analysis has, we believe, wider applicability for R&D applications in the social sciences.

Profile of Successful Implementation

The data used in constructing this profile were collected from the final summary log. The FSL was chosen for analysis as it indicated the field staff member's final perception of factors influencing his implementation process. It also gave us his evaluation of the weighting or importance of various factors.

The information from the FSLs was recorded into four general categories:

1. *Key Community Groups* contacted during the implementation (i.e., public agencies, private agencies, voluntary associations, and reasons for contact);
2. *Key Individuals* contacted (i.e., agency staff, staff of other agencies, clients, etc., and reasons for these contacts);
3. *Facilitating Factors* in implementation (i.e., personal commitment, support of agency staff, client and community interest);

4. *Limiting Factors* in implementation (i.e., lack of time, lack of clarity in the agency, lack of knowledge in the community).

Facilitating and limiting factors can be defined as any factors that serve to influence the practitioner in his or her ability to obtain his or her goal(s) successfully. These factors were divided into four major categories or "sectors": *personal* (the practitioner, himself), *organization* (sponsoring agency), *client,* and *community.* Pertinent variables are reported according to two types of indicators:

1. A relatively high percentage of practitioners stated that this item was one of three most important facilitating or limiting conditions within the particular sector;
2. A relatively high intensity of facilitation or limitation is indicated by the practitioners on a scale ranging from "non" (0) to a "great deal" (4).

In this sub-analysis, we sought trends and parameters in process variables among those implementations that were judged to have reached "complete" or "almost-complete" attainment of intended outcomes. Descriptive data were given regarding such areas as the number of individuals and groups typically contacted in a given implementation, and the reasons for contacting different individuals and groups. In this way, it is possible to hypothesize those variables to be addressed by practitioners implementing (replicating) this guideline. In addition, we gave ranges for these variables among successful implementations. This will suggest likely "tolerances" or parameters to practitioners who wish to use the guideline; for example, the fewest number and the largest number of groups or individuals that he is likely to contact in implementing the guideline. Hopefully, this should provide him with a mental set or posture of anticipation as he initiates the guideline implementation. The analysis question asked here is: among the very large number of process variables studied, which particular ones may be isolated and associated with high levels of goal attainment?

Multivariate Analysis of Process Variables in High vs. Low Goal Attainment

In this analysis we attempted to "tease out" variables particularly associated with high goal attainment by comparing the "complete" attainment cohort with all others. The relatively new methodology of discriminant analysis was employed, not only to indicate which variables were associated with greater attainment, but also to signify the statistical significance of these variables and aspects of interaction among them. We hoped to arrive at a hierarchy or ranking of importance among process variables associated with successful implementation. See the project technical report (Rothman, Teresa and Erlich, 1977) for further details.

Multivariate Analysis of Antecedent Variables in High vs. Low Goal Attainment

For this analysis a plan virtually identical to that above was designed, but here the domain was antecedent variables and their relative influence on outcome rather than process variables. Antecedent variables pertain to baseline factors in the initial implementation setting. Antecedent variables were obtained from baseline instruments filled out by the field staff pertaining to personal, organizational, community, and client attitudes and characteristics. It was our intent to determine, for example, whether initial attitude toward a guideline might influence one's success in using it.

An adjective checklist, a questionnaire, dealing with attitudes toward guidelines, collected information on factors that could conceivably influence practitioners' predilection to use guidelines in the field. The checklist was a form of the semantic differential, an instrument that attempts to measure (unbiased) attitudes toward a concept (the guideline.) It was developed by C. E. Osgood (1957). The attitudes are referred to as *dimensions,* of which there are four: (1) meaningfulness, (2) ethics, (3) power, and (4) implementability of the guideline. These dimensions were measured on an interval scale from 1–4 on a pre-test and post-test basis.

Other antecedent variables were measured in questionnaires collecting information concerning factors that may generally influence community practice. One collected information concerning practitioner social values that may be related to social work's ideals as a profession. These values included public aid, personal freedom, personal goals, social causation, pluralism, secularism, self-determination, positive satisfaction, social protection, innovation-change, social welfare, and cooperation towards group goals. Other antecedent data collected on field staff included personal attributes, professional attitudes, and political beliefs. We were unable to discern in this study clear relationships between antecedent variables and outcomes using guidelines.

Comparative Analysis Across Guidelines

Each of the above analyses is guideline specific. We also elected to examine data comparatively across guidelines. This procedure was not part of the R&D process, but represented an excursion into research and theory that was a by-product of development. It was our hunch that by examining data across guidelines, it might be possible to ascertain, for example, whether certain process factors were related to a given type of intervention, or if they held regardless of the type of intervention. We considered the possibility that those variables that were present and significant in this particular sample for all four guidelines (as, for example, certain types of facilitating or limiting factors) might well be generic features of community intervention. If this could be verified, then we would be identifying factors that practitioners should become more attuned to in their work environments, and that students in professional schools should be trained to develop the capabilities for recognizing and manipulating.

LIMITATIONS AND POTENTIALS OF THE ANALYSIS

These, then, are the basic features of the quantitative data analysis plan. There are some limitations that ought to be underlined: the absence of rigid operational controls, the relatively small N (from a statistical standpoint, not from a field work point of view), the use of mainly self-reporting data-gathering instruments, and the large number of interrelated variables being investigated. All of these are formidable constraints, especially from a traditional research perspective.

There is another way to view these matters, however. We were concerned with R&D involving a complex process of social intervention—and attempted to gain understanding of this phenomenon *in its complexity*. Through such understanding we could mold effective strategies and techniques for dealing with social problems. Our point of departure was knowledge utilization and the development of effective practice tools. We attempted to adapt research methods and procedures to those purposes rather than to confine our objectives and activities to conventional social science norms and acceptable methodological approaches.

The product of our development methods—a handbook for practitioners—was described and illustrated earlier (Chapter 9). The diffusion and social marketing methods employed to disseminate the handbook have also been presented.

ASSESSING THE PRODUCT

The diffusion studies pointed to a high degree of acceptance of the handbook by practitioners, and a high level of use of it in the agency practice situation. This is one criterion of success. Two additional means of product evaluation were employed and will be noted briefly here.

As rated by our panel of experts, fifteen of twenty-one field staff members achieved a success rating of four or five, complete or almost complete success in implementing the innovation guideline. Comparable success ratios were experienced on the other three guidelines examined in the field test (seventeen of twenty on one, fourteen of nineteen on another, and sixteen of eighteen on the third). It is, therefore, reasonable to infer a fairly high level of goal attainment using the prototype version of the handbook before improvements had been incorporated.

Comparable data on outcomes for similar goals without use of the handbook are not available. This leaves the question of how ultimately to appraise this success. It is certainly possible that success may have been affected by other contextual and supportive features of the project, external to the handbook itself. However, there was a definite trend in the direction of success, and we believe this trend is persuasive.

Questionnaire responses were obtained from practitioners who used the handbook as their main training tool in a 2-½-day workshop, sponsored by a continuing education organization. The responses of the handbook-using group (N = 12) were compared with responses on the same questionnaire given to almost one thousand practitioners who attended forty-five other workshops dealing with a wide range of topics and employing a wide range of training tools and methods in the same continuing education symposium. The external organization workshop staff employed a rating scale of from 1 to 5 to gauge reactions. On this scale, 1 indicated the most favorable response, and 5 the least favorable. The degree to which the handbook was able to bridge the gap between theory and practice is suggested by comparing the response patterns of the handbook-using group with the others:

questionnaire item:	handbook using group: mean	all other groups: mean
Applicability to practice (aggregate)	1.25	1.89
Content was applicable to my work	1.25	1.82
Material presented was not too general and abstract for me to use in my work	1.42	1.96
It will be possible for me to utilize the knowledge and skills I have obtained in this workshop	1.08	1.90

In all cases the handbook-using group responded in a more favorable direction to application-related questions. This indicates that research-derived action principles can be perceived to be of direct utility by practitioners when conveyed in such a product. While our staff did not have access to the original data in order to test the significance of the differences, the consistency of the trend in the direction must certainly be viewed as highly suggestive.

These sources of evidence, taken together, lend general encouragement to the R&D means for converting research into practice. We think they are sufficient to encourage further experimentation along these lines. The results are not altogether surprising. Ordinarily, students and practitioners are given only a research finding or a generalization. They are expected to proceed the remainder of the way to application on their own. Occasionally, this is augmented by provision of an abstract application strategy. It is obvious that a great number of additional linking functions and conversion aids, including user-ready products, are necessary to make application of research and theory expeditious or even possible.

This case study has demonstrated some of these linking functions and their methodological counterparts. We trust that it has conveyed a measure of the promise we believe is inherent in social R&D for the application of social research and the creation of practical tools to enhance practice in the human services fields. To return to Urban's remark at the beginning of this section, perhaps some skeptics have been convinced that the rhetoric of social R&D can be reduced to workable procedures and products. The others should continue to press their criticisms. The presentation has also suggested difficulties and flaws in social R&D at this early stage in its evolution. Progress in science and technology takes time and repetitious, cumulative experience. Shared results among additional experimenters will serve to facilitate advances in methodology and to generate more elegant case studies, hopefully in the middle-range future.

BIBLIOGRAPHY

GOPAL, M. H., *An Introduction to Research Procedure in Social Sciences.* New York: Asia Publishing House, 1964.

MESSICK, SAMUEL, "Evaluation of Educational Programs as Research on the Educational Process." Paper presented at the American Psychological Association meeting, Washington. D.C., 1969.

OSGOOD, C. E., *The Measurement of Meaning.* Urbana: The University of Illinois Press, 1957.

PELZ, DONALD, "Creative Tensions in the Research and Development Climate." *Science,* 157, no. 3785 (July 14, 1967), 160–165.

ROBERTS, EDWARD B., "Facts and Folklore in Research and Development Management." *Industrial Management Review,* 8, no. 2 (Spring 1967), 5–18.

ROTHMAN, J., JOSEPH G. TERESA, *Fostering Participation and Promoting Innovation* Itasca, Ill.: F. E. Peacock Publishers, Inc., 1978.

THOMAS, EDWIN J., "Research and Service in Single-Case Experimentation: Conflicts and Choices," *Social Work Research and Abstracts,* 14, no. 4 (Winter 1978), 20–31.

TRIPODI, TONY, PHILLIP FELLIN, and IRWIN EPSTEIN, *Social Program Evaluation: Guidelines for Health, Education and Welfare Administrators.* Itasca, Ill.: F. E. Peacock Publishers, Inc., 1971.

WEISS, C. H., *Evaluation Research: Methods of Assessing Program Effectiveness.* Englewood Cliffs, N.J.: Prentice-Hall, Inc., 1972.

Index